The State of Social Safety Nets 2015

The State of Social Safety Nets 2015

WORLD BANK GROUP

ISBN (paper): 978-1-4648-0543-1
ISBN (electronic): 978-1-4648-0544-8
DOI: 10.1596/978-1-4648-0543-1

Cover photo: © Gary Yim / Shutterstock.com. Used with the permission of Gary Yim / Shutterstock.com. Further permission required for reuse.
Page 6: © Robin Nieuwenkamp / Shutterstock.com. Used with the permission of Robin Nieuwenkamp / Shutterstock.com. Further permission required for reuse.
Page 20: © 1,000 Words / Shutterstock.com. Used with the permission of 1,000 Words / Shutterstock.com. Further permission required for reuse.
Page 32: © Zvonimir Atletic / Shutterstock.com. Used with the permission of Zvonimir Atletic / Shutterstock.com. Further permission required for reuse.
Page 42: © Gail Palethorpe / Shutterstock.com. Used with the permission of Gail Palethorpe / Shutterstock.com. Further permission required for reuse.
Page 62: © Malgorzata Kistryn / Shutterstock.com. Used with the permission of Malgorzata Kistryn / Shutterstock.com. Further permission required for reuse.
Page 72: © Jayakumar / Shutterstock.com. Used with the permission of Jayakumar / Shutterstock.com. Further permission required for reuse.

Cover and interior design: Karol A. Keane, Keane Design, Inc.
Library of Congress Cataloging-in-Publication Data has been requested.

Contents

Appendixes

Boxes

Figures

Map

Tables

Foreword

The need for social safety nets is a critical concern for governments across the globe and for the billions of men, women, and children striving to improve their livelihoods. As interest in and the use of social safety nets keep growing, countries struggle to make social safety net interventions more effective and to integrate them better in their overall social protection and labor systems.

This report documents the state of the social safety net agenda in low- and middle-income countries. In recent years, a true policy revolution has been under way. The statistics in this report capture this revolution and reveal it in many dimensions at the country, regional, and international levels. This latest edition of a periodic series draws heavily on the survey and administrative data in the World Bank's Atlas of Social Protection: Indicators of Resilience and Equity (ASPIRE), a comprehensive international database.

The effort to collect data through ASPIRE has resulted in capturing and bringing together a large body of data that was not previously available. Today, 131 countries out of 157 in the ASPIRE database have in-kind transfers, specifically in the form of school feeding. This fundamental transfer, ubiquitous in low-income countries, is quite important in middle-income countries as well. But while school feeding programs have been around for a long time, the emerging trend for many countries is to increasingly move toward cash-based assistance. Cash transfers are present in 130 countries, with the most rapid growth occurring in Africa. There, 40 countries now have unconditional cash transfer programs in place—almost double the number in 2010.

Why this growth? Why this commitment to make social safety nets part of the development policy architecture in low- and middle-income countries alike? Because social safety nets work. Their value has been demonstrated not from anecdotal evidence, but from extensive and robust evaluations often conducted with the same rigorous standards guiding, for example, medical research. Importantly, an increasing share of these evaluations is being undertaken in some of the most challenging and lowest-income contexts around the world.

How much do social safety nets cost? Costs range between 1.5 percent and 1.9 percent of gross domestic product in low- and upper-middle-income countries, respectively. Total spending on social safety nets in 120 developing countries is US$329 billion—approximately twice the amount needed to lift people out of extreme poverty. Different countries have made different choices in terms of financing their social safety nets for different social, economic, historical, and political reasons. Differences in budgetary choices tend to translate into differences in program performance across contexts; thus, for the same amount of resources, countries can achieve differing impacts. Therefore, one important question to explore is what countries are doing to improve the efficiency of social safety net programs as a system. This report provides an attempt to set realistic benchmarks for countries to assess the performance of their social safety nets in terms of coverage, spending, and impacts on reducing poverty.

Many countries have made strides in connecting poor and vulnerable people to different programs—with respect to not only social protection, but also jobs and other social interventions such as health and education. The agenda has become one of unlocking countries' potential, with the building of systems playing a big role. However, overlaps among programs persist and coordination remains limited in most cases. Establishing effective management, information, and evaluation systems; introducing accurate registries of beneficiaries; devising a proper way of verifying people's identity; adopting reliable payment mechanisms; ensuring appropriate institutional arrangements; and handling other administrative concerns all stand between an array of programs and effective interventions. Yet the system's agenda is very dynamic—not only because it is underpinned by ever-improving technologies, but also because of the way economies are evolving and increasingly urbanizing, among other trends. How social safety nets are implemented in response to urban poverty and what are the special features of social safety nets in urban areas are some key questions that this report starts to explore, as informed by ongoing analytical and practical work by the World Bank and by various governments.

We are excited to offer you the full range of data and analysis that inform this report, and we look forward to producing, sharing, and disseminating the latest global, regional, and country-level developments in the crucial field of social safety nets, through this 2015 edition and the ones to come.

Arup Banerji
Senior Director, Social Protection and Labor Global Practice
The World Bank Group

Acknowledgments

This report was prepared by a team led by Maddalena Honorati, together with Ugo Gentilini and Ruslan Yemtsov. The other members of the core team were Veronica Silva and Philip O'Keefe. Overall guidance was provided by Arup Banerji, Senior Director of the Social Protection and Labor Global Practice; Anush Bezhanyan, Practice Manager, Social Protection and Labor Global Practice; and Omar Arias, Lead Economist, Social Protection and Labor Global Practice. We gratefully acknowledge the research assistance provided by Marina Novikova and Wouter Takkenberg. We thank Raiden Dillard, Alies van Geldermalsen, and Ngoc-Dung Thi Tran for support on design, layout, and formatting.

The team is grateful to Francesca Bastagli, Margaret Grosh, Phillippe Leite, Cem Mete, and Edmundo Murrugarra, who contributed feedback and suggestions throughout the process.

The special highlights featured in the report were produced with inputs from Mook Bangalore, Carlo Del Ninno, Marianne Fay, Stéphane Hallegatte, Matthew Hobson, Suleiman Namara, Mirey Ovadiya, Robert Palacios, Patrick Premand, Nina Rosas Raffo, Adrien Vogt-Schilb, and Giuseppe Zampaglione.

The ASPIRE team—including Stefanie Brodmann, Paula Cerutti, Aylin Isik-Dikmelik, Oleksiy Ivaschenko, Ana Sofia Martinez, Cem Mete, Victoria Monchuk, Claudia Rodriguez Alas, Joana Silva, and Frieda Vandeninden—offered valuable technical support.

Special thanks to country teams for validating program data on spending and number of beneficiaries, including Pablo Ariel Acosta, Afrah Alawi Al-Ahmadi, Ghassan N. Alkhoja, Colin Andrews, Diego Angel-Urdinola, Philippe Auffret, Ashiq Aziz, Shrayana Bhattacharya, Andras Bodor, Gbetoho Joachim Boko, Hugo Brousset Chaman, Lucilla Maria Bruni, Robert S. Chase, Aline Coudouel, Benedicte Leroy De La Briere, Carlo del Ninno, Rony Djekombe, Heba Elgazzar, Randa G. El-Rashidi, Lire Ersado, Endashaw Tadesse Gossa, Melis Guven, Samira Ahmed Hillis, Oleksiy Ivaschenko, Quanita Ali Khan, Silvana Kostenbaum, Dima Krayem, Phillippe Leite, Rene Antonio Leon Solano, Emma Mercedes, Emma Mistiaen, Khalid Ahmed Ali Moheyddeen, Victoria Monchuk, Monsalve Montiel, Claire V. Morel, Fitsum Z. Mulugeta, Michael Mutemi Munavu, Suleiman Namara, Nga Nguyet Nguyen, Surat F. Nsour, Philip O'Keefe, Foluso Okunmadewa, Azedine Ouerghi, Jyoti Maya Pandey, Peter Pojarski, Aleksandra Posarac, Aneeka Rahman, Jasmine Rajbhandary, Laura B. Rawlings, Setareh Razmara, Dena Ringold, Nina Rosas Raffo, Haneen Ismail Sayed, Anita M. Schwarz, Ahmad Shaheer Shahriar, Oleksiy A. Sluchynskyy, Julia Smolyar, Carlos Soto, Victoria Strokova, Shalika H. Subasinghe, Fanta Toure, Maurizia Tovo, James Tumwine, John Van Dyck, Rashiel Velarde, Andrea Vermehren, Giuseppe Zampaglione, and Eric Zapatero.

The External and Corporate Relations Publishing and Knowledge Division coordinated the design, typesetting, printing, and dissemination of the print and electronic versions of this report. Special thanks go to Steve Pazdan, Nancy Morrison, Paola Scalabrin, and Karol Keane. Thanks also to Muhamad Al Arief, our senior communications officer.

Structure of the Report

This report is the second edition of a series of periodic publications that monitor the state of safety nets. It does so by presenting key global safety net statistics on coverage, spending, policies, institutions, administration, and a range of performance-based dimensions. The 2015 edition of *The State of Social Safety Nets* presents a richer and more comprehensive set of data compared with the 2014 edition. The two editions are not strictly comparable because of different methods and data (see appendix A). The report is structured around five sections:

- Section 1 reviews key global safety net features based on the report's inventory of programs.
- Section 2 presents levels and patterns in countries' social safety net spending.
- Section 3 takes stock of key policy, institutional, and administrative developments.
- Section 4 discusses results on a range of performance indicators, including a snapshot of main results related to coverage and adequacy of safety net transfers and impact evaluations.
- Section 5 explores several emerging issues and practices of social safety nets in urban contexts—this year's special feature.

Each section contains a highlight that focuses on a special topic, and a set of seven appendixes presenting inventories, data, statistics, and resources complete the report.

Abbreviations

ADB	Asian Development Bank
ASPIRE	Atlas of Social Protection: Indicators of Resilience and Equity (World Bank)
AUP	asentamiento urbano precario (precarious urban settlement)
CCT	conditional cash transfer
CIT	conditional in-kind transfer
EAP	East Asia and Pacific
ECA	Europe and Central Asia
ECD	early childhood development
ECLAC	Economic Commission for Latin America and the Caribbean (United Nations)
ESSPROS	European System of Integrated Social Protection Statistics database (European Union)
HIC	high-income country
ILO	International Labour Organization
LAC	Latin America and the Caribbean
LIC	low-income country
LMIC	lower-middle-income country
MENA	Middle East and North Africa
MIC	middle-income country
MIS	management information system
OECD	Organisation for Economic Co-operation and Development
PMT	proxy-means-testing
PPP	purchasing power parity
PSNP	productive safety net program
SAR	South Asia region
SOCX	Social Expenditure Database (OECD)
SP	social protection
SPL	social protection and labor
SSA	Sub-Saharan Africa
SSN	social safety net
UCT	unconditional cash transfer
UIT	unconditional in-kind transfer
UMIC	upper-middle-income country
UN	United Nations
WFP	World Food Programme

Executive Summary

The objective of *The State of Social Nets* is to compile, analyze, and disseminate data and developments at the forefront of the social safety net agenda.[1] This series of periodic reports is part of broader efforts to monitor progress in the implementation of the World Bank 2012–22 Social Protection and Labor Strategy against the strategic goals of increasing coverage, especially among the poor, and enhancing integrated social protection and labor systems.[2]

This second edition of *The State of Social Safety Nets* examines trends in coverage, spending, and program performance based on the World Bank Atlas of Social Protection: Indicators of Resilience and Equity (ASPIRE) updated database. The report documents the main safety net programs that exist globally and the ways countries use them to alleviate poverty and build shared prosperity. Expanding on the 2014 edition, the analysis based on household survey data covers 44 additional countries and includes updated administrative information on spending and number of beneficiaries for 136 countries. This edition also includes a new section featuring a special theme, urban safety nets.

Interest in and use of social safety nets keep growing. Today's world of social safety nets is complex: an average developing country now has about 20 social safety net programs. As of 2015, every country in the world has at least one social safety net program in place. In the 136 countries for which beneficiary data are available in the World Bank's ASPIRE database, 1.9 billion people are on beneficiary rolls of social safety net programs, of which 44 percent receive in-kind transfers, 37 percent receive cash-based transfers, and 19 percent receive fee waivers.

While the number of countries with traditional social safety net programs—school feeding and in-kind transfers—remains stable, cash transfers are becoming more popular. In the past year, new information has become available for 11 countries with unconditional cash transfers (UCTs). In Africa, 40 countries (out of 48 in the region) have UCTs, a doubling since 2010. Twelve more countries have introduced the more institutionally demanding conditional cash transfer (CCT) programs. CCTs are now present in 64 countries, a dramatic increase from 2 countries in 1997 and 27 in 2008. Public works aimed at income transfers have been implemented in 94 countries—many of them are in conflict-affected and fragile states.

Despite remarkable progress over the past half decade, most of the poor remain outside the social safety net system, especially in lower-income countries. Low- and lower-middle-income countries have the lowest coverage levels of poor people in their societies, and the least ability to direct resources to those most in need. Only one-quarter of the poorest quintile are covered by social safety net programs in those contexts. The proportion grows to 64 percent in upper-middle-income countries. The coverage gap is particularly acute in Sub-Saharan Africa and South Asia, where most of the global poor live. In these regions, only one-tenth and one-fifth of the poorest 20 percent have access to social safety nets, respectively. Urban areas have serious gaps in coverage, at all income levels. While 285 million poor people live in cities in developing countries, reaching them presents special challenges, including identifying, targeting, communicating with, and enrolling perspective beneficiaries.

The outreach to the poor is increasing mostly through cash transfer programs. CCTs are playing a key role in expanding social safety net coverage of the poor in upper-middle-income countries, while school feeding programs and public works provide the greatest coverage in lower-income countries—although limited.

Countries at all levels of income are investing in social safety nets. Low-income and middle-income countries devote approximately the same level of resources to social safety nets (1.5 and 1.6 percent of gross domestic product [GDP], respectively), while richer countries spend 1.9 percent of GDP on them. However, some lower-income countries allocate more funds than the global average. For example, Sierra Leone commits 4.8 percent of GDP to safety nets and Lesotho spends 6.6 percent, while Georgia, a lower-middle-income country, spends 7 percent of GDP. This suggests that spending on safety nets reflects not just income, but policy priorities, history, composition of the overall social protection systems, and contextual factors (such as being a fragile state). Cash transfers constitute the highest share of spending in all regions except Sub-Saharan Africa, where food and in-kind transfers are the dominant component (comprising 27 percent of total safety net spending, on average). Among cash-based transfers, social pensions account for the highest share of expenditures, followed by poverty-targeted transfers.

Countries are investing in social safety nets to reap the benefits of human capital development and income-generating activities. Empirical evidence based on rigorous impact evaluations keeps growing and offering new insights on the transformational role of social safety nets. Since 2014, an additional 23 impact evaluations (building on 145 reviewed until then) have been published. More than half of them focus on Sub-Saharan Africa. Newer studies confirm the positive and significant impacts of cash transfers on school enrollment and attendance; increased live births in safer facilities; improved prenatal and postnatal care; regular growth monitoring of children during critically important early ages; and enhanced food security. The studies also delve deeper into the productive impacts of cash transfers, demonstrating how predictable cash transfers enhance households' investment in activities to generate agricultural and nonagricultural income. Cash transfers also have major positive spillover effects on the local economy of target communities. Evidence collected from the "From Protection to Production Project" in Africa shows that these programs have a nominal income multiplier ranging from US$1.34 to US$2.52 for each US$1.00 transferred.

Impacts on reducing the poverty gap depend on how well the poor are covered and on the adequacy of benefits, among other factors. Countries typically strike a balance within a given budgetary framework between expanding coverage and providing more adequate transfers to a smaller group of beneficiaries. For example, Mauritius and Hungary achieve the same poverty reduction effect with quite different combinations of adequacy and coverage. Higher levels of spending are typically associated with higher impacts on poverty; however, even within similar budgets, some countries do better than others at each level of spending. This pattern allows performance to be benchmarked against countries at the cost-effectiveness "frontier." Successful countries are reducing the poverty gap by more than 50 percent compared to income levels before the transfer. When countries are spending less than the global average on their safety nets, they find that impacts on poverty reduction are lower, with only 10–20 percent of the poverty gap eliminated.

In most countries, the size of safety net transfers is not adequate to close the poverty gap, particularly in low-income countries. The average level of cash benefits is only 10 percent of the poor's consumption across low-income countries. It represents 21 percent of the poor's consumption in lower-middle-income countries and 37 percent in upper-middle-income countries. Transfer amounts represent approximately one-fifth of the income needed to close the poverty gap in low-income countries and half the income needed in lower-middle-income countries. On average, they are adequate to lift a poor person out of poverty only in upper-middle-income countries.

The targeting of social safety nets is generally pro-poor, but there is room for improvement. CCTs are the best targeted programs, devoting as much as 50 percent of benefits to the poorest quintile in the case of the large-scale CCT programs in Latin America and 46 percent in the case of more recently established programs (such as the Pantawid in the Philippines). Social pensions and UCTs are less well targeted to the poor, although by design a number of them are categorical programs (or programs that use specific categories or population groups to define benefit eligibility, such as children allowances or universal social pensions for all citizens above a certain age).

To increase the efficiency of safety nets, better-coordinated systems are required. Protecting the poor and the vulnerable and allowing them to avail themselves of opportunities requires integrated systems, necessitating multiple social protection programs to work together. A coherent system starts with a plan and a policy framework to guide multiple social protection interventions. In recent years, the number of countries with a solid social protection framework in place has grown considerably. As of 2015, 77 countries have a social protection policy in place, while 31 countries are currently planning or formulating one. This planning and policy work is key to ensuring a coherent strategic framework that can guide multiple social protection interventions.

The adoption of social and beneficiary registries is growing steadily. At least 21 countries have a fully institutionalized social registry. An additional 26 countries, including many in Sub-Saharan Africa, are in the process of building registries. At least 26 countries have fully operational beneficiary registries, while another 16 are currently developing theirs. These registries range from serving a single program to 80 different programs, as in Chile.

Spending efficiency can be improved by strengthening the institutional capacity, coordination, and programs' administration and evaluation. The efficient implementation of social protection systems requires tools that facilitate the selection of beneficiaries, service delivery, and monitoring of both processes and outcomes. Countries are increasingly investing in management information systems and targeting approaches of varying complexity and sophistication, allowing more efficient management of safety net programs.

There is growing interest in the role that safety nets can play in urban areas, including the emergence of a first generation of urban programs. At least a dozen countries are undergoing an iterative process of experimentation, learning, and organic adaptation of programs to urban areas, in terms of both operational "nuts and bolts" (or basic elements for a program to be implemented) and strengthening integration to other sectors. For example, in Mexico, about 40 percent of the beneficiaries of Prospera (formerly Oportunidades) live in urban and peri-urban areas, up from 7 percent at the early stages of roll-out in 1997–98. In China, urban Dibao beneficiaries rose from 0.85 million in 1996 to 21.4 in 2013. Lessons from the first years of introduction and scale-up will help inform learning within and across countries in cutting-edge areas for the social protection agenda.

Future editions of *The State of Social Safety Nets* series will continue to stay up to date with the latest innovations and progress in the ever-changing landscape of social safety nets around the world.

As countries continue to roll out, expand, and refine their social safety nets and integrate them into social protection systems, there will be new developments in policy, program design, administration, and evaluation. New and updated data—from both surveys and administrative data—will provide ongoing snapshots of the latest available information on the efficiency and effectiveness of safety nets in reducing poverty and building shared prosperity.

Notes

1. *Social safety nets* are noncontributory measures designed to provide regular and predictable support to poor and vulnerable people. These are also referred to as safety nets, social assistance, or social transfers and are a component of larger social protection systems.

2. The World Bank 2012–2022 Social Protection and Labor Strategy (www.worldbank.org/spstrategy) states that the "overarching goals of the strategy are to help improve resilience, equity, and opportunity for people in both low- and middle-income countries through integrated social protection and labor systems, increasing coverage of social safety net programs, especially in lower-income countries, and improved evidence."

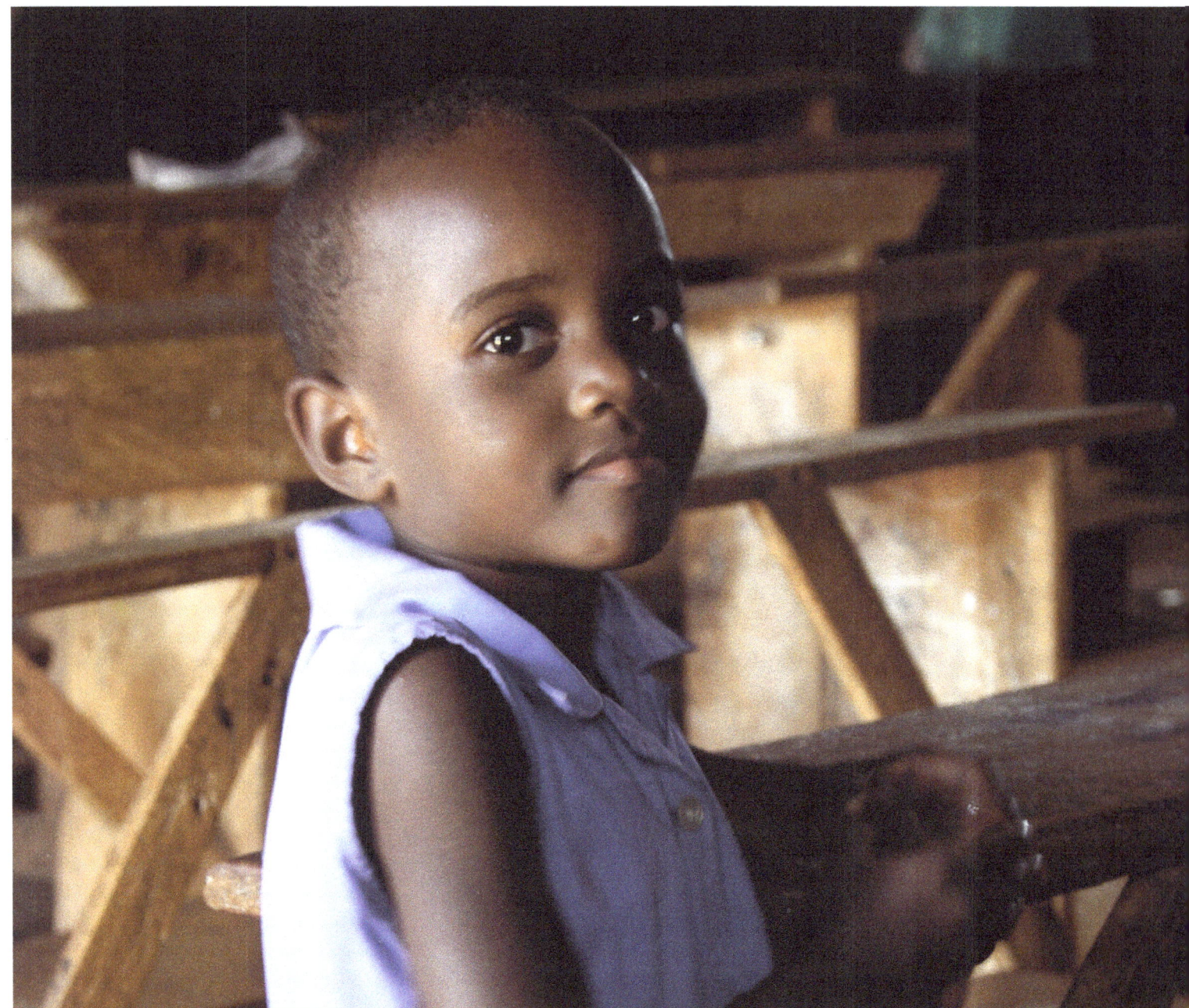

Section 1.

Inventory of Social Safety Net Programs

This section examines the coverage of social safety nets, both across the total population and among the poor. To do so, the analysis is based on the most recently available administrative data in the World Bank Atlas of Social Protection: Indicators of Resilience and Equity (ASPIRE) database and on updated coverage indicators from household surveys. The analysis starts with the definition of social safety net programs of various forms and presents their distribution across regions and income groups. This is followed by an examination of enrollment rates and coverage rates. Enrollment rates are defined as the number of beneficiaries on the rolls of all social safety net programs, as a percent of the population. Coverage rates refer to the actual number of recipients of social safety nets in cash, in-kind, or near-cash as percent of total population.[1] The analysis chiefly draws from administrative data on program numbers of beneficiaries in the ASPIRE database and is complemented by data from other international agencies.

Definitions

Social safety nets are noncontributory measures designed to provide regular and predictable support to poor and vulnerable people. They are also referred to as *safety nets*, *social assistance*, or *social transfers*, and are a component of larger social protection systems.

In general, *social protection*[2] also includes *social insurance*, such as health insurance, as well as labor market programs. Figure 1.1 positions social safety nets within this group of programs and transfers and provides examples of programs that fall under the remit of social safety nets and possible areas of overlap with other social protection components.

In this report, social safety net programs have been examined in line with international standards as noncontributory programs in cash or in kind[3] meant to support the poor and vulnerable. However, because of the way countries may define their safety net universe, the review also considers measures that provide access to various essential public services, including basic services such as health, education, and housing through fee waivers.[4]

The review does not consider generalized subsidies as part of safety nets, which in most cases include regressive interventions tied to fuel and energy consumption. Box 1.1 defines the resulting types of social safety net programs considered in the analysis.

Based on such an approach, the report identified 589 programs in 145 developing countries, economies, and territories (out of the 157 surveyed, of which 136 have detailed program-level data on number of beneficiaries enrolled) (see appendixes A and B).[5] For each program, appendix C reports the number of beneficiaries and the program-specific source of information.

Types and Coverage of Safety Net Programs

The use of social safety net instruments keeps growing around the world, especially the use of cash-based programs (see box 1.2). The expansion of cash transfers is particularly evident in Sub-Saharan Africa. For example, in 2010, about half the countries in the continent (21) had some form of unconditional cash transfers (UCTs) in place; by 2014, new information had become available showing that the number of countries implementing UCTs had almost doubled to 40. Globally, the number of countries with conditional cash transfers (CCTs) increased dramatically from 27 in 2008 to 64 in 2014. Public works have been implemented in 94 countries—many of them fragile and conflict-affected situations (figure 1.2).

Every country has at least one social safety net program in place. School feeding programs and UCTs are the most prevalent type of transfer: they are present in 131 and 130 countries, respectively. In almost one-quarter of the cases, or 37 countries, the cash transfers are in the form of social pensions. Public works are the

The use of social safety net instruments keeps growing around the world, especially the use of cash-based programs.

■ Main Messages for Section 1

- The portfolio of social safety net programs is large and diverse. A developing country runs about 20 different safety net programs, on average. Cash transfers and school feeding programs are present in almost all countries.
- Worldwide, 1.9 billion people are enrolled in social safety net programs.
- The world's five largest social safety net programs are all in middle-income countries and reach over 526 million people.
- Cash transfers are becoming more popular and increasingly complex. Conditional cash transfer programs are now present in 64 countries, a dramatic increase from 2 countries in 1997 and 27 countries in 2008.

Figure 1.1 How social safety nets fall within social protection and labor systems

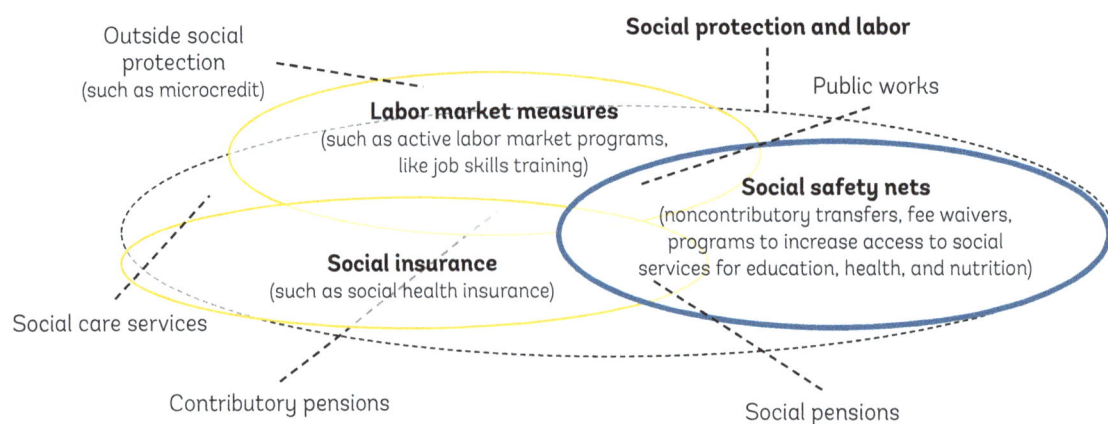

Box 1.1 **Types of Safety Nets**

This report considers six types of social safety net programs: conditional cash transfers, unconditional cash transfers, school feeding programs, unconditional in-kind transfers, public works, and fee waivers.

Conditional cash transfers (CCTs) are periodic monetary benefits to poor households that require beneficiaries to comply with specific behavioral requirements to encourage investments in human capital (such as school attendance, immunizations, and health checkups). The report includes under the category of CCTs any cash transfer program that has a conditionality component in its operation manual, even if it is weakly conditioned or weakly enforced (*soft conditionalities*). Examples include programs that combine one or more conditions, such as ensuring a minimum level of school attendance by children, undertaking regular visits to health facilities, or attending skills training programs. CCTs also include school stipend programs to cover school fees and other costs of schooling. The Philippines' Pantawid program falls under this category.

Unconditional cash transfers (UCTs) provide cash without particular co-responsibilities for beneficiaries; they may spend the cash as they wish. Examples embrace various cash transfer programs targeted to particular categories of people, such as the elderly (also known as *social pensions*); family allowances, including birth grants and supplements for adult dependents; and cash transfers specifically targeted to children, including orphan and foster family allowances. The Hunger Safety Net Program in Kenya is an example. Although sometimes similar, UCTs differ from CCTs since they are not conditioned on pre-established behavioral requirements.

School feeding programs. Like CCTs, school feeding requires forms of compliance, such as ensuring a certain level of monthly school attendance. However, the form of transfer is in kind. Sometimes these programs also include "take-home" food rations for children's families. An example is Brazil's Programa Nacional de Alimentacao Escola.

Unconditional in-kind transfers allow the distribution of food or other in-kind transfers without any form of conditionality or co-responsibility. Examples include the provision of fortified food supplements to malnourished pregnant women and children. The Programa Nacional de Reabilitação Nutricional in Mozambique provides a comprehensive nutrition rehabilitation program for children and adults who are severely malnourished.

(continued)

Box 1.1 *(Continued)*

Public works programs (PWs) engage participants in manual, labor-oriented activities such as building or rehabilitating community assets and public infrastructure. Examples include seasonal labor-intensive works for poor and food insecure populations. Public works implemented under the Productive Safety Net Program in Ethiopia illustrate this type of safety net.

Fee waivers assist households in meeting the cost for a defined class of services, particularly related to education, health, and housing. Waivers can apply to either partial or discounted fees, as well as to other charges or expenditures. The Capitation Grant Program in Ghana, which helps households access primary health care services at no cost for them, epitomizes this category.

next most common type of assistance and are in place in 94 countries. CCTs continue to expand. They are present in almost half the countries (64) in the sample (figure 1.3).

There is great diversity in program portfolios. In particular, 62 percent of countries (98) have at least four program types; 33 countries have two or three types; and 26 countries have only one or none of the types (appendix C). Diversification is greater in Latin American and Caribbean, Eastern European, and Central Asian countries, while the portfolio of programs tends to be more concentrated on two or three intervention types in East Asia and Pacific and the Middle East and North Africa.

The prevalence of program types varies by regions and by countries' income levels. Table 1.1 reports the number of countries in each region with at least one program of a given

type. Almost all countries in Europe and Central Asia—29 out of 30—have a UCT program. Unconditional in-kind transfers and public works are most prevalent in Africa, where 42 and 39 countries (out of 49), respectively, have such programs. CCTs, historically a trademark of the Latin America region, are expanding in all regions, especially in Africa, where soft conditionalities in the form of sensitization campaigns to encourage access to social services and community-based trainings to promote positive behavioral changes have been introduced within cash transfer programs, as in Burkina Faso, Cameroon, the Republic of Congo, Ghana, Niger, Tanzania, and Togo.

The prevalence of program types differs by countries' income levels. Both conditional and unconditional in-kind transfers are equally prevalent among low-income countries, middle-

Box 1.2 What "Conditionality" Really Implies

The dichotomy between unconditional and conditional cash transfers is not sharp; rather, there is a great deal of variation in the intensity of the conditionality. Conditional cash transfers (CCTs) may vary considerably in terms of level of planning, monitoring, and enforcement of compliance. For example, Baird, De Hoop, and Özler (2013) distinguish four categories of conditionalities with respect to education-related conditions: (1) explicit conditions on paper and/or encouragement of children's schooling, but no monitoring or enforcement (an example is Ecuador's Bono de Desarollo Humano); (2) explicit conditions, monitored with

minimal enforcement (examples are Brazil's Bolsa Familia and Mexico's PROSPERA); (3) explicit conditions with monitoring and enforcement of enrollment condition (an example is Cambodia's CESSP Scholarship Program); and (4) explicit conditions with monitoring and enforcement of attendance condition (examples are Malawi's SIHR CCT arm and China's Pilot CCT program).

Their main finding is that programs that are explicitly conditional, monitor compliance, and penalize noncompliance have substantively larger effects on children's school enrollment.

Source: Baird, De Hoop, and Özler 2013.

Figure 1.2 Social safety net programs have been rising steadily

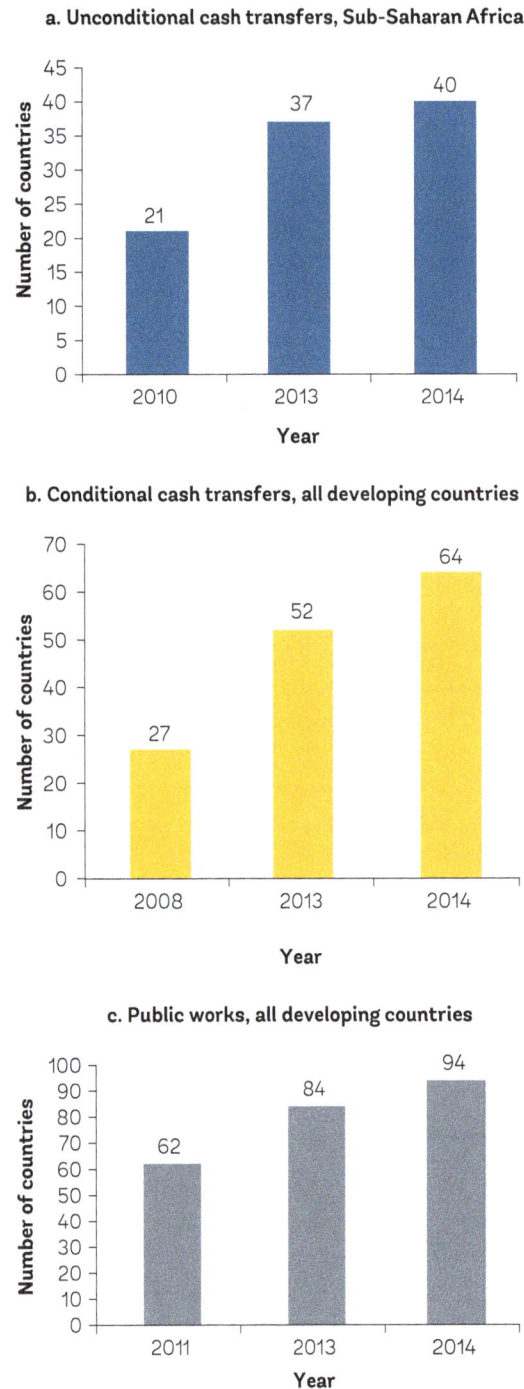

a. Unconditional cash transfers, Sub-Saharan Africa

b. Conditional cash transfers, all developing countries

c. Public works, all developing countries

Sources: World Bank for 2013–14 based on ASPIRE database; see appendix C of this report for specific sources. For unconditional cash transfers in 2010, see Garcia and Moore 2011. Data for 2008 for conditional cash transfers are from Fiszbein and Schady 2009. For public works up to 2011, the number refers to countries as reported in Subbarao and others 2013.

the world are concentrated in low-income and lower-middle-income countries (table 1.2).

By 2014, more than 1.9 billion people in the developing world—about a third of the population in these countries—were beneficiaries of social safety net programs, according to the administrative data at the program level for 136 countries analyzed in this report. This large number is driven in part by very large programs in the largest countries such as China and India.

Cash transfers are the largest programs worldwide in terms of flagship programs. However, in terms of combined beneficiary numbers, in-kind assistance and fee waivers continue to dominate. Almost one-third of the global client load of safety net programs, or around 600 million people, is accounted for by in-kind and food transfers; 14 percent by school feeding (reaching 276 million people); and another 19 percent by fee waivers and targeted subsidies (reaching 381 million people). UCT and CCT programs, including public works, combined reach 718 million people, 36 percent of global capacity. Again, this result is driven by several very large in-kind programs. However, when looking at the largest programs only by type, cash transfer programs account for over 50 percent of the beneficiaries in social safety net programs as of 2014.

The five largest social safety net programs in the world account for about half of global coverage, reaching over 526 million people. They are all in middle-income countries. The Chinese Dibao is the largest UCT program, reaching about 75 million individuals. With coverage of almost 78 million people per year, the Janani Suraksha Yojana in India is the largest CCT in the world. Three Indian programs are among the largest in each of the types. Beyond CCTs, the School Feeding Program (reaching 105 million people) and the Mahatma Gandhi National Rural Employment Guarantee Scheme (reaching 182 million people) are the largest-scale social safety nets globally. The Child Support Grant in South Africa is the largest social safety net in Africa, followed by Ethiopia's Productive Safety Nets Program (table 1.3).

The coverage of individual flagship programs varies greatly, ranging from less than 1 percent of the population in some countries to over 40 percent in Malaysia, Moldova, Turkey, and El Salvador (table 1.4).

In most countries, some beneficiaries of social safety net programs benefit from multiple forms

income countries, and upper-middle-income countries. Among other instruments, in-kind assistance and public works are concentrated at the lower part of the country income spectrum: two-thirds of public works programs around

Figure 1.3 School feeding programs are the most prevalent type of social safety net

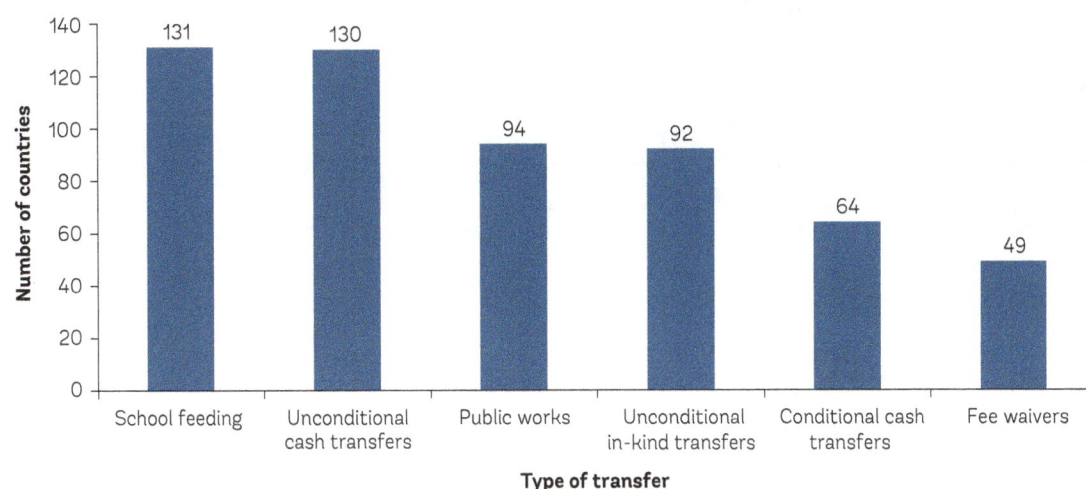

Source: ASPIRE; see appendix C.

Table 1.1   Number of Countries with at Least One Type of Social Safety Net Program, by Region
Number of countries

Program type	Region						Total of countries with at least one program
	Africa	East Asia and Pacific	Europe and Central Asia	Latin America and the Caribbean	Middle East and North Africa	South Asia	
Conditional cash transfers	18	7	7	22	5	4	63
Unconditional cash transfers	41	11	29	28	14	7	130
Unconditional in-kind transfers	42	7	8	24	7	4	92
School feeding	45	12	23	28	16	7	131
Public works	39	9	17	17	7	5	94
Fee waivers	12	7	14	10	3	3	49
Total number of countries in respective region	48	21	30	29	19	8	157

Source: ASPIRE, appendix C.

of social safety nets. The provision of different benefits can be measured through enrollment rates of beneficiaries to different programs.[6] Globally, over 68 countries (about half of those included in the analysis) have low enrollment rates—including programs with well below 20 percent of their total population (figure 1.4). This means that, by definition, they cannot include all of the poorest in at least one of their programs (an example is Senegal). Conversely, countries whose rate is above 100 percent provide some form of double benefit to their citizens. Those multiple benefits can be a desirable and positive feature when interventions respond to different household needs or provide pathways to graduation. In other cases, such overlaps may signal gaps and inefficiencies (as in Georgia, Latvia, Moldova, Sri Lanka, and Turkey). This issue is discussed further in section 4.

Cash transfer programs account for about half the total social safety net beneficiary rolls. They range from being the predominant form of social safety net (in Malaysia, Moldova, Trinidad and Tobago, and Vietnam) to being practically absent in safety net systems with both extensive (Mozambique, Niger, Sri Lanka) and low coverage (Bhutan, Cambodia, Guinea). Despite these extremes, most countries rely on both cash and noncash forms of social safety nets to reach their beneficiaries. Fragile and conflict-affected situations tend to rely on social safety net programs more than other areas. In

Table 1.2 Number of Countries with at Least One Type of Social Safety Net Program, by Country Income Group

Number of countries

Program type	Income group				Total of countries with at least one program
	Low-income	Lower-middle-income	Upper-middle-income	High-income	
Conditional cash transfers	14	22	21	6	63
Unconditional cash transfers	28	42	44	16	130
Unconditional in-kind transfers	29	33	25	5	92
School feeding	31	42	42	16	131
Public works	30	35	23	6	94
Fee waivers	8	17	19	5	49
Total number of countries in respective income group	33	50	53	21	157

Source: ASPIRE, appendix C.

these settings, social safety nets help prevent common and damaging coping strategies, such as selling assets, which affected populations resort to in time of stress (see highlight 1, on fragile and conflict-affected situations).

Social safety nets can counteract shocks if programs can be scaled up rapidly after a shock. In 2014–15, a range of countries have used those interventions as a first-line response to large natural disasters. Growing

Table 1.3 Top Five Social Safety Net Programs, by Scale

Conditional cash transfers		
Country	Program name	Beneficiaries (millions)
India	Janani Suraksha Yojana	78
Brazil	Bolsa Familia	49
Mexico	Prospera	26
Philippines	Pantawid	19
Colombia	Familias en Accion	12

Unconditional cash transfers		
Country	Program name	Beneficiaries (millions)
China	Di-Bao	75
India	IG National Old Age Pension Scheme	21
Indonesia	Bangtuan Langsung Tui	16
Malaysia	BR1M	15
South Africa	Child Support Grant	11

Unconditional in-kind/near-cash transfers		
Country	Program name	Beneficiaries (millions)
Turkey	Gida Yardimi	9
Mexico	Milk grant benefit	6
China	Wubao	6
Sudan	General food distribution program	5
Ghana	Free uniforms/books	5

(Table continues next page)

Table 1.3 Top Five Social Safety Net Programs, by Scale
(Continued)

School feeding		
Country	**Program name**	**Beneficiaries (millions)**
India	School feeding	105
Brazil	Program de Alimentacao Escolar	47
China	School feeding	26
South Africa	School feeding	9
Egypt, Arab Rep.	School feeding	7

Public works programs		
Country	**Program name**	**Beneficiaries (millions)**
India	MGNREG	182
Ethiopia	PSNP[a]	7
Morocco	INDH	4
Russian Federation	Regional public works	2
Bangladesh	EGPP	1

Fee waivers		
Country	**Program name**	**Beneficiaries (millions)**
Indonesia	Jamkesmas, including Jampersal	86
China	Medical assistance	42
Philippines	PhilHealth	39
Turkey	Green card	36
Ukraine	Housing and utility allowances	5

Source: ASPIRE, appendix C.
Note: Numbers refer to *individual* beneficiaries. In cases where number of beneficiaries data are reported at the household level, the official average household size is used to approximate an individual beneficiary: Brazil = 3.47; Malaysia = 3 (approximate); Philippines = 4.6; Turkey = 3.8; Ukraine = 2.7.
a. About 80 percent of Productive Safety Nets Program (PSNP) beneficiaries participate in public works.

Table 1.4 Top Five Social Safety Net Programs, Share of Population
Percent of total population

Conditional cash transfers		
Country	**Program name**	**Percent of population**
Honduras	Bono 10,000	29
Colombia	Familias en Accion	25
Brazil	Bolsa Familia	24
Mexico	Prospera	21
Philippines	Pantawid	21

Unconditional cash transfers		
Country	**Program name**	**Percent of population**
Malaysia	BR1M	51
Yemen, Rep.	Social Welfare Fund	31
Azerbaijan	Targeted social assistance	29
Georgia	Targeted social assistance	25
Estonia	Subsistence benefit	24

(Table continues next page)

Table 1.4 Top Five Social Safety Net Programs, Share of Population (Continued)

Unconditional in-kind/near-cash transfers		
Country	**Program name**	**Percent of population**
El Salvador	Programa de Agricultura Familiar	42
Niger	Saving Lives	23
Senegal	CSA	21
Ghana	Free exercise books	18
Yemen, Rep.	Emergency Food and Nutrition Support	18

School feeding		
Country	**Program name**	**Percent of population**
Swaziland	School meal program	26
Timor-Leste	School feeding program	24
Brazil	Program de Alimentacao Escolar	24
El Salvador	Alimentacion Escolar	23
Lesotho	School feeding program	21

Public works programs		
Country	**Program name**	**Percent of population**
India	MGNREG	15
Sierra Leone	Rural Public Works	13
Morocco	INDH	12
South Sudan	Food-for-assets	8
Malawi	Public works program	8

Fee waivers		
Country	**Program name**	**Percent of population**
Turkey	Green card	48
Moldova	Heating allowance	46
Philippines	PhilHealth	40
Indonesia	Jamkesmas, including Jampersal	34
Latvia	Housing benefit	22

Source: ASPIRE, appendixes B and C.
Note: Numbers refer to program *individual* beneficiaries as percent of total population, as reported in appendix B. In cases where data on number of beneficiaries are reported at the household level, the official average household size is used to approximate an individual beneficiary: Brazil = 3.47; Ecuador = 5.0; Estonia = 2.3; Georgia = 2.66; Moldova = 3.0; Philippines = 4.6; Turkey = 3.8.

investments are being made to embed ex ante disaster prevention into safety net approaches, especially in areas prone to recurrent covariate shocks. In other cases, crises are also evolving in nature, with safety nets responding to new and complex forms of widespread epidemics, such as in the case of Ebola in West Africa (box 1.3).

Figure 1.4 Enrollment rates in social safety net programs vary by country, with over half not enrolling even the bottom fifth of the population

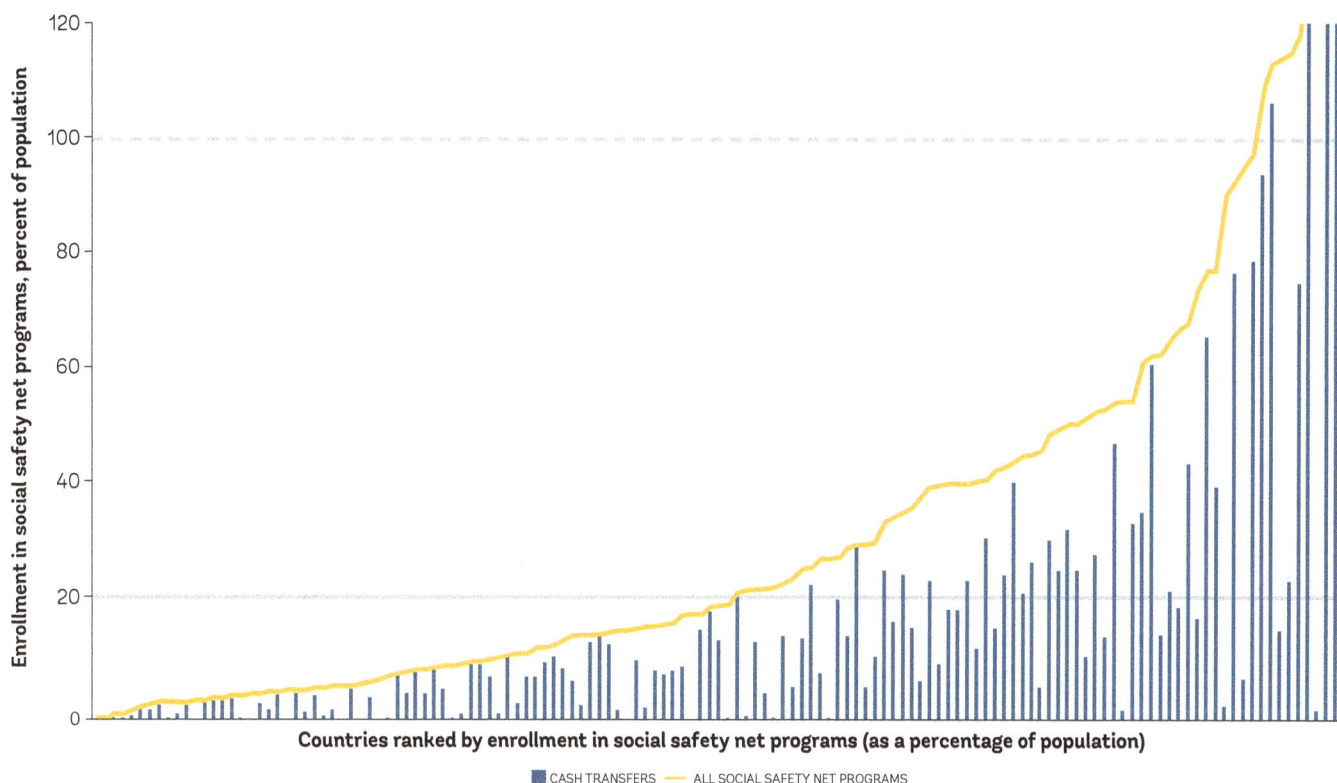

Source: ASPIRE (administrative data for 136 countries).
Note: Enrollment rates are defined as the number of beneficiaries on the rolls of all social safety net programs, as a percent of the population. Beneficiary rolls are based on administrative data. Enrollment rates include double counting of beneficiaries; as such, they should not be interpreted as a measure of coverage (hence totals may add up to more than 100 percent).

Box 1.3   Response to the Ebola Outbreak in West Africa

In 2014, the most widespread epidemic of the Ebola virus disease in history spread across several West African countries. It struck Guinea in December 2013 and then crept into Liberia and Sierra Leone. By February 2015, the World Health Organization (WHO) reported a total of 23,729 confirmed, probable, and suspected cases of Ebola, and 9,604 deaths. Sierra Leone endured the worst impact. Since the outbreak, more than 1,300 foreign medical personnel have been deployed in these countries. The outbreak has severely crippled the health system and is having drastic economic impacts, with continued job losses, and schools were not set to reopen until early 2015. Fear of Ebola has hampered trade, shuttered businesses, and restricted travel in the affected countries. As a result, many households have been forced to take short-term actions to cope, which can have substantial long-term effects on welfare. The World Bank Group estimates that these countries will lose at least US$1.6 billion in forgone economic growth in 2015 as a result. Guinea, Liberia, and Sierra Leone are being supported with immediate responses to the health and food security concerns. Provisions have been made for treatment and care to contain and prevent the spread of infections, help communities cope with the economic impact, and improve public health systems.

Ebola Impact, Recovery, and Scaling Up of Social Protection

Like other epidemics, the main impacts of the Ebola crisis are indirect economic

(continued)

Box 1.3 *(Continued)*

impacts as people have changed their behaviors (a behavioral response). For instance, many people stopped working because they were afraid or they faced restrictions on movements. Liberian and Sierra Leonean households surveyed in late 2014 and January 2015 report having sold assets, sold or slaughtered livestock, borrowed money, sent children to live with relatives, drawn down savings, or delayed investments in order to cope (World Bank 2015). Declines in employment are evident both among wage workers and the nonfarm self-employed in urban areas, especially in Free Town.

To mitigate the negative impacts, governments of the affected countries, with support from many international donors, are improving food security in the worst affected areas and are rapidly scaling up existing safety net programs, particularly cash transfers and public works programs. The World Bank Group has supported efforts to rapidly expand delivery of cash transfers in all three countries, totaling US$14 million. It is devoting another US$32 million to scaling up safety nets, with a continued emphasis on building the administrative and delivery capacity of systems, especially in Liberia and Sierra Leone. Beyond safety nets, substantial World Bank Group resources in the three worst-affected countries and Guinea-Bissau have been redirected toward logistics, community sensitization, disease surveillance, and data collection systems to monitor the socioeconomic impacts of the disease to inform the Ebola response going forward.

In Liberia and Sierra Leone, existing delivery mechanisms for safety net programs, including e-payments, will be used to scale up and deliver targeted cash transfers in affected areas. Since February 2015, the Sierra Leone government, with World Bank Group support, has been scaling up complementary cash transfer interventions to mitigate the socioeconomic impacts of Ebola. Some 5,000 youth have participated in public works, and more than 10,000 beneficiaries have been enrolled in two cash transfer programs. In February 2015, the Liberian government launched a public works project to reach over 10,000 poor youth, plus a cash transfer program targeting 10,000 extremely poor labor-constrained individuals and households affected by Ebola. In Guinea, the cash-for-work activity of the Productive Safety Nets Project has continued operating throughout the Ebola epidemic, providing 12,000 temporary jobs as of January 2015. The United Nations, together with other development partners, including the World Bank Group, is initiating an Ebola Recovery Assessment (ERA) covering Guinea, Liberia, and Sierra Leone. The assessment aims to identify a post-Ebola recovery agenda connecting and building upon the ongoing response effort.

Source: World Bank 2015.

Notes

1. *In-kind transfers* provide additional resources to beneficiary households by making food or other goods and services available to them at no cost when they need it most, in such forms as food rations, supplementary and school feeding programs, and emergency food distribution. *Near-cash transfers* include food stamps, coupons, or vouchers that may be used by households to purchase food (or other commodities or services that are subsidized through this mechanism) at the authorized retail locations or providers.

2. Definitions of social protection abound. Generally, *social protection and labor* refer to the set of policies and programs aimed at preventing or protecting all people against poverty, vulnerability, and social exclusion throughout their life cycles, with a particular emphasis on vulnerable groups. Social protection can be provided in cash or in kind, through noncontributory schemes, providing universal, categorical, or poverty-targeted benefits such as social assistance or social safety nets, contributory schemes with social insurance being the most common form, and by building human capital, productive assets, and access to productive jobs. The definition in the report is consistent with the definition from the World Bank Social Protection Strategy 2012–2022: "Social protection and labor systems, policies, and programs help individuals and societies manage risk and volatility and protect them from poverty and destitution—through instruments that improve resilience, equity, and opportunity."

3. Although vouchers or near-cash transfers have a number of commonalities and differences with cash and in-kind modalities, vouchers are considered in the report as part of a broader set of in-kind transfers.

4. Fee waivers may involve a partial or full reduction in a fee or price, hence requiring beneficiaries to cover part of the service or commodity cost (in cases of extreme hardship, the service or commodity is provided for free). In a strict sense, therefore, those measures are not entirely noncontributory (beneficiaries must contribute by paying part of the price in most cases). However, they are commonly considered part of the national safety net portfolio in this report.

5. See appendix A for a description of the methodology used and definitions of social protection concepts and programs. See appendix B for the sample of countries, economies, and territories analyzed in this report, and their income group according to the most recent World Bank classification (2015).

6. The measure clearly includes multiple instances of double-counting of beneficiaries; as such, it cannot be interpreted as a measure of coverage.

References

Baird, S., J. De Hoop, and B. Özler. 2013. "Income Shocks and Adolescent Mental Health." *Journal of Human Resources* 48 (2): 370–403.

Fiszbein, A., and N. Schady. 2009. "Conditional Cash Transfers: Reducing Present and Future Poverty." World Bank Policy Research Report, World Bank, Washington, DC.

Garcia, M., and C. M. T. Moore. 2011. *The Cash Dividend: The Rise of Cash Transfer Programs in Sub-Saharan Africa*. Directions in Development Series. Washington, DC: World Bank.

Subbarao, K., C. del Ninno, C. Andrews, and C. Rodríguez-Alas. 2013. *Public Works as a Safety Net: Design, Evidence, and Implementation*. Directions in Development Series. Washington, DC: World Bank.

World Bank. 2015. *The Socio-Economic Impacts of Ebola: Results from a High Frequency Cell Phone Survey in Sierra Leone and Liberia*. Washington, DC: World Bank.

Less than one-fifth of the world's population lived in fragile and conflict-affected situations in 2010, yet these areas were home to about one-third of the world's poor (World Bank 2011).[1] The prevalence of poverty in fragile situations is double that in nonfragile situations. This high prevalence is both a by-product and a cause of fragility.

It is important to recognize "fragility" as a dynamic and multidimensional concept. Fragility extends over a broad spectrum of circumstances that manifest in a range of countries, economies, and territories, including the Arab Republic of Egypt, Iraq, Myanmar, Sierra Leone, Timor-Leste, and the Republic of Yemen. Perhaps a better way of approaching fragility is to differentiate among contexts by considering an entity's level of resilience, as suggested in the literature. Resilience is defined as the capacity of a political and social system to adapt to shocks (see OECD 2008 and World Bank 2011). Unlike the more amorphous concept of fragility, this is a highly useful concept, in that it is more aligned with the process any entity—a person, a family, a community, or a country—needs to go through when facing multiple challenges.

Safety net programs and policies in fragile and conflict-affected situations have a particularly difficult role of balancing short-term emergency needs (in response to conflict or natural disaster) with longer-term needs of reducing chronic poverty and inequality. Beyond the income support function, safety net schemes also have an important social stability function. By establishing regular and predictable support, these schemes are able to initiate or reestablish a form of social contract between the authorities and the people, and reinstate some level of trust and mutual confidence between citizens and government.

Social safety nets are among the main instruments for building resilience and for protecting the poor in fragile, conflict-, and violence-affected situations.

Though interest exists in building safety net systems, most interventions in fragile and conflict-affected situations remain somewhat ad hoc and opportunistic. The most prevalent types of programs are school feeding, food, in-kind, and near-cash transfers, followed by public works programs. In weak enabling environments—which are prone to frequent emergencies and sporadic and/or regional violence, and must contend with weak governments—social safety nets often make use of community structures, particularly to facilitate access to services and to implement public works, livelihood support, or school feeding programs.

Three main lessons can be drawn from recent experience. First, institutional/human capacity is a main determinant of the design of social protection and labor (SPL) programs in fragile and conflict-affected situations. Despite continued social and security unrest, for instance, the Republic of Yemen has rapidly and successfully scaled up its Social Welfare Fund. From an initial coverage of 100,000 beneficiaries in 2001, it expanded to 1.5 million households during the 2011 political crisis, while its budget grew from US$4 million at the onset (2001) to around US$300 million in

2012. This program clearly shows that with moderate capacity and an average enabling environment, rapid scale up is possible, provided there is political will.

Second, building programs by utilizing existing social institutions or community-based approaches can help ensure program success, impact, and sustainability. In fragile and conflict-affected situations, service delivery channels can be replaced with a less formal organization/body. This approach has been successful in different contexts, including Angola, Rwanda, Togo, and the Republic of Yemen. When designing and delivering SPL policies/programs, these realities should be taken into account, particularly the interface between the government and other actors. Appropriate roles should be assigned to existing social and institutional structures such as community, religious, and nongovernmental organizations. All have valuable links to hard-to-reach groups. Villages in Togo, for instance, have long-standing school feeding programs that made use of *femmes-mamans,* female vendors who prepare food for beneficiary school children. Using this existing informal social mechanism has been a successful approach for a low-capacity setting—and has reached a large number of beneficiaries. A nutritional assessment has shown that the school meals being served are providing between 60 and 90 percent of the daily caloric intake needed for primary school–age children.

Third, an incremental approach to building cohesive social assistance policies appears to work even in the most fragile environments. Many fragile and conflict-affected situations have nascent programs that have built on experience, such as starting reforms around a single program in West Bank and Gaza, and building administrative systems around it. Moreover, administrative reforms are often easier and less controversial than policy-related ones, and help build evidence about efficiency gains and impact. Making use of technology to improve coverage and governance also helps, such as using smart cards, mobile technology, and banking systems effectively for monitoring and payments, as in Lebanon and Sierra Leone. Focusing on building registries and management information system platforms is crucial and provides large efficiency gains in the face of shocks. The World Bank supported such efforts in Kosovo and the Republic of Yemen. Focusing on moving toward poverty-based targeting and consolidating social assistance benefits to be targeted through one mechanism, as done in the Republic of Yemen, has the potential to yield good results.

Note
1. This highlight is based on Ovadiya and others 2015.

References

OECD (Organisation for Economic Co-operation and Development). 2008. *Concepts and Dilemmas of State Building in Fragile Situations: From Fragility to Resilience.* Paris: OECD.

Ovadiya, M., A. Kryeziu, S. Masood, and E. Zapatero Larrio. 2015. "Social Protection in Fragile and Conflict-Affected Countries: Trends and Challenges." Social Protection and Labor Discussion Paper 1502, World Bank Group, Washington, DC.

World Bank. 2011. *World Development Report 2011: Conflict, Security, and Development.* Washington, DC: World Bank.

Section 2.
Spending on Social Safety Nets

This section presents key patterns in aggregate social safety net spending and its composition by program type. In a departure from last year's edition, total social safety net spending is derived from program-level data. To enhance comparisons across countries, program data on spending are aggregated in harmonized categories based on classifications and methodology in the World Bank Atlas of Social Protection: Indicators of Resilience and Equity (ASPIRE) database. The definition of social safety net spending extends to conditional and unconditional cash transfers; food and in-kind transfers; school feeding; public works; fee waivers; and other forms of social safety nets, including social care services. General subsidies for energy, electricity, and food are excluded.

The analysis is based on data drawn from a total of 120 countries. The most recent data on spending generally span 2010 to 2014 (see appendix D for a complete summary of spending data, years, and data sources by country).[1] Program-level data in ASPIRE presented here are based primarily on data collection efforts by the World Bank, but also rely on international databases maintained by the Asian Development Bank, the United Nations Economic Commission for Latin America and the Caribbean (ECLAC), HelpAge, and the World Food Programme (WFP).

Spending Patterns

Developing countries spend an average of 1.6 percent of gross domestic product (GDP) on social safety net programs; the median country spends 1.1 percent. Considerable resources are committed globally to fight extreme poverty worldwide, as revealed by an examination of aggregate spending on social safety nets (excluding general price subsidies) in a sample of 120 countries with available data. Safety net spending is higher than the global average in Europe and Central Asia and in Sub-Saharan Africa, where some countries exceed the average spending level of the members of the Organisation of Economic Cooperation and Development (OECD) (figure 2.1).[2] The combined spending on social safety nets amounted to about US$329 billion between 2010 and 2014. This sum is twice the amount needed to provide every person living in extreme poverty with an income of US$1.25 a day.

Low-income and middle-income countries devote approximately the same level of resources

to social safety nets (1.5 and 1.6 percent of GDP, respectively), while richer countries spend 1.9 percent of GDP on average. However, there is considerable variation across countries, especially among lower-income countries (figure 2.2). Despite having fewer resources for social safety nets, some lower-income countries allocate considerably more funds than the 1.6 percent average for developing countries. For example, the maximum social safety net spending in low-income countries is 4.8 percent of GDP in Sierra Leone and 6.6 percent in Lesotho; it is 7 percent of GDP in Georgia, among lower-middle-income countries. These levels greatly exceed the highest level among the high-income countries in the sample: 3.6 percent, in Croatia.

Country income levels only partly explain the higher spending levels; various other factors shape the pattern of spending on safety nets, including policy preferences, fragile contexts, reliance on social insurance schemes, and legal provisions. Figure 2.3 shows a weak relationship between spending and country income, suggesting that resources spent on social safety nets may reflect policy choices instead of pure economic factors and level of development. Countries with similar GDP per capita may spend very different shares of GDP on social safety nets; conversely, countries with similar levels of social safety net spending may have different GDP per capita. For example, the Arab Republic of Egypt spends one-fifth as much on social safety nets of what a country with a similar income such as Georgia spends, Mongolia spends six times more than Indonesia, while Burundi spends five times more than Burkina Faso. On the other hand, Kenya, a low-income

Spending on social safety nets in 120 developing countries totaled US$329 billion— twice the amount needed to provide every person living in extreme poverty with an income of US$1.25 a day.

■ Main Messages for Section 2

- Safety nets are affordable at all levels of income. Low-income and middle-income countries devote about the same level of resources to social safety nets (1.5 and 1.6 percent of GDP, respectively), while richer countries spend 1.9 percent of GDP.
- Cash transfer programs constitute the highest share of spending in all regions except in Sub-Saharan Africa, where food and other in-kind transfers dominate.
- The efficiency of spending can be improved by strengthening institutional capacity, coordination, program administration, and evaluation.

Figure 2.1 Countries and territories spend 1.6 percent of GDP on social safety net programs, on average, although the level varies by region

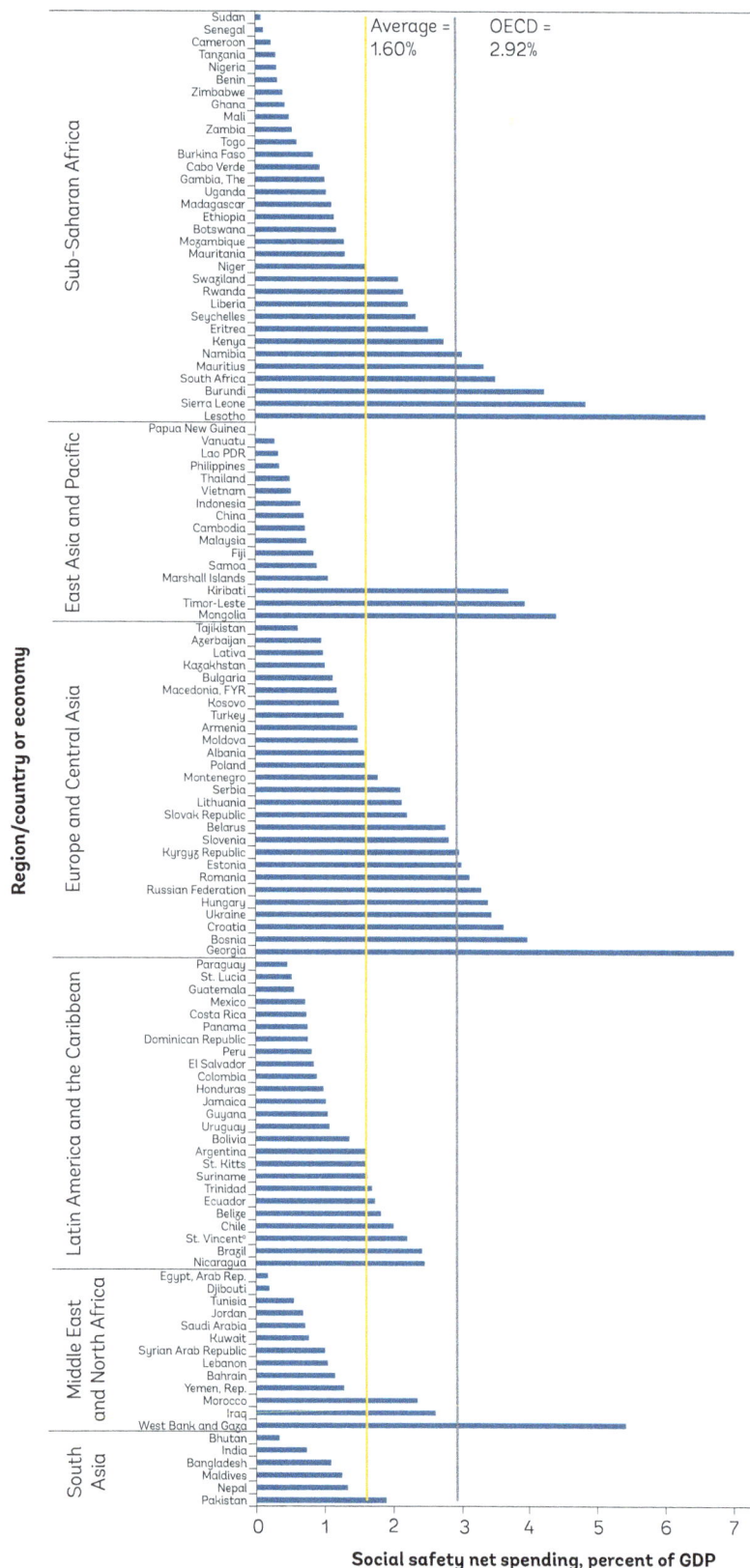

Region/country or economy

Average = 1.60%   OECD = 2.92%

Sub-Saharan Africa: Sudan, Senegal, Cameroon, Tangania, Nigeria, Benin, Zimbabwe, Ghana, Mali, Zambia, Togo, Burkina Faso, Cabo Verde, Gambia, The, Uganda, Madagascar, Ethiopia, Botswana, Mozambique, Mauritania, Niger, Swaziland, Rwanda, Liberia, Seychelles, Eritrea, Kenya, Namibia, Mauritius, South Africa, Burundi, Sierra Leone, Lesotho

East Asia and Pacific: Papua New Guinea, Vanuatu, Lao PDR, Philippines, Thailand, Vietnam, Indonesia, China, Cambodia, Malaysia, Fiji, Samoa, Marshall Islands, Kiribati, Timor-Leste, Mongolia

Europe and Central Asia: Tajikistan, Azerbaijan, Lativa, Kazakhstan, Bulgaria, Macedonia, FYR, Kosovo, Turkey, Armenia, Moldova, Albania, Poland, Montenegro, Serbia, Lithuania, Slovak Republic, Belarus, Slovenia, Kyrgyz Republic, Estonia, Romania, Russian Federation, Hungary, Ukraine, Croatia, Bosnia, Georgia

Latin America and the Caribbean: Paraguay, St. Lucia, Guatemala, Mexico, Costa Rica, Panama, Dominican Republic, Peru, El Salvador, Colombia, Honduras, Jamaica, Guyana, Uruguay, Bolivia, Argentina, St. Kitts, Suriname, Trinidad, Ecuador, Belize, Chile, St. Vincent[a], Brazil, Nicaragua

Middle East and North Africa: Egypt, Arab Rep., Djibouti, Tunisia, Jordan, Saudi Arabia, Kuwait, Syrian Arab Republic, Lebanon, Bahrain, Yemen, Rep., Morocco, Iraq, West Bank and Gaza

South Asia: Bhutan, India, Bangladesh, Maldives, Nepal, Pakistan

Social safety net spending, percent of GDP

Source: ASPIRE, based on most recent spending data available between 2010 and 2014 (appendix D).
Note: Average spending on social safety nets for the Organisation for Economic Co-operation and Development (OECD) countries is based on the Social Expenditure Database (SOCX) by combining "family" and "other social policy functions" as the closest approximation to noncontributory safety nets, as defined in this report. Bars report country total social safety net spending as a percent of GDP in the respective year.
a. Data for St. Vincent include data for the Grenadines.

country, spends as much on social safety nets as Slovenia, a high-income country.

The limited coverage of social insurance instruments (such as contributory pensions, and health and unemployment insurance) explains the greater use of universal noncontributory pensions and government-sponsored health insurance schemes. Social pensions—regular cash transfers paid by governments to older members of the population and not directly linked to prior contributions—are becoming important elements of public pension policy in varied forms in a growing number of countries and contribute to increasing safety net spending in cases such as Georgia, Mongolia, Lesotho, and Timor-Leste (see highlight 2, on social pensions). Georgia does not have a contributory public pension scheme and provides a flat universal pension to all elderly citizens, financed with general revenues, together with disability benefits. Within Georgia's social protection system, spending on social pensions represents almost 90 percent of overall expenditures.[3] In Mongolia, since 2010 the Human Development Fund has provided assistance to all citizens for pensions and health care. The very high level of spending in Lesotho is almost entirely due to its universal pension program, which provides generous benefits to the elderly. Similarly in Timor-Leste, the universal social pension provided to all citizens over the age of 60 accounts for a large share of social safety net spending.

Countries recovering from conflict or recognizing the need to rebalance social dynamics may have more generous social safety net systems (see highlight 1, on fragile and conflict-affected situations). Despite their diversity in terms of institutional capacity and economic development, Bosnia, Burundi, Kiribati, Sierra Leone, Timor-Leste, and West Bank and Gaza are all facing ongoing political conflict and fragility. As shown in figure 2.3, these countries share high levels of social safety net spending compared to their GDP, as governments have relied on social safety net instruments to foster social cohesion and recovery after periods of civil strife and turmoil. In Timor-Leste, the growing fiscal space from oil-fund revenues explains the rapid increase in the social assistance budget. Sierra Leone, another post-conflict country with considerable natural wealth, has a similar social safety net program, although it is mostly financed by external donors. In the West Bank and Gaza, spending on the main safety net, the cash transfer program, has increased substantially over the past four years, reflecting the strong political will to set up a well-targeted program able to respond effectively to poor people's emergencies in a context of violence and instability.

Spending Composition

Unconditional cash transfers (UCTs) account for most of the total spending on safety nets, while low-income countries allocate more resources to in-kind transfers and public works programs.[4] Figure 2.4 shows the average spending as a share of GDP by program category and income group, reflecting the policy choices on the portfolio of safety net programs, as well as different country capacity to deliver transfers. Low-income countries spend more on average on food and in-kind transfers (0.7 percent of GDP), public works (0.34 percent of GDP), and school feeding programs (0.22 percent of GDP), compared to other countries. As country income grows and capacity increases, unconditional cash benefits account for higher average levels of spending: 1.16 percent of GDP in lower-middle-income countries; 1.11 percent of GDP in upper-middle-income countries; and 1.37 percent of GDP in high-income countries.

Not surprisingly, fragile countries and small states generally have higher spending than average, spending more on food, in-kind, and public works programs (figure 2.4). Food rations in Iraq

Figure 2.2 Variations in social safety net spending are higher in lower-income countries

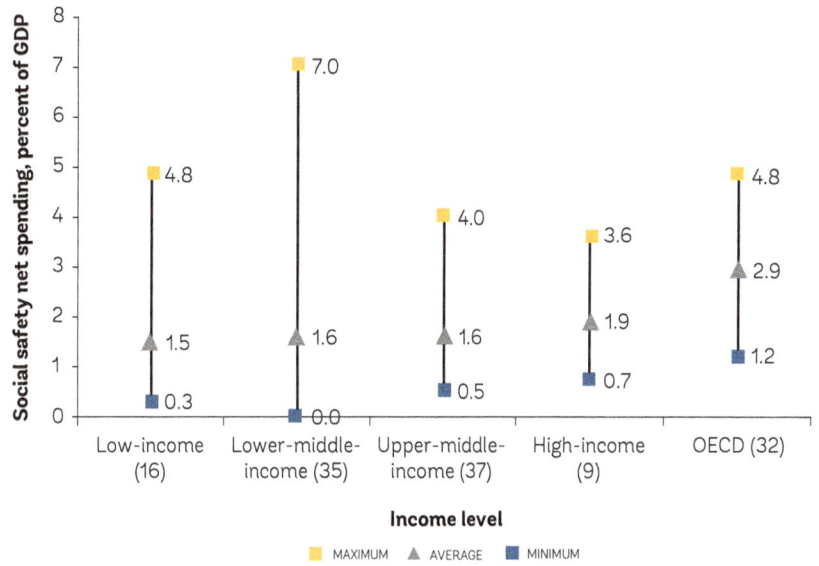

Source: ASPIRE, based on most recent spending data available between 2010 and 2014; see appendix D. Data for OECD countries refer to 2011 and are based on the SOCX database.
Note: The number of countries with available data per income group is indicated in parentheses. Comparisons between ASPIRE and SOCX should be interpreted with caution as the definition of social safety nets is not fully consistent. Social safety net spending for OECD countries here is approximated by the sum of the "family" and "other social policy" social protection functions, as defined in the SOCX Database.

(an upper-middle-income country) account for 2.2 percent of GDP. Cash transfers are high in fragile lower-middle-income economies such as Bosnia (4 percent of GDP) and West Bank and Gaza (4.7 percent of GDP). Given the small size of their economies and the higher fixed admin-

Figure 2.3 Spending on social safety nets is weakly associated with income levels

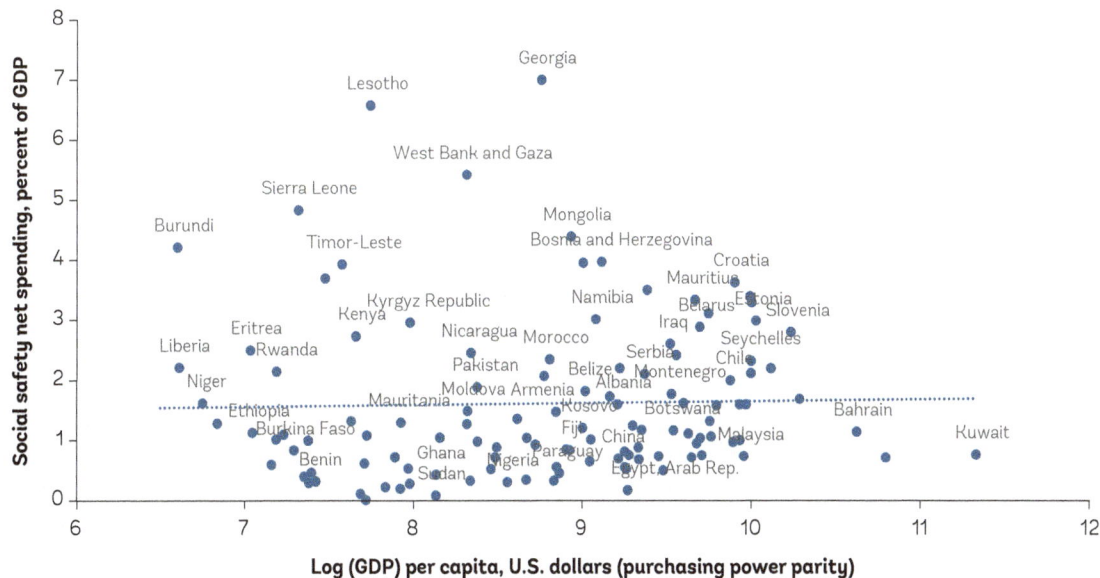

Source: ASPIRE, based on most recent spending data available between 2010 and 2014 (appendix D), and average GDP per capita in terms of purchasing power parity in U.S. dollars during the same period.

Figure 2.4 The composition of social safety net spending varies by income level and the enabling environment

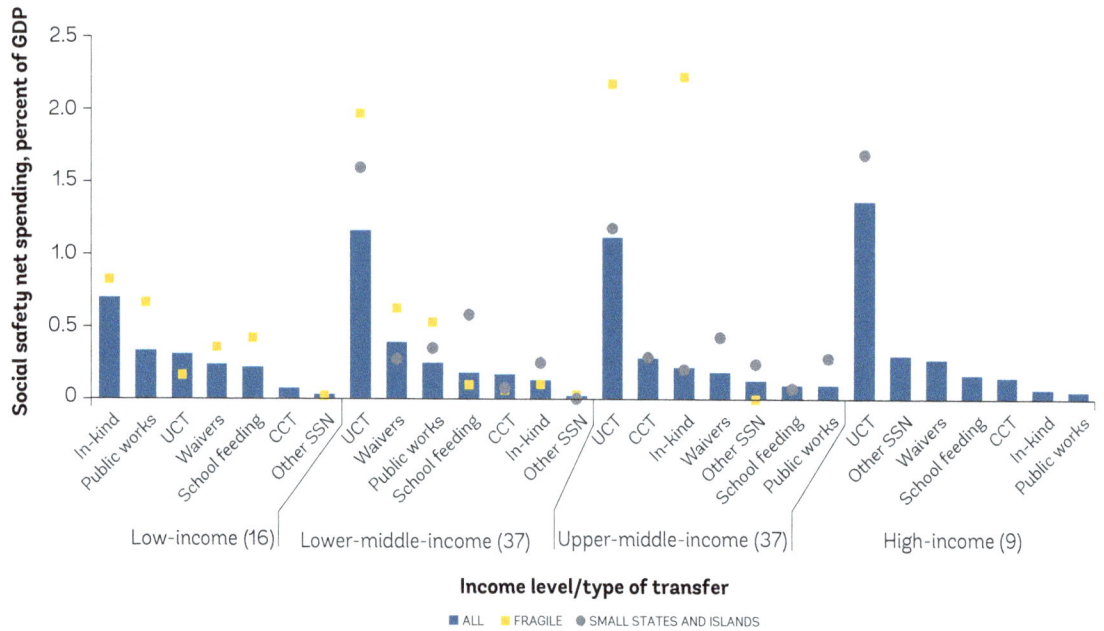

Source: ASPIRE.
Note: The number of countries with available data per income group is indicated in parentheses. Thirteen countries in the sample are defined as "fragile," based on the World Bank 2015 Harmonized List of Fragile Situations. Nineteen are small states, defined by the World Bank as those countries with total population below 1.5 million. Fourteen are small islands, as defined by the World Bank. CCT = conditional cash transfer; SSN = social safety net; UCT = unconditional cash transfer.

Figure 2.5 Spending composition varies by program type across regions
Percent of total social safety net spending

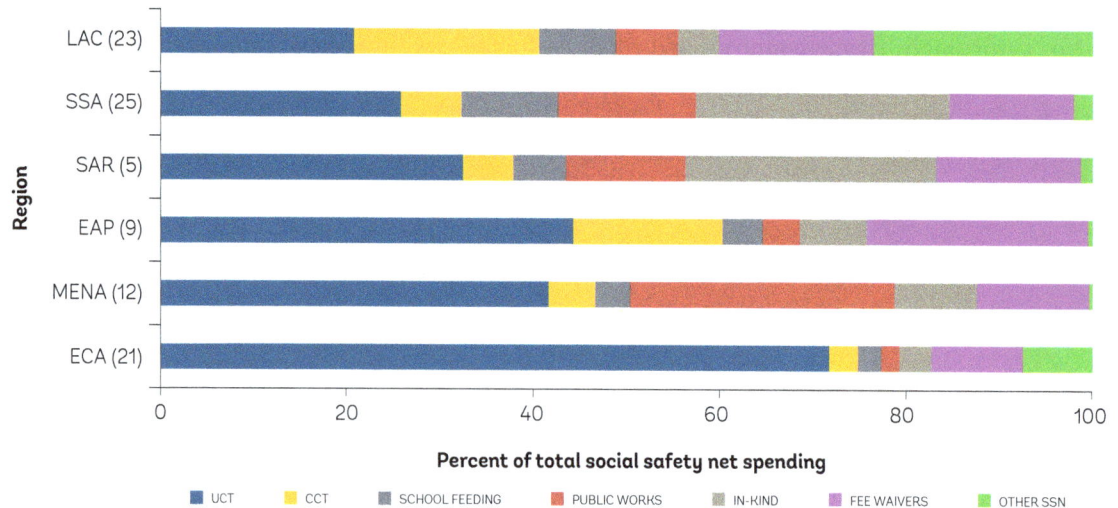

Source: ASPIRE.
Note: The number of countries with available data in each region is indicated in parentheses. CCT= conditional cash transfers; SSN = social safety net; UCT = unconditional cash transfers. Regions: EAP = East Asia and Pacific; ECA = Europe and Central Asia; LAC = Latin America and the Caribbean; MENA = Middle East and North Africa; SAR = South Asia; SSA = Sub-Saharan Africa.

istration cost relative to their GDP, small states and islands tend to spend more on safety nets than average, as do Namibia (2.4 percent) and Seychelles (1.9 percent).

Spending composition varies by region, with different degrees of diversification across pro-

gram types. Spending in Europe and Central Asia is more concentrated on cash transfers (unconditional), which account for more than 70 percent of safety net budgets. By contrast, spending is most diversified across different program types in Latin America and the Carib-

Figure 2.6 Old-age social pensions make up the highest share of worldwide spending on cash transfers

Percent of spending on unconditional cash transfers

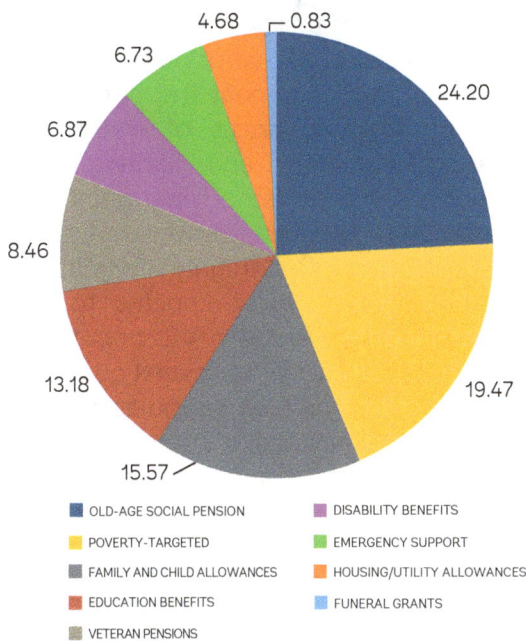

- OLD-AGE SOCIAL PENSION
- POVERTY-TARGETED
- FAMILY AND CHILD ALLOWANCES
- EDUCATION BENEFITS
- VETERAN PENSIONS
- DISABILITY BENEFITS
- EMERGENCY SUPPORT
- HOUSING/UTILITY ALLOWANCES
- FUNERAL GRANTS

Source: ASPIRE.

Note: Average country spending on each type of transfer as share of total spending on unconditional cash transfers, based on the latest program spending value available between 2010 and 2014.

bean, Sub-Saharan Africa, and South Asia, reflecting regional differences in program portfolios (figure 2.5). UCTs constitute the highest share of spending in all regions except Sub-Saharan Africa, where food and in-kind transfers persist (as in 2014) as the dominant component (making up 27 percent of total safety net spending on average). Conditional cash transfers (CCTs) are becoming increasingly larger in safety net budgets outside Latin America and the Caribbean, where they were pioneered. On average, CCTs account for about 20 percent of total spending in Latin America; 16 percent in East Asia, driven by the at-scale Pantawid Pamilyang Pilipino Program (accounting for 67 percent of budget) in the Philippines, and Decree 43 in Vietnam (38 percent of the budget in 2010). Fee waivers, in the form of discounted education and health services, represent the second largest share of total spending in East Asia (24 percent), and the third largest share in Latin America and the Caribbean (16 percent). Public works represent the second highest spending share in the Middle East after UCTs (more than 40 percent of the total

budget in Djibouti, Morocco, and the Republic of Yemen). Their relative spending share is also considerable in South Asia and Sub-Saharan Africa, where public works are most commonly implemented.

Old-age social pensions account for the highest share of cash transfer expenditures globally, followed by poverty targeted cash transfers. Programs that provide UCTs in cash have the similar characteristics of allowing recipients to use the cash transfer to purchase the goods preferred; however, they differ in their eligibility conditions, benefit size, and periodicity. Nine types of UCTs are defined in the ASPIRE database: noncontributory old-age pensions (both means-tested and universal); poverty-based cash transfers (mostly means-tested); family and children allowances (including birth grants and universal benefits for children below a certain age); education benefits (scholarships) in cash; veterans benefits; disability benefits; emergency cash support (often one-time); housing/utility allowances in cash; and funeral grants. Figure 2.6 shows the relative average shares of each type of UCT, reflecting the heterogeneity of country social protection systems. Globally, spending is quite diversified across types, with larger shares of resources going to old-age social pensions (24 percent of total cash spending); poverty-targeted cash transfers (19.5 percent); categorical family and child allowances—which are most common in Eastern Europe and former Soviet Union countries (15.6); and education benefits (13.2 percent). Veteran benefits (8.5 percent), disability benefits (6.9 percent), and emergency support (6.7 percent) account for slightly less than equal shares.

Energy and electricity subsidies crowd out social safety net spending in several countries. General price subsidies[5] play a key redistributive role and often represent the main form of safety net (box 2.1). In many Middle Eastern and North African countries, spending on energy subsidies (over 4 percent of GDP, on average) is greater than spending on social safety net programs (around 1.4 percent of GDP) (see figure 2.7). Spending on energy subsidies is more than three times higher than safety net spending in Nigeria, Cameroon, and Ecuador. Electricity subsidies also account for a substantial portion of government spending. Lower-income countries such as the Kyrgyz Republic, Mozambique, and Zambia spend

Box 2.1 Spending on Fuel Subsidies Is Often Greater than Spending on Social Safety Nets

Several countries have fuel subsidies that account for a substantial portion of government spending (data on energy and electricity subsidies spending are available for about 65 countries). Regardless of the level of income, spending on fuel subsidies is highest in the Middle East and North Africa region and may crowd out public spending on social safety nets and pro-poor policies.

Even lower-income countries such as the Kyrgyz Republic, the Republic of Yemen, and Cameroon spend about 9.0, 6.0, and 4.0 percent of GDP, respectively, on energy and electricity subsidies, compared to 3.0, 1.0, and 0.2 percent of GDP on social safety net programs (figure B2.1.1).

In oil-exporting countries, fuel subsidies are used as policy instruments to distribute oil revenues across the citizenry. Energy subsidies benefit the population through reduced prices of energy for heating, transport, and lighting, and through lower prices of energy-intense goods and services. However, energy subsidies are often highly inequitable, as they yield greater benefits to the upper-income groups in the population (IMF 2013). Studies from several countries have shown that fuel subsidies are regressive and ineffective in terms of protecting the poorest (Silva, Levin, and Morgandi 2013).

Figure B2.1.1 Fuel subsidies exceed social safety net spending in some countries

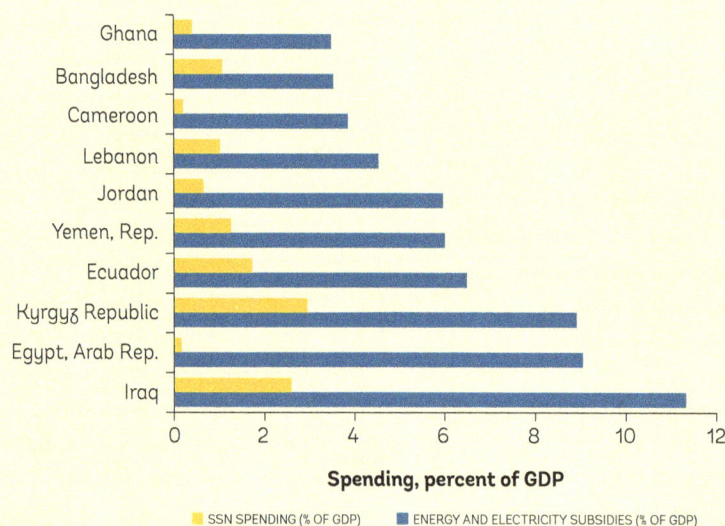

Spending, percent of GDP

SSN SPENDING (% OF GDP)   ENERGY AND ELECTRICITY SUBSIDIES (% OF GDP)

Sources: ASPIRE; IMF 2013.
Note: SSN = social safety net.

more on electricity subsidies (5.4, 4.9, and 4.8 percent of GDP, respectively) than on safety net programs (3.0, 1.3, and 0.5 percent of GDP, respectively). While smaller in size than energy subsidies, spending on food subsidies balances out safety net spending. Iraq, the Syrian Arab Republic, and Egypt spend 3.3, 2.8, and 2.4 percent of GDP, respectively, on food subsidies, compared to 2.6, 1.0, and 0.2 percent on social safety nets, respectively. In Africa, Mauritania and Zambia spend 1.9 and 1.5 percent, respec-

tively, on food subsidies, compared to social safety net spending of 1.3 and 0.5 percent of GDP, respectively. In Asia, the food public distribution system (PDS) in India and the Raskin food subsidy scheme in Indonesia account for 0.6 and 0.3 percent of GDP, respectively, compared to 0.73 and 0.65 percent spending on safety nets, respectively.

The share of social safety net spending devoted to poverty-targeted programs[6] decreases as countries get richer. Figure 2.8 shows that in a subsample of 67 countries for which information on program targeting methods is available, low-income countries spend on average 75 percent of the budget allocated to social safety nets on targeted programs; lower-middle-income countries spend 70 percent; upper-middle-income countries spend 58 percent; and high-income countries equally share the budget between targeted and nontargeted programs. This trend may reflect the combination of limited budgets and high needs in poorest countries, with the consequent policy choice of prioritizing the poorest of the poor and channeling resources through targeted programs.

On average, higher safety net spending increases redistribution; however, the effectiveness of spending also depends on how well programs are targeted to the poor. Figure 2.9 plots countries' benefit spending as a percentage of household consumption against poverty reduction achieved as a result of social safety net transfers (assuming household consumption falls by the transfer amount in the absence of safety nets).[7] Higher levels of spending are typically associated with greater impacts on poverty; however, poverty-reducing effects depend on the adequacy of benefits and on how well the poor are covered so that resources are distributed progressively. Successful countries are reducing the poverty gap by more than 50 percent compared to income before the transfer. When countries spend less than average on their safety nets, impacts on poverty reduction are less pronounced, with only 10–20 percent of the poverty gap eliminated. Even with similar budgeted expenditures, some countries do better than the others at each level of spending, allowing for performance benchmarking against countries at the cost-effectiveness "frontier."

Hungary tops the chart by having the largest poverty reduction effects, but it also has the highest level of spending. Moving from the left to the right (with the same cost of the social safety net), the efficiency of spending improves. This potential for improvement is marked by arrows. Countries that are furthest to the right represent the "frontier," or benchmark performance for their level of spending.

However, the analysis in figure 2.9 represents only part of the budget for the safety nets: the cash transfer component that reaches the final beneficiaries. In addition, all social safety nets have a significant administrative budget, which

Figure 2.7 Half the world spends more on subsidies than on social safety nets, on average

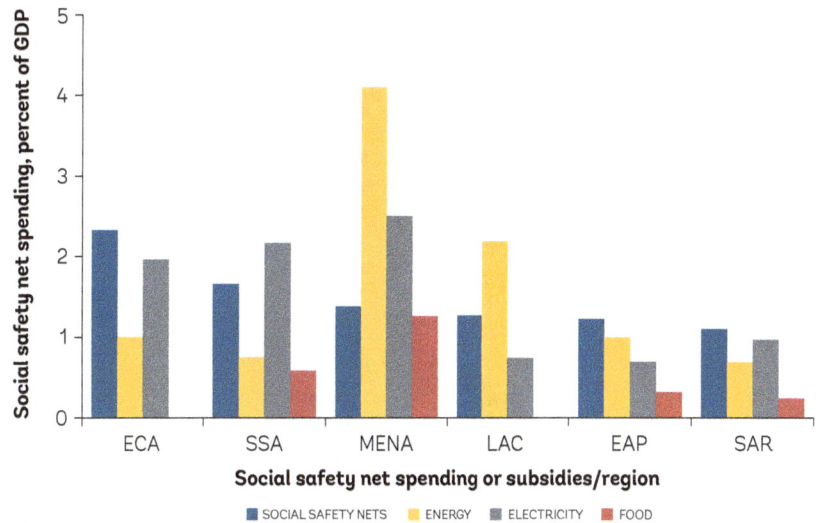

Sources: ASPIRE; IMF 2013; Sdralevich and others 2014.
Note: Data on food subsidies are not available for all countries. Regions: EAP = East Asia and Pacific; ECA = Europe and Central Asia; LAC = Latin America and the Caribbean; MENA = Middle East and North Africa; SAR = South Asia; SSA = Sub-Saharan Africa.

Figure 2.8 Lower-income countries devote a higher share of their social safety net budgets to targeted programs

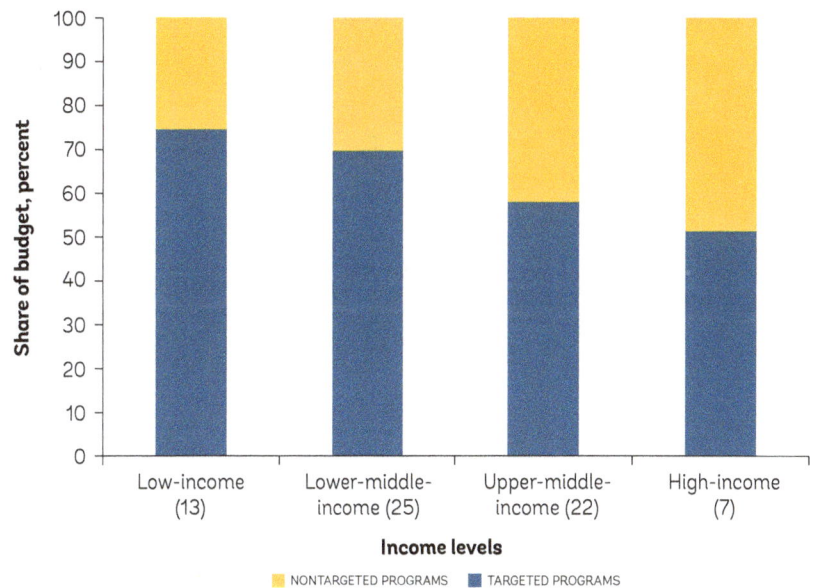

Source: ASPIRE.
Note: Targeted programs refer to programs that by design select beneficiaries using means-tested, proxy-means-tested, community-based, geographical targeting, and self-targeting approaches. Nontargeted programs refer to universal and categorical programs. The number of countries for which data are available is indicated in parentheses.

also needs to be taken into account while comparing the efficiency of various programs and types of spending. For example, both Hungary and Mexico do well in terms of the transfer budget, but Mexico achieves that high level of transfer while spending 0.7 percent of GDP on social safety nets, while Hungary spends more

Figure 2.9 Many countries are below the cost-efficiency frontier of social safety nets

Poverty gap reduction and cost of SSN benefits as percent of household consumption

Source: ASPIRE.

Note: The poverty gap reduction and the cost of SSNs are both estimated based on representative household surveys; see appendix F of this report. The cost of SSNs as percent of household consumption is derived by multiplying the average SSN transfer adequacy by the number of beneficiary households. Arrows indicate improving efficiency of spending. The dotted line represents the cost-efficiency frontier for a given level of benefit spending. The countries furthest to the right represent the "frontier," or benchmark performance for their level of spending. SSN = social safety net.

than 1 percent of GDP. This suggests a higher efficiency of the administrative system in Mexico than in Hungary.

Notes

1. For 21 countries of the 120 included in the analysis in this section, only aggregate data on safety net spending are available; for those 21 countries, data are not disaggregated by program.

2. Comparisons with the OECD average should be interpreted with caution, as the definition of social safety nets may not be fully consistent across countries. The definition of social safety nets in the OECD's Social Expenditure Database (SOCX) and the European Commission's European System of Integrated Social Protection Statistics (ESSPROS) database is confined to social protection functions, notably old-age, disability, unemployment, active labor market programs, health, family, survivorship, housing, and other social policy. Despite the common Classification of the Functions of Government (COFOG) framework for social spending, challenges remain comparing ASPIRE with the OECD/European Union classification.

3. If only targeted social assistance was counted as social safety net spending in Georgia, its level of spending

would not be different from other countries with similar income: around 0.6 percent of GDP.

4. Social safety nets can be classified as a transfer in the form of cash, food, near-cash, and services, and with conditionality of provisions (conditional or nonconditional). This report classifies six types of social safety nets: unconditional cash transfers, conditional cash transfers, food and in-kind, school feeding, cash and food-for-work, and fee waivers. For the purpose of the spending analysis in this section, spending on other social safety nets not elsewhere classified, including social care services, is grouped in a separate "other SSN" category. Unconditional cash transfers include means-tested and categorical noncontributory cash benefits for families, children, and orphans; disability benefits; and social pensions to the elderly.

5. *General price subsidies* are measures that keep prices for consumers below market levels, and thus benefit households through lower commodities prices. General subsidies are universal in the sense that all consumers have access to the same commodities at the same price. The analysis focuses on three types of general subsidies: energy, electricity, and food subsidies. *Energy subsidies* include government interventions and subsidized sales of petroleum products, including gasoline and diesel used for transport. *Subsidies*

for electricity lower prices for generating electricity for agricultural use, kerosene used for lighting and heating, and liquefied petroleum gas used for cooking. *Universal food subsidies* are government interventions to lower the price the general population pays for staple foods. Governments may also provide universal access to food or other commodities through subsidized sales at public distribution centers or designated private outlets on a first-come, first-served basis.

6. *Targeted programs* refer to programs that by design select beneficiaries using means-tested, proxy-means-tested, community-based, geographical targeting, and self-targeting approaches. *Nontargeted programs* refer to universal and categorical programs.

7. Obviously, immediate impacts on poverty reduction are not the only benefits of social safety nets; they also have significant longer-terms impacts in terms of building human capital and assets. The design of social safety net programs in countries may deemphasize poverty reduction and concentrate on other parameters. Work is continuing to devise and benchmark the effectiveness of social safety nets in their efforts to achieve full and longer-term impacts on poverty reduction, while enhancing livelihoods and economic growth.

References

IMF (International Monetary Fund). 2013. *Energy Subsidy Reform: Lessons and Implications*. Washington, DC: International Monetary Fund.

Sdralevich, M. C. A., M. R. Sab, M. Y. Zouhar, and G. Albertin. 2014. *Subsidy Reform in the Middle East and North Africa: Recent Progress and Challenges Ahead.* Washington, DC: International Monetary Fund.

Silva, J., V. Levin, and M. Morgandi. 2013. *Inclusion and Resilience: The Way Forward for Social Safety Nets in the Middle East and North Africa*. Washington, DC: World Bank.

Weblinks

ASPIRE (The Atlas of Social Protection: Indicators of Resilience and Equity), World Bank, www.worldbank.org /aspire/.

COFOG (Classification of the Functions of Government), United Nations Statistics, http://unstats.un.org/unsd /cr/registry/regcst.asp?Cl=4.

Database of Conditional Transfer Programs (Programas de Transferencias Condicionadas), ECLAC (Economic Commission for Latin America and the Caribbean of the United Nations), http://dds.cepal.org/bdptc+/.

ESSPROS (European System of Integrated Social Protection Statistics), European Union, http://ec.europa.eu /eurostat/web/social-protection/data/database.

Social Pension Database, HelpAge International, http:// www.pension-watch.net.

SOCX (Social Expenditure Database), Organisation for Economic Co-operation and Development (OECD), http://www.oecd.org/social/expenditure.htm.

Social pensions are regular cash transfers paid by governments to older members of the population. Unlike pensions via social insurance, there is no link between the transfer paid and prior payment contributions, typically payroll tax deductions. The use of the word "social" implies that the objective of these pensions is primarily related to redistribution and addressing poverty, which distinguishes them from other noncontributory pensions, such as special veterans' pensions and civil service pensions. Within this overarching definition, parameters of social pension design vary considerably, including age of eligibility, citizenship and residency criteria, and whether or not they are means-tested.

Despite their long history, social pensions have come to prominence only over the last two decades. Of the 101 countries that have a social pension (according to the HelpAge International Social Pension 2014 database), around half have been introduced since 1990. The pace of introduction is also accelerating. Since 2000, 32 countries have introduced social pensions, compared to 18 in the previous decade.

The expansion of social pensions has been characterized by interesting differences across regions. In no other region has the recent interest in social pensions been more marked than in Latin America and the Caribbean (Rofman, Apella, and Vezza 2014). The main social pension in the region initially was the rural pension in Brazil. Argentina, Chile, Guyana, Suriname, Uruguay, and a handful of Caribbean islands, including Jamaica, also had some form of social pensions, but these (social pensions) were largely means-tested to a small portion of older people. Today, every country in South America has put in place a social pension, as have most Central American countries, with the exception of Honduras and Nicaragua. Social pensions have expanded particularly rapidly in some countries. Ecuador introduced a social pension as part of its Bono de Desarollo Humano program in 2003, which has expanded to cover over half of people aged 65 and above. In Mexico, the introduction of a universal pension in Distrito Federal (Mexico City) in 2003 was expanded to all persons aged 70 and above in rural areas, and more recently to all Mexicans over 65 with no other pension income. Many existing social pensions have also undergone significant reform in recent years. In 2008, Chile transformed its poverty-targeted Pensiones Asistenciales (PASIS) scheme and minimum guarantee for its contributory scheme into a solidarity pension aimed at the bottom 60 percent of the income distribution. In the same year, Bolivia's universal Bonosol pension evolved into the Renta Dignidad, with a lower eligibility age, increased benefits, and more regular payments.

The pace of introducing new social pension programs, and the expansion of programs, has increased greatly.

Sub-Saharan Africa, and particularly the southern tip of the continent, is home to some of the largest scale social pension schemes introduced to date. In the early 1990s, following the end of apartheid, the social pension schemes in South Africa and Namibia were reformed so that all older people—regardless of race—would receive benefits on the same terms (Devereaux 2001). These schemes appear to have influenced the neighboring countries of Botswana (1996), Lesotho (2004), and Swaziland (2005) to introduce social pensions that cover all, or most, older people over a set age. In most of these countries, these social pensions are part of wider systems of near-universal grants (including for disability and orphans) that have been described as a "Southern Africa model" of social protection (Niño-Zarazúa and others 2010).

Many South Asian countries can be considered to have been pioneers in the recent extension of social pensions. Bangladesh, India, and Nepal all introduced social pensions in the mid- to late-1990s. The programs in Bangladesh and India were originally targeted to a small minority of older people, but have since been gradually expanding coverage (Begum and Wesumperuma 2012; ISSA 2013). Nepal introduced a virtually universal pension for older people in 1995 with a high eligibility age of 75 that was reduced to 70 in 2008, with a lower age for specific groups including Dalits (Untouchables) (NEPAN 2011). Nevertheless, these programs still remain modest in terms of coverage and benefit levels.

In the East Asia and Pacific region, means-tested social pension schemes exist in Indonesia (essentially a pilot), Malaysia, the Philippines, Thailand, and Vietnam, and universal schemes exist in Brunei Darussalam, Kiribati, and Samoa. Thailand's scheme has seen one of the most dramatic transformations since 2009, when it was extended from a means-tested program to all older people over age 60 except for government pensioners (Suwaranda and Wesumperuma 2012). Since 2008, Timor-Leste has provided a universal pension to all citizens over the age of 60. The most important extension of pension coverage in the region—and possibly in global history—has been the introduction of a New Rural Social Pension scheme in China since 2009. The program falls within a contributory social insurance scheme in which older people receive a monthly pension on the condition that their own children are contributing to the system. This makes the scheme noncontributory to the extent that it does not require prior contributions from the recipient, but the condition on children's contributions makes it unique to our knowledge. Since its introduction, 133 million people over the age of 60 have received payments from the scheme—or about 60 percent of the population 60 and over (ISSA 2013).

Meanwhile, the declining coverage of contributory pensions in Europe and Central Asia has created a coverage gap that has led to increasing discussion of how social pensions could fill the gap. In contrast to most other low- and middle-income countries, the legacy of almost universal formal employment during the Soviet period means that most countries have near-universal pension systems based on payroll contributions. Nevertheless, a sharp increase in informal employment in the region, teamed with pension reforms aimed at creating a closer link between contributions and benefits, means that the proportion of the workforce contributing to a pension is rapidly decreasing (Mikkonen-Jeanneret and others 2011). The role of social pensions will become increasingly important if these countries are to maintain the universal coverage of their pension systems. Georgia is one country that appears to have already recognized this trend by converting its contributory social insurance system into a basic universal social pension in 2006 (UN HRC 2010). Other countries do have social pensions, but these are often limited to a tiny minority of the population. For example, fewer than 1 to 2 percent of those over 60 are covered in the Kyrgyz Republic and Moldova.

References

Begum, S., and D. Wesumperuma. 2012. "Overview of the Old Age Allowance Programme in Bangladesh." In *Social Protection for Older Persons: Social Pensions in Asia*, edited by S. W. Handayani and B. Babajanian, 187–213. Manila: Asian Development Bank.

Devereaux, S. 2001. "Namibia: Social Pensions in Namibia and South Africa." IDS Discussion Paper 379, Institute of Development Studies, Brighton, England.

ISSA (International Social Security Association). 2013. *Pension Schemes Witnessed about 130 Million New Members within One Year.* Geneva: International Social Security Organization.

Mikkonen-Jeanneret, E., R. Rayapova, and N. Yefimov. 2011. *Off the Grid: Exploring the Expanding Informal Economy and Threats to Old-Age Social Protection in Kyrgyzstan and Tajikistan.* London: HelpAge International.

NEPAN (Nepal Participatory Action Network). 2011. *The Effectiveness of Non-contributory Social Pension in Nepal: Participatory Research Report.* Kathmandu, Nepal: NEPAN.

Niño-Zarazúa, M., A. Barrientos, D. Hulme, and S. Hickey. 2010. "Social Protection in Sub-Saharan Africa: Will the Green Shoots Blossom?" MPRA Paper 22422, Munich Personal RePEc Archive (MPRA), University Library of Munich, Germany.

Rofman, R., I. Apella, and E. Vezza, eds. 2014. *Más allá de las Pensiones Contributivas.* Washington, DC: World Bank.

Suwaranda, W., and D. Wesumperuma. 2012. "Development of the Old-Age Allowance System in Thailand: Challenges and Policy Implications." In *Social Protection for Older Persons Social Pensions in Asia,* edited by S. W. Handayani and B. Babajanian. Manila: Asian Development Bank.

UN HRC (United Nations Human Rights Council). 2010. *Report of the Independent Expert on the Question of Human Rights and Extreme Poverty.* Report A/HRC/14/31. New York: UN HRC.

Section 3.
Policy, Institutions, and Administration

This section describes different approaches that social protection policies and strategies use to organize a variety of social safety net interventions. The discussion is based on data gathered from 136 countries through internal policy monitoring and reporting materials. Appendix E provides the collective source of information for this section.

Policies and Strategies

Countries are increasingly formulating national social protection policies or strategies to reduce or eliminate poverty. While social safety net interventions have existed since the start of organized governance, comprehensive policies and strategies for poverty reduction began to be developed in the 1990s following the Copenhagen Social Development Summit. In the 2000s, governments began recognizing social protection as a new government sector and prioritizing the creation of social protection policies and strategies.

More than half the countries surveyed have an approved social protection policy or strategy in place. A total of 77 countries, or 57 percent of the 136 surveyed countries, have a social protection policy in place; another 31 countries (or 23 percent) are planning or formulating a policy. In only 20 percent of surveyed countries (or 28 countries), no information was reported or available on policy monitoring systems or from literature reviews (figure 3.1).

Approved national social protection strategies are more common among higher-income countries. Table 3.1 provides a detailed breakdown of the status of social protection policies by income groups and regions. About 80 percent of upper-middle-income countries (40 out of 55) have a comprehensive social protection strategy in place, with 5 countries developing one. The share is much lower among lower-middle-income countries and low-income countries: about half. However, many low-income countries are moving toward a coherent framework and are in the process of developing a national policy or strategy. Sub-Saharan Africa is the region most active in creating or preparing social policy frameworks at this time, with 15 countries (or 31 percent) planning or preparing a policy or strategy. This highlights the increasing focus on implementing safety net systems in Sub-Saharan Africa recently. The share of existing social protection strategies is highest in Europe and Central Asia.

There are three distinct types of overall social protection strategies across countries. In about 19 percent of countries, the social protection policy is incorporated in a wider poverty reduction strategy or plan, and frequently forms a pillar of a wider country development strategy, including to address overarching issues such as climate change and disaster risk management (see highlight 3, on climate change, poverty, and the importance of leveraging social protection). In 16 percent of countries, specific laws covering only social safety nets have been enacted. In the majority of cases (88 countries, or 65 percent), however, countries have developed a comprehensive social protection strategy or plan covering social safety net programs, labor programs, and pensions (figure 3.2).

Sector-specific strategies are becoming more common worldwide, with social protection no longer falling under wider development frameworks. This result suggests that increasingly policies are geared toward social protection priorities. In all regions, the majority of policies are pure social protection strategies, except in the Middle East and North Africa, where policies are incorporated into a broader development or poverty reduction strategy. In low-income and lower-middle-income countries, the proportion of countries with social protection

Social protection national strategies and policies are in place in 77 countries and developing in another 31. Meanwhile, countries are enhancing coordination mechanisms to implement social protection strategies across government bodies.

■ Main Messages for Section 3

- Stand-alone social protection strategies are becoming more common worldwide. The majority of countries have developed comprehensive social protection strategies or plans covering social safety net programs, labor programs, and pensions.
- The implementation of comprehensive social protection policies demands institutional arrangements among a variety of institutions, agencies, and entities in different sectors. The specific coordination mechanisms to oversee social protection strategies vary across countries, though all face common challenges.
- Countries have developed management information systems of varying complexity and sophistication. Social registries, beneficiary registries, and monitoring and evaluation systems are among the most commonly used tools to support the administration and management of social protection systems.

Figure 3.1 Status of social protection policies or strategies as of 2014

Percent of countries

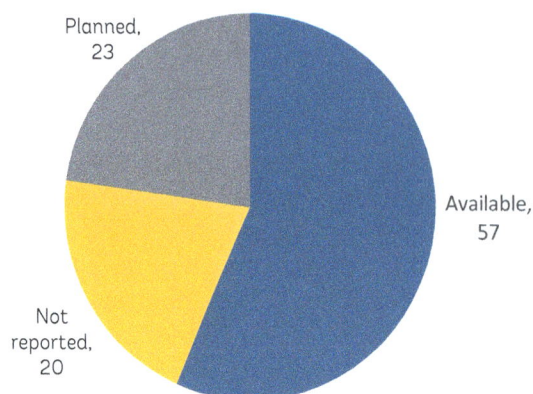

Planned, 23

Available, 57

Not reported, 20

Source: World Bank internal monitoring reports 2014.

Figure 3.2 Existing social protection policy or strategy as of 2014, by type

Percent of countries

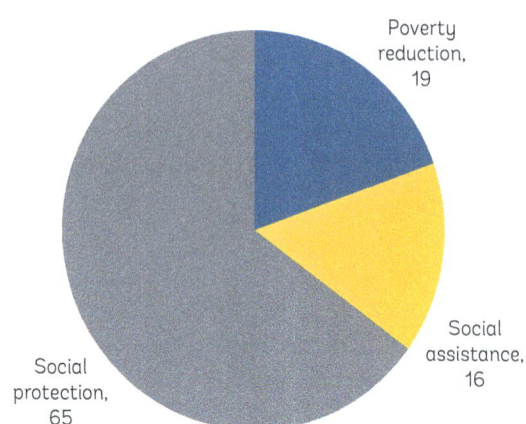

Poverty reduction, 19

Social assistance, 16

Social protection, 65

Source: World Bank internal monitoring reports 2014.

Table 3.1 Social Protection Policy/Strategy as of 2014, Low- and Middle-Income Countries

Number of countries

Income group and region	Status			Total
	Active	**Planned**	**Not reported**	**Total**
Income group				
Low-income	16	16	3	35
Lower-middle-income	21	10	15	46
Upper-middle-income	40	5	10	55
Total, middle-income	61	15	25	101
Region				
East Asia and Pacific	7	4	9	20
Europe and Central Asia	17	2	4	23
Latin America and the Caribbean	17	4	7	28
Middle East and North Africa	7	1	1	9
South Asia	2	5	1	8
Sub-Saharan Africa	27	15	6	48
Total	77	31	28	136

Source: World Bank internal monitoring reports.
Note: The total number of low-income and middle-income countries with available data on national social protection policy/strategy is 136.

strategies is about 75 percent. National strategies focusing only on social safety nets are more common in Sub-Saharan Africa (table 3.2).

Institutions

Given the multisectoral nature of social protection, governments are continuing to institutionalize mechanisms and bodies to enhance and strengthen coordination of social protection strategies across different ministries, agencies, and regional and local bodies. The design

and implementation of policies demand institutional arrangements and joint actions with other public sectors involved in the strategy, often including social development, health, education, and employment. This section describes and highlights some key changes taking place within the institutional context.

The wider the scope of the strategy and greater the diversity of agencies with a role to play in implementing it, the greater the number of actors in the collective body and the more

Table 3.2 Type of Policy/Strategy for Countries with Active Social Protection Policy/Strategy as of 2014, Low- and Middle-Income Countries

Number of countries

Income group and region	Type of policy/strategy			Total
	Poverty reduction	Social safety nets	Social protection	
Income group				
Low-income	2	2	12	16
Lower-middle-income	4	1	16	21
Upper-middle-income	9	9	22	40
Total, middle-income	13	10	38	61
Region				
East Asia and Pacific	2	1	4	7
Europe and Central Asia	5	1	11	17
Latin America and the Caribbean	3	3	11	17
Middle East and North Africa	4	1	2	7
South Asia	0	0	2	2
Sub-Saharan Africa	1	6	20	27
Total	15	12	50	77

Source: World Bank internal monitoring reports.
Note: The total number of low-income and middle-income countries with an active national social protection policy/strategy is 77.

complex decision making processes become. Challenges are rife, including the need to maintain a functional decision-making body across sectors that can monitor the implementation of the strategy. Different levels of state administration lead to different levels of interagency coordination, as shown in figure 3.3.

Usually, one chief ministry coordinates and leads the strategy. In most cases, the coordinating role is assigned to the ministry most directly linked to social protection, such as the Social Development Ministry, Social Inclusion Ministry, or the National Authority for Social Security. In these cases, the coordinating ministry summons entities to participate in the implementation of the strategy. For example, in Brazil, the Ministry for Social Development and Fight Against Hunger coordinates Brazil's strategy. In Kenya, coordination is divided between three ministries: the Ministry of Labor, the Ministry of Social Security and Services, and the Ministry of Devolution and Planning. In Romania, the Ministry of Labor coordinates the delivery of most social assistance programs, yet the processes of accountability remain the responsibility of the coordinating ministry and not of other committees or commissions. In the cases when coordination responsibilities fall

Figure 3.3 Most countries use one lead coordinating ministry to coordinate social protection policies

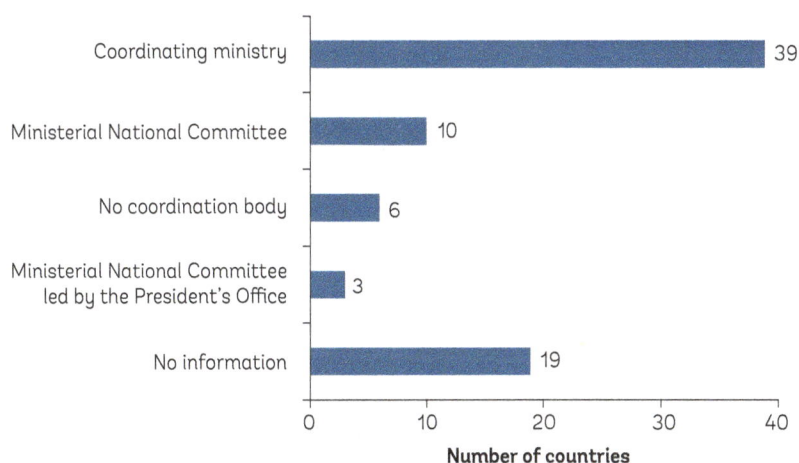

Source: World Bank internal monitoring reports 2014.
Note: The total number of low-income and middle-income countries with an active national social protection policy or strategy is 77.

under existing social ministries or with newly created ministries, like the Ministry of Development and Social Inclusion in Peru, the same entity in charge of planning and monitoring the strategy is often tasked with its implementation. This arrangement presents important management challenges.

Another method of coordination is through a coordinating commission or committee, often

Table 3.3 Key Coordination Bodies of Social Protection as of 2014, Low- and Middle-Income Countries

Number of countries

Income group and region	Coordination body					
	None	Coordinating ministry	National Committee (NC)	NC led by President's Office	Not reported	Total
Income group						
Low-income	1	7	3	3	2	16
Lower-middle-income	4	12	2	0	3	21
Upper-middle-income	1	20	5	0	14	40
Total, middle-income	5	32	7	0	17	61
Region						
East Asia and Pacific	1	3	3	0	0	7
Europe and Central Asia	0	7	1	0	9	17
Latin America and the Caribbean	1	10	3	0	3	17
Middle East and North Africa	1	4	0	0	2	7
South Asia	1	0	0	0	1	2
Sub-Saharan Africa	2	15	3	3	4	27
Total	6	39	10	3	19	77

Source: World Bank internal monitoring reports.
Note: The total number of low-income and middle-income countries with an active national social protection policy/strategy is 77.

called a Ministerial National Committee. The committee is created specifically to coordinate the strategy. In many cases, this committee lies directly under the presidency. For example, in Benin, the Comité Socle de Protection Sociale is responsible for coordination related to the social protection strategy. Although it is chaired by the Ministry of Development, the committee is housed under the direct leadership of the president of the republic. Because of their proximity to the president, these types of committees often have stronger convening and coordination powers than they would otherwise have. In many other cases, the committee may fall under a ministry such as the Ministry of Planning, the Ministry of Finance, or the Ministry of Labor. These interministerial coordination bodies typically operate with an executive secretary in charge of coordination tasks. Ministries and agencies that are part of the committee or commission collaborate in an effort to achieve the goals set out within the strategy. Such committees have a more deliberate function than an advisory one; among their duties is monitoring the commitments that each of the participating institutions have made to implement the strategy. Table 3.3 presents a breakdown of different coordination bodies.

It is also vital that social protection strategies are coordinated with broader government programs and priorities in other social sectors such as education and health, to ensure long-term success, and to encourage promotion of human capital through early childhood development, skills development, and access to jobs. Research on the interaction of early childhood development initiatives combined with cash transfer programs have found that strengthening these linkages can provide significant gains in achieving social protection objectives.

Administration

The effective implementation of a social protection system requires tools that facilitate the selection of beneficiaries, the delivery of services, and the monitoring of both processes and outcomes. Thus interest and investment in systems to manage information concerning potential beneficiaries of social protection programs is growing. Countries have generated management information systems (MIS) of varying complexity and sophistication, allowing more efficient management and effective results of social protection programs (table 3.4).

Three main mechanisms support the administration and management of social protection

Table 3.4 Social Protection and Labor System Administration Tools as of 2014
Number of countries

Income group and region	Administration tools			Total
	Basic monitoring tools	Social registry	Beneficiary registry	
Income group				
Low-income	23	9	1	35
Lower-middle-income	29	21	19	46
Upper-middle-income	41	17	25	55
Total, middle-income	70	38	44	101
Region				
East Asia and Pacific	11	4	4	20
Europe and Central Asia	18	7	7	23
Latin America and the Caribbean	24	17	19	28
Middle East and North Africa	7	5	5	9
South Asia	5	2	1	8
Sub-Saharan Africa	28	12	9	48
Total	93	47	45	136

Source: World Bank internal monitoring reports.
Note: The total number of low-income and middle-income countries with available data is 136. The same country could have more than one administration tool.

systems: the registration of potentially eligible individuals or households for the allocation of social benefits (*social registry*); the registration of beneficiaries of social protection interventions (*beneficiary registry*); and *monitoring and evaluation systems*. These instruments should ease the functioning of social protection systems and increase the levels of management efficiency and effectiveness.

The use of data to improve service delivery is still not widespread. About 68 percent of countries report that they regularly use monitoring tools to track progress on program performance. These tools can range from information systems to track budgets, the number of beneficiaries, and key performance indicators to complex and integrated management information systems; process evaluations to identify implementation issues and propose strategies to address key bottlenecks; and systematic, periodic impact evaluations to assess whether programs are achieving their intended outcomes. Social registries, used for targeting purposes, are present or being created in 47 countries, while 45 countries have implemented beneficiary registries for a specific program or across social protection programs (figure 3.4).

Support for social and beneficiary registries has grown considerably in recent years. At least

Figure 3.4 Many countries lack social protection and labor system administration tools
Number of countries

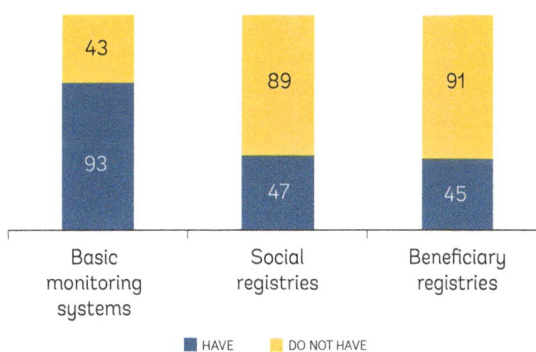

Source: World Bank internal monitoring reports 2014.

21 countries have a fully institutionalized social registry. An additional 26 countries, including many in Sub-Saharan Africa, are in the process of building one. At least 29 countries have fully operational beneficiary registries, while an additional 16 are developing them. These registries range from serving a single program, as in Armenia, to 80 different programs in Chile. A selection of operational registries can be found in table 3.5. A selection of registries under development can be found in table 3.6.

Table 3.5 Selected Examples of Operational Social and Beneficiary Registries

Country	Name	Managing institution	Number of households (thousands)	Number of programs served
Social registries				
Belize	Single Identification System of Beneficiaries (SISB)	Ministry of Economic Development	3.5 (2013)	—
Bolivia	Beneficiary Registry of Social Programs	Ministry of Development Planning	—	4
Brazil	Cadastro Unico	Ministry of Social Development and Fight against Hunger	25,000	20
Cabo Verde	Unique Registry	—	—	2
Chile	Integrated System of Social Information (SIIS)	Ministry of Social Development	4,200	80
Colombia	Integrated Information System of Social Protection (SISPRO)	Ministry of Health and Social Protection	3,000	31
Costa Rica	Sistema de Identificación de la Población Objectivo (SIPO)	IMAS (Agency for Social Benefits)	1,420[a]	3
Ecuador	Social Registry and Registry of the Social Programs (RIPS)	Ministry Coordinator of Social Development	—	—
Guatemala	Registro Unico de Usuarios Nacional (RUU-N)	Ministerio de Desarrollo Social (MIDES)	2,600	108
Honduras	Unique Registry of Participants (RUP)	National Information Center for Social Sector, under the Government's Office	3,350	18
Indonesia	—	National Team for the Acceleration of Poverty Reduction (TNP2K) Secretariat	25,000	3
Lesotho	National Information System for Social Assistance (NISSA)	Ministry of Social Development and Fight against Hunger	40 (as of July 2013)	3 planned, 1 as of July 2013
Macedonia, FYR	Cash Benefits Management Information System (CBMIS)	Ministry of Labour and Social Protection	—	1
Mauritius	Social Register of Mauritius (SRM)	Various ministries	41 (as of June 2013)	4
Mexico	Cuestionario Unico de Informacion Socioeconomica for SEDESOL	Various ministries	7,400	—
Pakistan	National Socio Economic Registry (NSER)	Benazir Income Support Program (BISP)	27,000	30
Panama	Unified Registry of Beneficiaries (RUB)	Ministry of Social Development (MIDES)	178.3[a]	11
Philippines	Listahanan or National Household Targeting System for Poverty Reduction (NHTS-PR)	Department of Social Welfare and Development	10,909	3
Romania	Integrated Information System for Administration of Social Benefits (SAFIR)	National Agency for Social Benefits	6,000[a]	14
Turkey	Social Assistance Information System (SAIS)	General Directorate of Social Assistance	8,000	17
Beneficiary registries				
Armenia	Family Benefit System	Ministry of Labor and Social Affairs	95	1
Azerbaijan	MIS of Ministry of Labor and Social Protection of Population (MLSPP)	Ministry of Labor and Social Protection of the Population	127	3
China	Registry of Beneficaries Dibao	—	78,000	1
Dominican Republic	Sistema Unico de Beneficiaros (SIUBEN)	Cabinet of Social Policy Coordination	6,059	10
Jamaica	Beneficiary Management Information System	Ministry of Labor and Social Security	375	—
Seychelles	Integrated MIS	Agency for Social Protection	—	5
South Africa	National Integrated Social Information System (NISIS)	South African Social Security Agency (SASSA)	22,000[a]	8

Source: World Bank internal monitoring reports.
Note: Data refer to the number of households unless noted otherwise. — = not available.
a. Data refer to a total number of beneficiaries.

Table 3.6 Selected Examples of Operational Social and Beneficiary Registries Being Developed

Country	Name	Managing institution
Bangladesh	Bangladesh Poverty Database	Ministry of Planning
Benin	Unique Registry	Permanent Executive Secretariat of the National SP Commission (11 ministries)
Cambodia	Poor ID	Ministry of Planning
Djibouti	Registre Unique	Pending
Dominica	National Beneficiary Information System (NBIS)	Ministry of Social Services, Community Development and Gender Affairs
El Salvador	Single Registry of Beneficiaries (RUP)	Pending
Georgia	System of Social Assistance	Minister of Labor, Health and Social Service Agency
Ghana	Ghana National Household Registry (GNHR)	Minister of Gender, Children and Social Protection
Jordan	National Unified Registry	Pending
Kenya	Integrated Registry of Beneficiaries	Ministry of Labor, Social Security and Services
Kyrgyz Republic	Pending	Ministry of Social Development
Lebanon	National Poverty Targeting Program	Ministry of Social Affairs
Mongolia	Intersectoral Database of Poor Households and Registry of Beneficiaries	Pending
Morocco	Unified Register	Pending
Nicaragua	Unique Registry of Participants (RUP)	Ministry of Family, Adolescence and Childhood (MIFAN)
Papua New Guinea	Pending	Department for Community Development
Paraguay	Single Registry of Beneficiaries	Pending
Peru	National Registry of Beneficiaries	Ministry of Development and Social Inclusion
Rwanda	Integrated Management Information System	Pending
Senegal	Unique registry	Délégation Générale à la Protection Sociale et la Solidarité Nationale
St. Lucia	Central Beneficiary Registry	Pending
Tajikistan	National Registry of Social Protection	Social Protection agency and Housing and Maintenance Department (HMD)
Tunisia	Unified Registry and Unique Identification System	Pending
Zambia	Single Registry of Beneficiaries	Pending

Source: World Bank internal monitoring reports.

Climate change will increase the frequency and intensity of extreme weather events.[1] As climate impacts increase over time, building the tools needed to manage the increased risks is an urgent task.

Social Protection to Mitigate Impacts of Climate Shocks

Climate impacts are expected to increase the flows of vulnerable people falling into poverty, directly through losses from flood or drought, and indirectly through impacts on health and disease. Climate impacts may also make it more difficult for people to escape poverty by slowing asset accumulation, reducing land and labor productivity, or affecting support systems (Hallegatte and others 2014).

Poor people will be disproportionally affected, as they often inhabit poor-quality housing and live on land that is marginal or prone to flooding. Moreover, they often hold assets in material form (rather than financial assets) and pursue occupations that are more vulnerable to climatic shocks, such as farming. The effects on welfare and prospects will depend not only on the direct impacts, but also on the ability of people and institutions to cope and adapt. Again, poor people are at a disadvantage. They have less access to the information, markets, and financial tools that support adaptation.

Social protection has the potential to play a significant role in minimizing the impacts of climate change on poor people.

Against this backdrop, social protection can be honed into a major tool to minimize the impacts of climate change on poor people. After a shock, social safety nets can be effective at counteracting adverse impacts if interventions are scaled up or introduced rapidly. When droughts in East Africa caused food shortages and famine in 2011, for instance, Ethiopia was the only country in the region where poverty did not increase. The Productive Safety Net Program (PSNP) expanded its coverage from 6.5 million to 9.6 million in two months, and increased the duration of benefits from six to nine months per year. Similarly, in Brazil, after massive floods and landslides hit in January 2011, causing 903 deaths and leaving 17,000 homeless, the Bolsa Familia program provided in-kind and cash benefits to 162,000 families in 279 municipalities within 10 days of the floods. Its central registry helped identify the affected families.

Social protection can also help before disasters strike. In this context, *adaptive social protection* (ASP) is an approach to help build resilience, with an emphasis on leveraging on existing systems. The Sahel region, for example, is extremely prone to risk. A multidonor initiative is underway to increase access to effective ASP for vulnerable populations in six Sahel countries: Burkina Faso, Chad, Mali, Mauritania, Niger, and Senegal. The aim is to increase community resilience and to leverage existing social protection programs for faster, more responsive support to marginalized households.

Social protection programs rely on four fundamental building blocks to scale up efforts to mitigate crises and shocks. The first building block requires that countries have a sufficient footprint of at least one program in place, with appropriate delivery systems that can be used as the basis of a disaster response. Such a program should be capable of scaling up after the disaster and allowing for adjustments. Examples of such programs with built-in mechanisms to scale up rapidly when a disaster strikes include the Temporary Employment Public Works Program (PET) in Mexico, the Floods Emergency Cash Transfer Program in Pakistan, and the Pantawid Pamilyang Pilipino Program (4P) in the Philippines. The Productive Safety Nets program in Ethiopia incorporates various innovative features, such as public works activities to strengthen climate resilience, a risk financing facility to help households cope better with transitory shocks, and the use of targeting methods that assist the community members most vulnerable to climate shocks.

The second building block requires the presence of sufficiently strong information systems to facilitate effective preparedness and timely response. Financing instruments and resources are the third building block. It is critical to have financing schemes arranged in advance of disasters so scalable social protection programs can be dispatched in a timely and efficient way. Such tools help governments shift from assistance following disasters to proactive budget planning before disasters strike. Bolsa Familia in Brazil is a case in point. The fourth building block is institutional coordination and capacity. Scalable social safety net programs require a high degree of institutional coordination and capacity if they are to function well after a disaster.

Note

1. This highlight is based on the forthcoming World Bank publication, *Climate Change and Poverty*.

References

Hallegatte, S., M. Bangalore, L. Bonzanigo, M. Fay, U. Narloch, J. Rozenberg, and A. Vogt-Schilb. 2014. "Climate Change and Poverty—An Analytical Framework." Policy Research Working Paper 7126, World Bank, Washington, DC.

World Bank. Forthcoming. *Climate Change and Poverty*. Washington, DC: World Bank.

Results and Evidence about Social Safety Nets

The ultimate goal of social protection and labor systems is to help individuals and societies manage risk and volatility by increasing their resilience to shocks; making societies more equitable by sharing resources to help the poor and vulnerable avoid destitution; and improving access to opportunities generated by economic growth.[1] Safety net interventions contribute to achieving all three goals: resilience, equity, and opportunity. This section focuses on the performance of social safety nets in improving the equity goal only; specifically, it examines the poverty reduction impacts. Poverty is of course multidimensional, and requires multiple interventions from multiple sectors and policies. As such, social safety nets are one of an array of instruments to address poverty, albeit a vital one.

The analysis in this section relies on indicators from the World Bank Atlas of Social Protection: Indicators of Resilience and Equity (ASPIRE) database, based on harmonized household survey data from 105 countries to estimate how social safety net transfers (cash, near-cash, and in-kind) help reduce poverty (see box 4.1). In particular, the performance of safety nets is measured against key indicators such as coverage, enrollment, adequacy, and benefit incidence (see figure 4.1). This analysis is supplemented with results from selected recent impact evaluation studies.

Performance of Social Safety Net Programs

To fully understand how to improve the efficiency of safety net systems and enhance their effectiveness in reducing poverty, it is important to assess program performance at each step of the results chain. The results chain depicts the series of logical steps of cause and effect that link inputs, activities, or processes with outputs and outcomes of an intervention to capture their effect on the desired development impacts. Figure 4.1 presents a simplified results chain of a safety net system.

Better coordinated systems are required to increase the efficiency of safety nets. Protecting the poor and the vulnerable and allowing them to avail themselves of opportunities necessitates multiple social protection programs working together, to minimize duplication and overlap. A coherent system starts with a policy framework to guide multiple social protection interventions. Countries at different levels of development have had some success in taking such a

systematic approach. For instance, Madagascar, Mali, Mauritania, and Niger are building social safety net systems comprised of public works and cash transfers, coordinated at the central and local level. All have been inspired by the Productive Safety Nets program in Ethiopia. At a different level of development, the Arab Republic of Egypt is building a system of coordinated programs that will cover the poorest households with conditional and unconditional cash transfers and public works, using its own experience of creating a registry of beneficiaries using smart cards, and learning from the lessons of implementing nationwide coordinated approaches in Mexico and Pakistan.

Process indicators that can measure the soundness and efficiency of the operational procedures of programs are critical to achieving positive impacts. In safety net interventions, the most common operational procedures are program outreach and application, selection of beneficiaries (*targeting*), enrollment, payment delivery, periodic verification of eligibility, and monitoring and evaluation.[2] Regular monitoring of these processes can identify potential bottlenecks and trigger corrective actions to improve implementation. For example, delays and irregularities in transfer payments in Ghana's Livelihood Empowerment Against Poverty (LEAP) program led to the program's inability to increase household consumption or reduce poverty.

Only one-third of the poor are covered by any type of social safety net globally. Extending coverage of the poor remains an important development priority.

■ Main Messages for Section 4

- A significant gap persists in terms of covering the poor with social protection. The coverage gap is particularly acute in the two regions where most of the world's poor live: Sub-Saharan Africa and South Asia.
- The typical cash transfer program in lower-income countries does not provide adequate income support, covering only 10 percent of the consumption of the average poor person.
- Global poverty reduction due to social safety nets is significant, including reducing the poverty gap by 15 percent. Those impacts are much stronger in higher-income countries than in low-income countries, where needs are greatest.
- New studies confirm the positive and significant impacts of social safety net programs on education, health, food security, and nutrition outcomes in early childhood. Studies also demonstrate that predictable cash transfers can enhance households' investment in activities to generate income and can spark positive spillover effects in local economies.

Box 4.1 ASPIRE Indicators Based on Household Surveys

The ASPIRE (Atlas of Social Protection: Indicators of Resilience and Equity) database, accessible online, includes key country- and program-level indicators for social protection and labor programs, including social safety nets, social insurance, and labor market programs. These are calculated using nationally representative household surveys, and are the result of a careful process of quality assurance, identification of programs in each country, grouping of different programs into standard categories, and harmonization of core indicators. When interpreting ASPIRE indicators, it is important to bear in mind that the extent to which information on specific transfers and programs is captured in the household surveys can vary considerably across countries. Moreover, household surveys typically do not capture the universe of social protection programs in the country, usually only the largest programs. As a consequence, ASPIRE indicators are not fully comparable across program categories and countries; however, they provide approximate measures of social protection system performance.

The database includes over 153 harmonized nationally representative household surveys from 1998 to 2014, covering 112 countries. ASPIRE indicators track total transfers or benefits' coverage, adequacy, and targeting performance. The latter is measured by benefit or beneficiary incidence in the total population and across quintiles of the welfare distribution. ASPIRE also includes estimates of the simulated impacts of social safety nets on poverty and inequality reduction and the degree of program overlaps. In order to compare countries, poverty is defined in relative terms within each country. In each country, the bottom 20 percent of the population in terms of consumption or income (after the safety net transfer) is defined as poor as a practical comparative approach. Coverage, targeting, and impacts on poverty are then assessed focusing on that very low-income group as the target for safety nets. According to World Bank data, world poverty—as measured with a common absolute standard of US$1.25/day in purchasing power parity—was 20.6 percent in 2010. Hence, focusing on the bottom 20 percent globally is consistent with the objective of eliminating absolute poverty. However, not all countries have poverty rates equal or close to 20 percent of the population; the population groups in need of assistance may be wider in some countries.

Source: www.worldbank.org/aspire.

Figure 4.1 Results chain of a safety net system

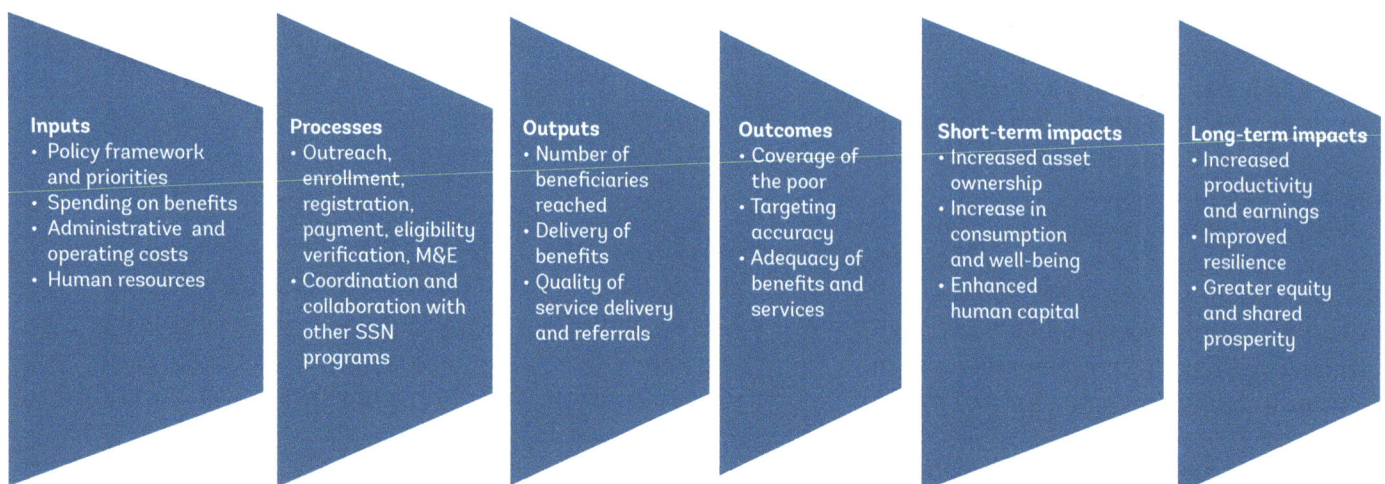

Inputs	Processes	Outputs	Outcomes	Short-term impacts	Long-term impacts
• Policy framework and priorities • Spending on benefits • Administrative and operating costs • Human resources	• Outreach, enrollment, registration, payment, eligibility verification, M&E • Coordination and collaboration with other SSN programs	• Number of beneficiaries reached • Delivery of benefits • Quality of service delivery and referrals	• Coverage of the poor • Targeting accuracy • Adequacy of benefits and services	• Increased asset ownership • Increase in consumption and well-being • Enhanced human capital	• Increased productivity and earnings • Improved resilience • Greater equity and shared prosperity

Note: M&E = monitoring and evaluation; SSN = social safety net.

Coverage

Globally, there continues to be a gap in terms of covering the poor. While strong differences exist across countries, on average, only one-third of the poor are covered by any type of social safety net (ASPIRE indicators based on household surveys; see box 4.1). The gap of coverage is particularly acute in the two regions where most of the global poor live: Sub-Saharan Africa and South Asia. Thus despite the extensive outreach of social safety net programs, most of the poor remain outside the system. Hence extending coverage of the poor remains an important development priority.

Outreach to the poor is increasing mostly through cash transfer programs. Figure 4.2 documents this trend and also shows that unconditional cash transfers (UCTs) and conditional cash transfers (CCTs) are playing a particular role in this expansion. At lower income levels, in-kind school feeding programs provide the largest, albeit limited, coverage. As country income increases, higher coverage is achieved through cash transfer programs. However, data also show that these programs provide only limited coverage of the poor. School feeding is not covering even 10 percent of the poor, on average, within the low-income countries where this program type has the highest coverage with respect to other program types.

Social safety nets play a key role in addressing the gap in the overall social protection coverage rates for poor countries, especially in South Asia and Sub-Saharan Africa. Globally for all regions, except Europe and Central Asia, social safety nets remain the main form of social protection in terms of coverage (figure 4.3). Extending the systems further will require different strategies in different countries and regions and will rely on a combination of instruments.

Enrollment

The better the ability of the social safety net system to enroll beneficiaries, the higher is the coverage rate of the poor. Table 4.1 shows a rather tight correlation between enrollment and coverage rates as captured by household surveys. However, there are some outliers and countries that complicate this comparison. In order to remain consistent, figure 4.4 uses household survey data to link coverage of the poor (measured as those beneficiary households in the poorest quintile of the respective national welfare distribution) to the social safety net system enrollment rates (measured as the sum of beneficiaries on the rolls of different types of safety net programs captured through the surveys).

There is a strong pattern between the beneficiary rolls of cash transfer programs and their

Figure 4.2 Coverage of the poor differs greatly by different types of safety nets and income groups

Coverage of the poor (poorest quintile)

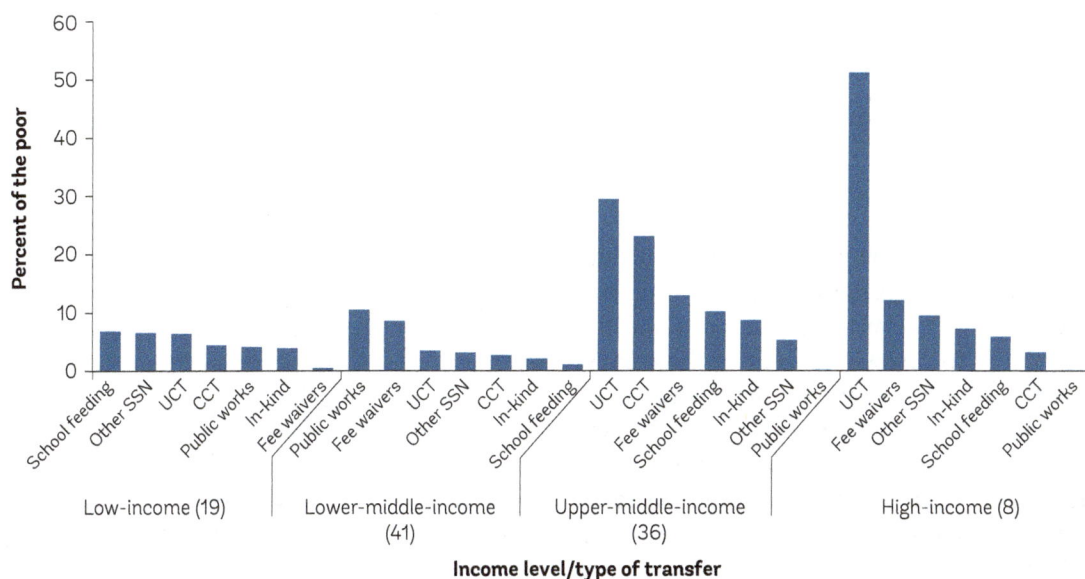

Sources: ASPIRE; see appendix G. Coverage rates are derived from household survey data, for the most recent year available per country.
Note: Coverage rates refer to the percent of poor receiving any social safety net transfer. Poor households are defined as those in the poorest quintile of countries' respective consumption/income distribution. The number of countries with available survey data for at least one program category in each income group is indicated in parentheses. CCT = conditional cash transfer; SSN = social safety net; UCT = unconditional cash transfer.

Figure 4.3 Coverage by different components of the social protection system varies by region

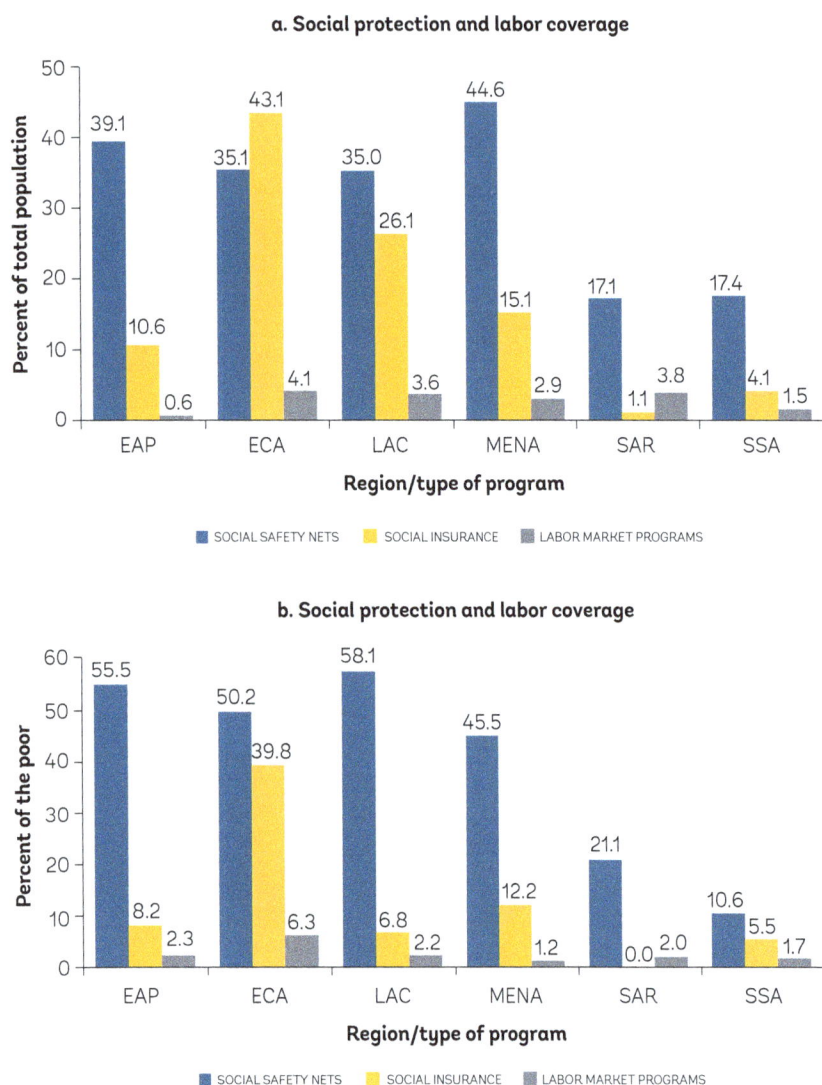

a. Social protection and labor coverage

b. Social protection and labor coverage

Sources: ASPIRE. Coverage rates are derived from household survey data, for the most recent year available per country.
Note: Poor households are defined as those in the poorest quintile of countries' respective consumption/income distribution. Aggregate statistics are based on countries with information on social safety net programs (105 countries). Regions: EAP = East Asia and Pacific; ECA = Europe and Central Asia; LAC = Latin America and the Caribbean; MENA = Middle East and North Africa; SAR = South Asia; SSA = Sub-Saharan Africa.

consumption levels below US$1.25/day per capita in purchasing power parity terms).

A critical level of enrollment is required to ensure coverage of the poor. No country achieves coverage of at least 50 percent of the poor if its overall enrollment rate is less than 20 percent. However, there are some variations across countries: 50 percent of the poor can be reached with very different enrollment rates: from about 20 percent of the population (as in Brazil) to more than double this size (54 percent, as in Ukraine). This implies very different budgets to achieve the same objective—and very different cost-efficiency in terms of poverty reduction.

No country covers 100 percent of the poor. There are significant differences in the way countries are capable of targeting their social safety net to the poor. Some countries (Chile, Ecuador, the Slovak Republic) have combined social safety net enrollment rates that exceed the size of their population (that is, some people are enrolled in more than one social safety net program). However, they still do not achieve 100 percent coverage of the poor. Targeting errors are inevitable in any program design, and even with universal programs, there are some groups that are particularly difficult to cover. While, for example, social safety net systems in Brazil, Malawi, and Turkey have approximately the same capacity in terms of percent of total population on the rolls, Malawi covers only about 20 percent of the poorest quintile, while Brazil and Turkey cover almost 60 percent (figure 4.4).

Adequacy

The contribution of safety net programs to total household consumption and poverty reduction varies substantially across country income levels. The average level of cash benefits covers only 10 percent of the consumption of the average poor person[3] across low-income countries. They cover almost twice that level (21 percent) in lower-middle-income countries, and almost four times as much (37 percent) in upper-middle-income countries. In terms of the extreme poor, the average size of the transfer is 30.6 percent of consumption of those below the absolute poverty line (US$1.25/day) among low- and middle-income countries (figure 4.5). According to World Bank data on global poverty, the average level of consumption among the poor in the developing world is 34.8 percent

actual coverage of the poor as country income increases. On average, lower-income countries have the lowest coverage of the poor and the least ability to direct resources to those most in need. In lower-income countries and lower-middle-income countries, only about 27 percent of the poorest quintile receive any form of social safety nets. This proportion grows to 64 percent in upper-middle-income countries and to 57 percent in the higher-income countries included in the analysis (table 4.1). Survey data suggest that social safety net coverage is capable of reaching half the extreme poor (those with below the US$1.25/day poverty line; this means that transfer amounts represent approximately one-fifth of the income needed to close the poverty gap in low-income countries, half the income needed in lower-middle-income countries, and is adequate as income support only in upper-middle-income countries.

Social pensions and family allowances are more generous, on average, than other safety net interventions, though there is variation across country income levels. UCT programs (including family allowances and benefits for orphans and vulnerable children) provide the highest income support in low-income countries: about 20 percent of consumption (figure 4.6). In upper-middle-income countries, there are no marked differences in adequacy among program types, which all provide between 20 and 25 percent of the poor's consumption, including categories such as social care classified under "other social safety nets." UCT and social pensions, broadly defined, include old-age and disability noncontributory pensions, and provide about 40 percent of the poor's consumption in upper-middle-income countries. Despite the small sample of countries, benefits paid for public works are higher as gross domestic product (GDP) per capita increases, consistent with minimum wage policies.

Benefit Incidence

The targeting of social safety nets is generally pro-poor. *Benefit incidence* captures the proportion of transfers that the poorest quintile receive as a percent of total transfers (appendix F). If this indicator is above 20 percent, the distribution tends to be pro-poor or progressive; if it is below 20 percent, the distri-

Figure 4.4 Higher coverage of the poor is associated with higher enrollment in social safety nets

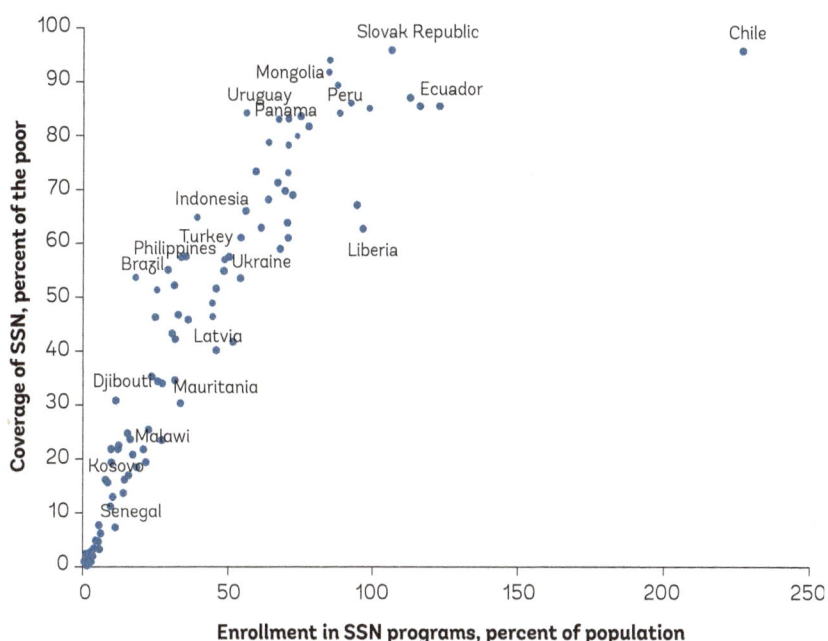

Sources: ASPIRE. Coverage rates and enrollment rates are both derived from household survey data, for the most recent year available per country.
Note: Enrollment rates are defined as the number of beneficiaries on the rolls of all social safety net programs, as a percent of the population (thus double counting is possible; hence total percentages may exceed 100 percent). Poor households are defined as those in the poorest quintile of the national welfare distribution. Aggregate statistics are based on countries/surveys with information on social safety net programs (104 countries). SSN = social safety net.

bution is regressive. The benefit incidence across program types varies, often reflecting the underlying extent to which programs target the poor rather than other social categories. CCTs are among the better targeted programs, directing more than 50 percent of spending to the poorest quintile in the case of the largest-scale CCT programs in Latin America, and 46 percent in the case of more recently established, at-scale programs such as the Pantawid

Table 4.1 Enrollment and Coverage of the Poor Rates, by Country Income Group

	Enrollment rates		Coverage of the poor	
Income group	All program types	Cash transfers only	All program types	Cash transfers only
Low-income	14.5	5.1	26.3	14.7
Lower-middle-income	26.0	9.1	27.6	16.6
Upper-middle-income	47.7	16.7	63.9	52.7
High-income	54.1	45.4	56.8	54.3

Source: ASPIRE.
Note: Enrollment rates are derived by summing up the number of beneficiaries of all safety net programs in the country as percent of total population; beneficiary rolls are based on administrative data. Enrollment rates include double counting of beneficiaries and as such, they should not be interpreted as a measure of coverage. The coverage of the poor indicator is expressed as the percentage of households in the poorest quintile of the national welfare distribution receiving any type of social safety net and cash transfer only, respectively, and is derived from household survey data, most recent year available per country, correcting for double counting of households. Cash transfers refer to both conditional and unconditional cash transfers (including social pensions) and public works.

Figure 4.5 The average transfer size does not fill the poverty gap

a. Cash transfers are not adequate in lower-income countries

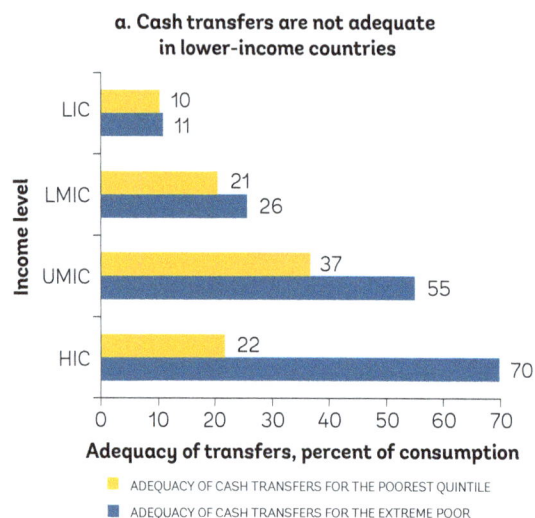

Adequacy of transfers, percent of consumption

- LIC: 10 / 11
- LMIC: 21 / 26
- UMIC: 37 / 55
- HIC: 22 / 70

Income level (vertical axis)

■ ADEQUACY OF CASH TRANSFERS FOR THE POOREST QUINTILE
■ ADEQUACY OF CASH TRANSFERS FOR THE EXTREME POOR

Source: ASPIRE.
Note: Adequacy of cash transfers for the poorest quintile (or extreme poor) is the total benefit amounts received by households in the poorest quintile (or extreme poor households) as percent of the total consumption or income of the poorest quintile (or the extreme poor). Extreme poor are those living on less than $1.25 a day at purchasing power parity (PPP) in 2005 U.S. dollars. Poorest quintile refers to the national consumption/income distribution. HIC = high-income countries; LIC = low-income countries; LMIC = lower-middle-income countries; UMIC = upper-middle-income countries.

b. The average size of cash transfers does not fill the poverty gap in low-income and lower-middle-income countries

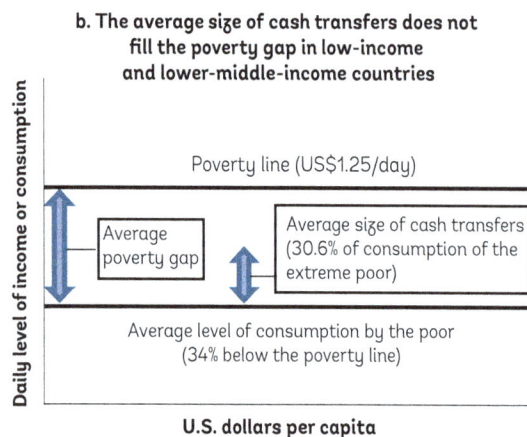

Daily level of income or consumption (vertical axis)

Poverty line (US$1.25/day)

Average poverty gap

Average size of cash transfers (30.6% of consumption of the extreme poor)

Average level of consumption by the poor (34% below the poverty line)

U.S. dollars per capita

Source: World Bank calculations based on ASPIRE; see appendix F.

in the Philippines. Figure 4.7 shows targeting performance of different types of programs (reflecting different targeting approaches), for first- and second-generation CCT programs. Targeting performance of social pensions and UCTs is weaker, as they may not be means-tested; indeed social pensions are universal in several countries (see highlight 2 on social pensions) and UCTs include categorical allowances and benefits.[4] Despite self-targeting, often adopted to select beneficiaries of public works, all quintiles of the population benefit equally, on average.

Impacts on Poverty Reduction

Social safety nets help achieve visible impacts in terms of reducing poverty and inequality. The simulated impact of all social safety nets on poverty headcount reduction[5] is 8 percent on average across 105 countries in the ASPIRE database (appendix F), which means that safety net transfers on average help reduce the poverty headcount rate by 8 percent, the value it would have been without safety nets. Poverty-reducing impacts are higher in higher-income countries (14 percent) than in low- (2 percent), lower-middle- (6 percent), and upper-middle- (10 percent) income countries. The reduction also differs by regions; it is largest in Europe and Central Asia (14 percent reduction) and smallest in South Asia (3 percent reduction). While informative about the scale of poverty, the headcount ratio does not measure how far the poor are from the poverty line (the *poverty gap*). Impacts on reducing the poverty gap are even higher, averaging 15 percent of the value of the poverty gap without safety nets. Patterns are similar across regions and income groups.

Impacts on reducing the poverty gap depend on how well the poor are covered and on the adequacy of benefits, among other factors. Countries differ considerably in how successful they are in closing the poverty gap, depending on the performance of each step along the results chain, from implementation to actual delivery (outputs), to outcomes achieved in terms of targeting accuracy and coverage of the poor. The combination of these factors explains the variation of poverty gap reduction across countries, and why this is due not only to the coverage of the poor and adequacy of benefits. While some countries have reduced poverty by more than 50 percent (Hungary, Mauritius, Poland), others have had negligible effects on poverty. Figure 4.8 maps poverty reduction effects to the two main factors: the coverage of the poor, and the adequacy of transfers. Obviously, the higher the coverage of the poor, the greater is the effect on poverty. But even achieving almost complete coverage while providing low transfers means that poverty reduction effects are low (as for Panama). Of course, when countries put relatively little weight on the role of safety nets in terms of both coverage and transfers (as in the case of Senegal), the poverty reduction effects are even smaller.

Even within similar budgetary allocation, some countries achieve higher poverty-reducing effects. This pattern provides a benchmark for assessing performance. The dotted lines in figure 4.8 represent different levels of resources committed to social safety nets, with higher lines corresponding to higher spending. Countries typically face a trade-off between expanding coverage and providing transfers with greater adequacy within a given budgetary envelope. For example, Hungary and Mauritius achieve the same poverty reduction effect with quite different combinations of adequacy and coverage. However, even within similar budget outlays, some countries are doing better than others.

Evidence from Impact Evaluations

Social safety nets are among the most rigorously evaluated interventions in development. Unlike ASPIRE indicators, impact evaluations estimate program impacts compared to rigorous counterfactuals (how individuals would have behaved without safety nets). Since the 2014 edition of *The State of Social Safety Nets*, at least 23 additional impact evaluations have been published,[6] over half of which were conducted in Sub-Saharan Africa (table 4.2). Some of the most notable evaluations published over the last year include the impact evaluation of the Pantawid Pamilyang Pilipino Program in the Philippines—one of the largest cash transfer programs in the world, serving over 4 million beneficiaries. In addition, a number of evaluations falling under the Food and Agriculture Organization's Protection to Production Program have added a significant evidence base to studies evaluating the potential productive impact of cash transfer programs in Sub-Saharan Africa on productive investments.

Rigorous evidence is being amassed at impressive speed, and is providing new insights into the transformational role of social safety net programs. Since 2011, more than 86 evaluations have focused on social safety net programs. About half focus on pilots and the rest examine established large-scale programs. Table 4.2 shows how Sub-Saharan Africa has overtaken Latin America as the most heavily evaluated region in the past four years. Table 4.3 summarizes the latest impact evaluation by country and intervention type. A large proportion (over 80 percent) continues to focus on

Figure 4.6 The adequacy of transfers for the poor varies by program type

Percent of consumption covered by transfers

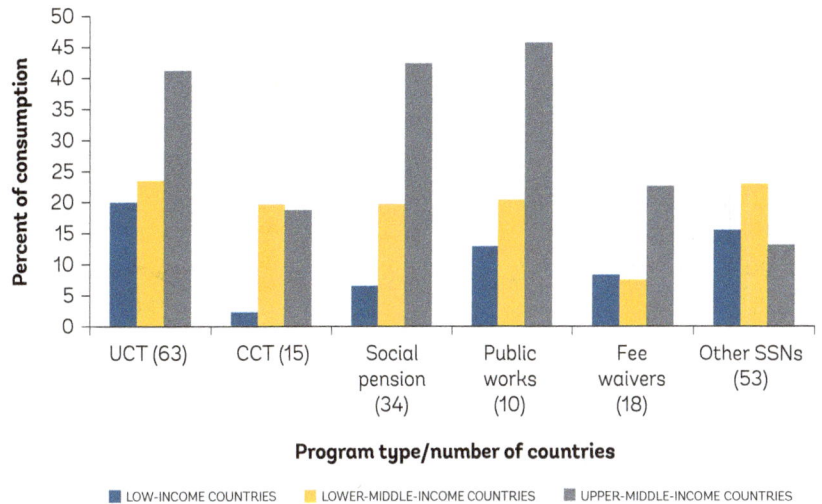

Program type/number of countries

■ LOW-INCOME COUNTRIES ■ LOWER-MIDDLE-INCOME COUNTRIES ■ UPPER-MIDDLE-INCOME COUNTRIES

Source: ASPIRE.
Note: Values refer to the average adequacy of transfers for the poor, defined as households in the poorest quintile of the national consumption/income distribution. Adequacy of transfers for the poorest quintile is the total benefit amounts received by households in the poorest quintile as percent of the total consumption or income of the poorest quintile. The number of countries for which data on the respective program type are available in national household surveys is indicated in parentheses. CCT = conditional cash transfer; SSN = social safety net; UCT= unconditional cash transfer.

cash transfers, including both conditional and unconditional programs. Other interventions evaluated include food transfers, early childhood development interventions (see highlight 4), and public works programs.

Most recent evidence confirms the positive and significant impact of cash transfers on education outcomes such as increased enrollment and attendance. Cash transfers, both conditional and unconditional, helped increase enrollment rates of primary and secondary children by 18 percentage points in Burkina Faso compared to a control group (families not receiving a transfer) and by 8 percent in Chile (figure 4.9).[7] Attendance rates, a key condition for many transfer programs, have also been improved for transfer beneficiaries, especially among secondary students (figure 4.10).

Results on health, nutrition, and food security continue to be positive and significant. In Peru, women of childbearing age enrolled in the Juntos cash transfer program were 91 percentage points more likely to have a doctor-assisted delivery compared to those not participating in the program (Perova and Vakis 2012). Evidence from Indonesia and the Philippines shows that cash transfer programs increased prenatal and postnatal care, regular

Figure 4.7 Conditional cash transfers are among the best targeted type of safety net

a. Targeting performance varies by targeting method used

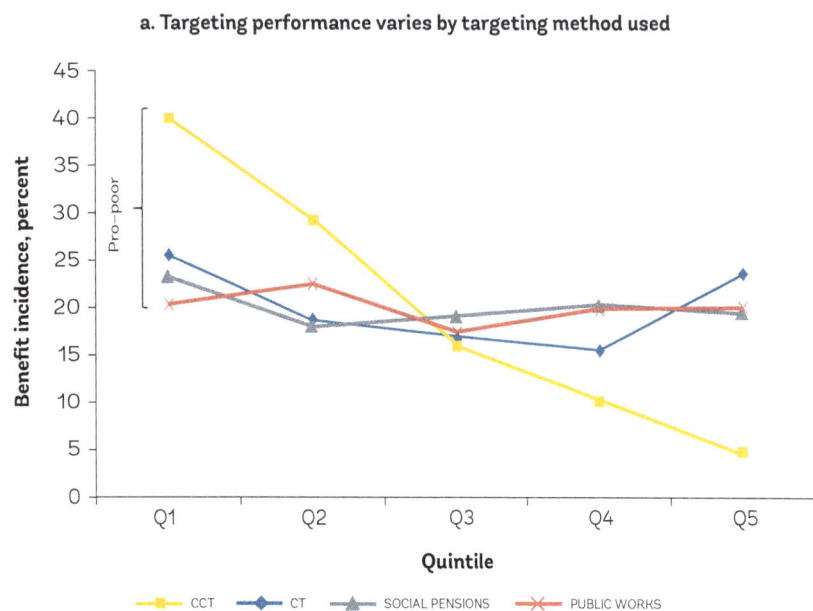

Source: ASPIRE.
Note: *Benefit incidence* refers to the sum of transfers received by individuals in each quintile of the national consumption/income distribution as a percentage of total transfers received by all individuals in the population. CCT = conditional cash transfer; CT = cash transfer; Q = quintile, with Q1 being the poorest 20 percent of the population and Q5 being the richest.

b. The targeting performance of conditional cash transfers in different countries varies considerably

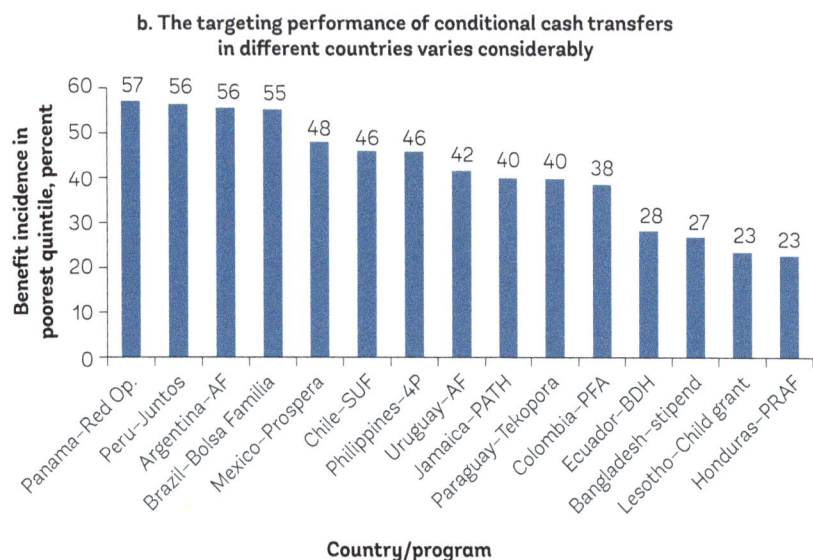

Source: ASPIRE.
Note: *Benefit incidence* refers to the sum of transfers received by individuals in the poorest quintile of the national consumption/income distribution as a percentage of total transfers received by all individuals in the population. 4P = Pantawid Pamilyang Pilipino Program; AF = Asignaciones Familiares; BDH = Bono de Desarrollo Humano; PATH = Programme of Advancement Through Health and Education; PFA = Programa Familias en Acción; PRAF = Programa De Asignación Familiar; Red Op. = Red de Oportunidades; SUF = Subsidio Único Familiar.

age-appropriate weighing, and facility-based deliveries for pregnant women and new mothers (World Bank 2011; Orbeta and others 2014). Safety net programs tend to increase the consumption of calories in the poorer households targeted, resulting in frequent direct health impacts on young children. For example, chil-

dren in households receiving a UCT in Lesotho were 16 percentage points less likely to be malnourished than similar children not receiving the transfers (Pellerano and others 2014). In Ecuador, a supplementary feeding program reduced child mortality in households exposed to the program for at least 8 months by 1.0 to 1.5 percentage points, from a baseline average rate of 2.5 percent (Meller and Litschig 2014).

A selection of impacts reviewed shows a significant impact of transfers on participants' household food security, especially in Kenya and Zambia. Programs in Brazil, Ecuador, Nicaragua, and Peru show large increases in the amount that families spend on food, compared to households that were not enrolled in safety net programs.[8]

While most of the recent evidence on safety nets revolves around cash transfers, new evidence has compared them to in-kind and near-cash transfers on a range of food security indicators. A review of 12 randomized and quasi-experimental studies (Gentilini 2014) comparing cash to food shows that differences between cash and food can be substantial for some indicators (food consumption and calorie availability), but in most instances the differences are not significant. Costs associated with cash transfers and vouchers tend to be substantially lower relative to food transfers. Yet the magnitude and direction of results can vary depending on methods used for a cost-effectiveness analysis.

Higher income from predictable cash transfers has helped households undertake productive investments in agricultural and nonagricultural activities to generate income. In many African countries, where safety net programs tend to target a large number of rural households, results show that the likelihood of beneficiary households owning livestock increased significantly. In Kenya, Lesotho, Mexico, and Zambia, the probability of participant households owning more expensive and more productive livestock—including cattle, draft animals, and pigs—increased (figure 4.11).[9] In addition, cash transfer programs have increased the likelihood of participant households owning agricultural tools by 32, 30, and 23 percentage points in Malawi, Zambia, and Ethiopia, respectively.[10] Studies in Nicaragua, Mexico, and Zambia indicate that beneficiaries are more likely to start up nonagricultural enterprises than those that do not receive transfers by 3, 4,

Figure 4.8 The poverty reduction effects of social safety nets depend on both the coverage of the poor and the adequacy of social safety net transfers

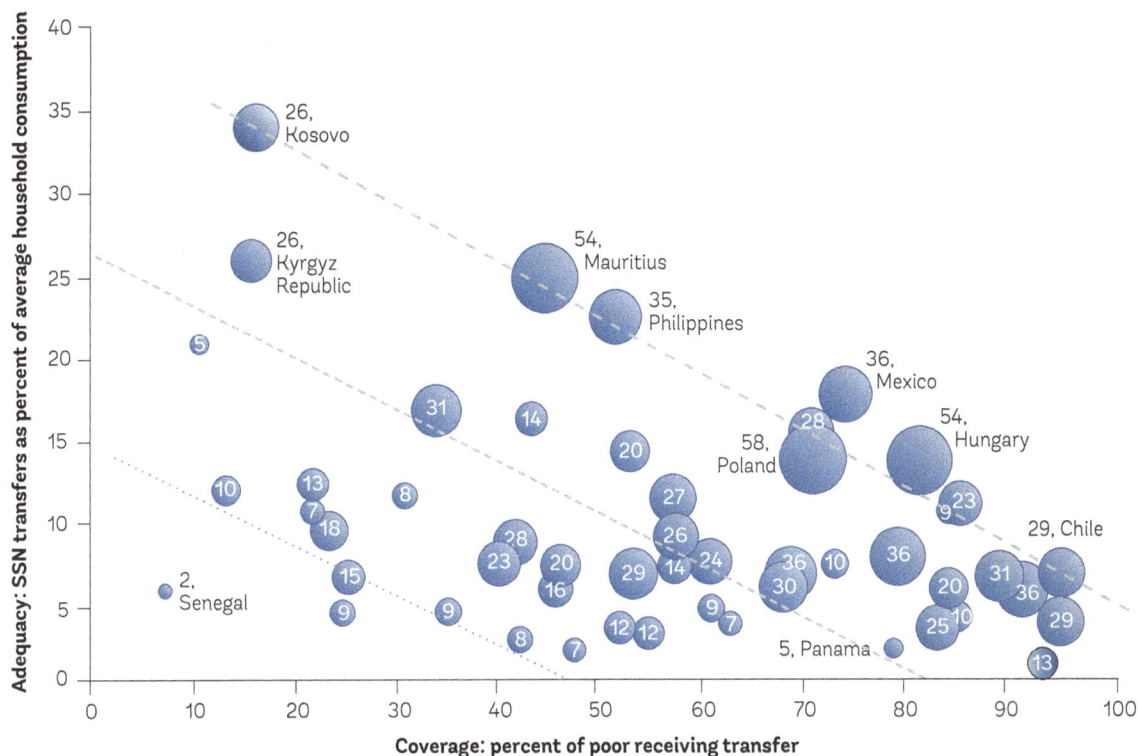

Source: ASPIRE; see appendix F.
Note: Coverage rates refer to the percent of poor receiving any social safety net transfer. The poor are defined as those households in the poorest quintile of the national consumption/income distribution. The size of the bubbles and the numbers inside the bubbles and next to country names indicate the percentage reduction in the poverty gap. The dotted and dashed lines represent different levels of resources committed to SSNs; higher lines correspond to higher spending. SSN = social safety net.

Table 4.2 Impact Evaluations, 1999–2015

Number of impact evaluations

Regions	2011–15	1999–2010
Sub-Saharan Africa	37	26
Latin America and the Caribbean	35	96
East Asia and Pacific	9	12
Middle East and North Africa	1	0
South Asia	3	13
Europe and Central Asia	1	6
Total	**86**	**153**

Sources: Authors' compilations (2011–15) and World Bank 2011 (1999–2010).
Note: Selection of studies for 2011-15 included rigorous impact evaluation studies published as journal articles, chapters in books, reports, or working papers. The search strategy relies on existing impact evaluation (IE) databases including 3IE's Impact Evaluation Repository, DIME's (Development IMpact Evaluation's) IE Working Paper Series, and the World Bank's Development Impact Blog series.

and 17 percentage points, respectively.[11] These microenterprises, such as carpentry businesses or food vendors, have the potential to result in significant long-term improvements in welfare.

This argument is further strengthened by the fact that evidence suggests that safety net programs do not reduce labor market participation. Over the last few years, program evaluations of social safety net interventions in Brazil, Chile, Honduras, Mexico, Nicaragua, and the Philippines have shown that such programs result in few (and insignificant) to no disincentives to labor market participation.[12]

Social safety nets can also lead to multiplier effects on local economies of targeted communities. A strong evidence base collected in the From Protection to Production Project[13] has found that cash transfer programs have major positive spillover effects on the local economy of targeted communities, with a nominal total income multiplier ranging from 1.08 to 2.52 dollars for each dollar transferred. This impact was found in eight different Sub-Saharan countries, including Zimbabwe (1.73) and Ghana (2.50).[14] Spillover effects stem from beneficiaries spending their transfers, often on goods or services from others inside and outside the local economy. In many cases, these are households not eligible to receive the cash transfer. As a result,

Table 4.3 Selected Recent Impact Evaluations of Social Safety Net Programs, 2014–15

Channel of impact	Country	Social safety net	Main findings	Year/Author
Early childhood development (ECD)	Indonesia	ECD	There is clear evidence that in project villages, the achievement gap between richer and poorer children, as measured by an array of child development outcomes and school enrollment, decreased in many dimensions.	Jung and Hasan 2014
Education	Cambodia	In-kind food, CCT	In most measures, similar impacts from receipt of food and cash scholarship were found. Both types of scholarship decreased the drop-out rate among recipient students.	Barker, Filmer, and Rigolini 2015
	Colombia	ECD	Psychosocial stimulation had significant positive effects on the language and cognitive development of children who received the home visits.	Attanasio and others 2015
	Nicaragua	CCT	Boys exposed to the program *in utero* and during the first two years of life have better cognitive outcomes when they are 10 years old than those exposed in their second year of life or later. For boys aged 9–12 in 2000 (and thus aged 19–22 in 2010), the short-term program effect of a half-grade increase in schooling was sustained into early adulthood, seven years after the end of the program. In addition, there were significant and substantial gains in both math and language achievement scores. Those boys of the same cohort in the early treatment group have higher earnings in the labor market than those in the late treatment group.	Barham and others 2014
Food security and nutrition	Zambia	UCT	Cash transfers improve household consumption, food consumption, diet diversity, and food security. Strong and significant heterogeneous impacts on reducing stunting were found among children who have access to clean water or more educated mothers.	Seidenfeld and others 2014
Health	Bangladesh	CCT	The pilot had a significant impact on the incidence of wasting (low weight-for-height) among children who were 10–22 months old when the program started. The pilot was also able to improve nutrition knowledge among mothers, including an increase in the proportion of beneficiary mothers who knew about the importance of exclusively breastfeeding infants until the age of 6 months.	Ferré and Sharif 2014
	Uganda	Food assistance	Significant positive impacts were found on nutritional status. Food assistance significantly increased the body mass index (BMI) by 0.6 kg/m2 and mid-upper arm circumference (MUAC) by 6.7 mm. When restricting the analysis to individuals with CD4 counts >0 cells/uL, food assistance resulted in large significant impacts.	Rawat and others 2014

(Table continues next page)

Channel of impact	Country	Social safety net	Main findings	Year/Author
Mixed	Ghana	Public works	The program had a positive impact on paid employment, food consumption expenditure, and food security for children. School attendance, particularly at the upper-secondary school level, increased among beneficiary households.	Osei-Akoto and others 2014
	Lesotho	UCT	The program helped increase the levels of expenditure on schooling, clothing, and footwear for children. The program also contributed to a significant reduction in the proportion of children 0–5 who suffered from an illness (generally flu or cold) in the 30 days prior to the survey. The Child Grant Program helped retain children 13–17 in primary school, particularly boys who would have otherwise dropped out.	Pellerano and others 2014
	Philippines	CCT	Pantawid Pamilya encourages the trial use of modern family planning methods. The program promotes facility-based deliveries and access to professional postnatal care and improves children's access to some key health care services. Among Pantawid beneficiaries, about 9 in 10 households are covered by the PhilHealth health insurance program. The program keeps older children in school. Children (10–14 years old) in the program work seven fewer days a month than children not in the program. Pantawid Pamilya increases households' investments in education and does not encourage dependency or spending more on vice goods, such as alcohol.	Orbeta Jr. and others 2014
	Philippines	CCT	Pantawid Pamilya is reaching most of its key objectives. The impacts found through this study are comparable to the levels of impact found in other CCT programs around the world at this stage of program maturity, particularly in terms of the program's achievements in improved use of health services and school enrollment.	Chaudhury, Friedman, and Onishi 2014
	Sierra Leone	Public works	Monthly incomes of participating households increased by 26 percent. Further, the program appears to have been a highly productive safety net. Program participation significantly increased the likelihood of creating enterprises and investing in homes and, in some cases, existing businesses. Beneficiary households increased their asset accumulation of small livestock.	Rosas and Sabarwal 2014
	Tanzania	CCT	Significant impacts are observed across a broad array of areas, including health, education, and various risk-reducing behaviors: use of health insurance, insurance expenditures, nonbank savings (for the poorest households), and the purchase of livestock such as goats and chickens. In addition, the program has led to significant increases in spending on certain children's goods (especially children's shoes).	Evans and others 2014

(Table continues next page)

Channel of impact	Country	Social safety net	Main findings	Year/Author
Productive investments	Lesotho	UCT	The program is associated with higher use of inputs, especially pesticides that prevented major crop losses after a severe outbreak of armyworms. The Child Grants Program contributed to increased production, both for the home garden and for main staple crops, including maize.	Daidone and others 2014
Program take-up	Colombia	Home visits from social workers	No consistent impact of the program was found, possibly because the way the pilot was implemented resulted in a very light treatment in terms of home visits.	Abramovsky and others 2014
Stimulating local economies	Ethiopia	UCT	Each birr (unit of Ethiopian currency) distributed in Hintalo-Wajirat generated an extra 1.52 birr via local market linkages, for a total income multiplier of 2.52. Similarly, each birr distributed in Abi-Adi generated an additional 0.35 birr, for a total income multiplier of 1.35. Simulations incorporating market constraints find a "real" income multiplier of 1.84 birr for Hintalo-Wajirat and 1.26 birr for Abi-Adi.	Kagin and others 2014
	Ghana	CCT	Transfers could lead to a relatively large income multiplier of GHS (Ghanaian cedi) 2.50. Adjusting for potential rising prices could lead to a lower real income multiplier of GHS 1.50.	Thome, Taylor, Kagin, and others 2014
	Zambia	UCT	The transfers could lead to a relatively large income multiplier of K (Zambian kwacha) 1.79. Eligible households receive the direct benefit of the transfer, while ineligible households receive the bulk of the indirect benefit.	Thome, Taylor, Davis, and others 2014
	Zimbabwe	UCT	Transfers could lead to relatively large nominal income multipliers of Z$ (Zimbabwean dollars) 1.73 and a real income multiplier that could be as low as Z$1.40.	Taylor and others 2014
Temptation goods	Mexico	In-kind food, CCT (although conditionality not enforced)	Households do not indulge in consumption of vices when handed cash. Furthermore, there is little evidence that the in-kind food transfer induced more food to be consumed than did the cash transfer of equal value.	Cunha 2014
	Peru	CCT	Food expenditures went up by 10–20 percent when beneficiaries received the cash transfer as opposed to when they did not have it. Additional evidence suggests that this increase is driven by higher consumption of candies, chocolates, soft drinks, and meals in restaurants, but not alcohol.	Dasso and Fernandez 2014

Source: Authors' compilations.
Note: CCT = conditional cash transfer; ECD = early childhood development; UCT = unconditional cash transfer.

for each dollar invested into a cash transfer program in Zimbabwe, 1.73 dollars in income was generated for the local economy. It is possible, however, that labor, capital, and land markets do not function optimally in these countries, meaning that prices could rise as a result of the transfer programs themselves, diluting the impact of this multiplier. Even after adjusting for any resulting local inflation, real multiplier effects are still higher than 1. Figure 4.12 presents both real and nominal multiplier effects.

While transfer programs raise consumption levels of food, health, education, and hygiene, there is no evidence that they also increase consumption of alcohol or tobacco. Programs in Africa, Latin America, and Eastern and Southern Asia all show no impact of transfer programs on the consumption of alcohol, tobacco, and gambling (Evans and Popova 2014). In fact, the evaluation of the Pantawid Program in the Philippines found that beneficiaries reduced their spending on alcohol by 39 percent in comparison to the control group (Chaudhury, Friedman, and Onishi 2014).

Several studies have measured the impact of interventions after five years or more,[15] indicating that impacts persist well after program exit.[16] In Nicaragua, seven years after treatment groups stopped receiving transfers, boys (now young men aged 19–22) in the early treatment group had still attained a half-year more in schooling than those who were exposed to the program three years later. Moreover, unlike long-term findings related to the Oportunidades (now Prospera) program in Mexico, the increase in grade attainment was accompanied with better literacy and math skills in comparison to the late treatment group. Yet in Colombia, a long-term analysis on the impact of Familias en Acción on test scores found no difference in the performance of poor high school graduates who were program recipients, compared to equally poor graduates who were not program recipients. Even four years after the control households were incorporated into the Opportunidades, the original beneficiary households had consumption levels that were 5.6 percent higher than the original nonbeneficiary households. This implies that the returns on investments made by the initial beneficiaries in the 18 months before the control households received benefits resulted in improved long-term living standards. A study on the impact of a supplemental feeding program in Guatemala found that boys who received a protein supplement between the ages of 0 and 2 had an hourly wage 25 years later that was US$0.67 higher than the control group: a 46 percent increase in average wages.

More research is needed in a number of areas, including the overall cost-benefit analysis of social safety net programs. The pace at which the evidence base on social safety nets continues to grow nonetheless remains impressive and continues to shed light on the transformational role these programs can have on the lives of program participants. New insights have found that safety net programs can also result in significant reductions in violence, including a sig-

Figure 4.9 Selected impacts of social safety nets on school enrollment rates

Percentage point increase compared to the control group

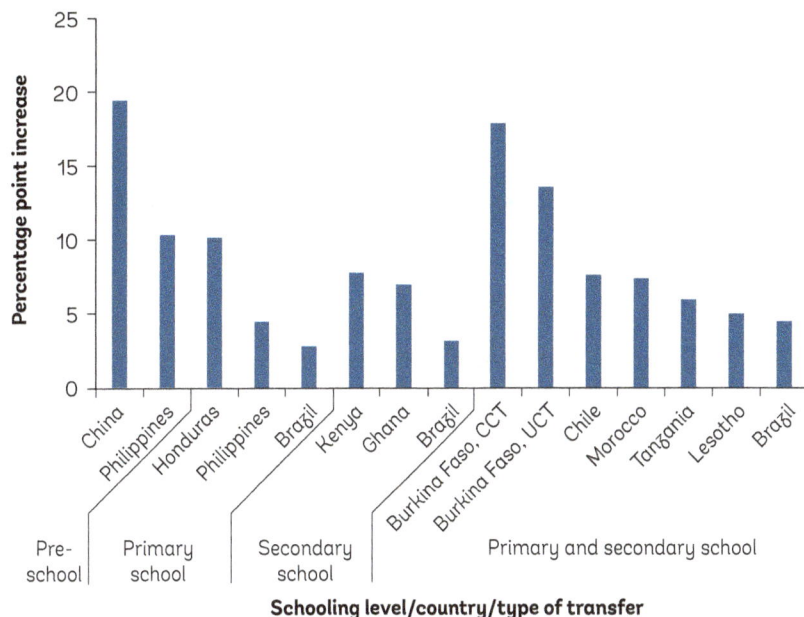

Source: World Bank, based on a review of selected impact evaluation studies.
Note: Percentage point increase in outcomes among program beneficiaries with respect to nonbeneficiaries (control group). CCT = conditional cash transfer; UCT = unconditional cash transfer.

Figure 4.10 Selected impacts of social safety nets on school attendance rates

Percentage point increase compared to the control group

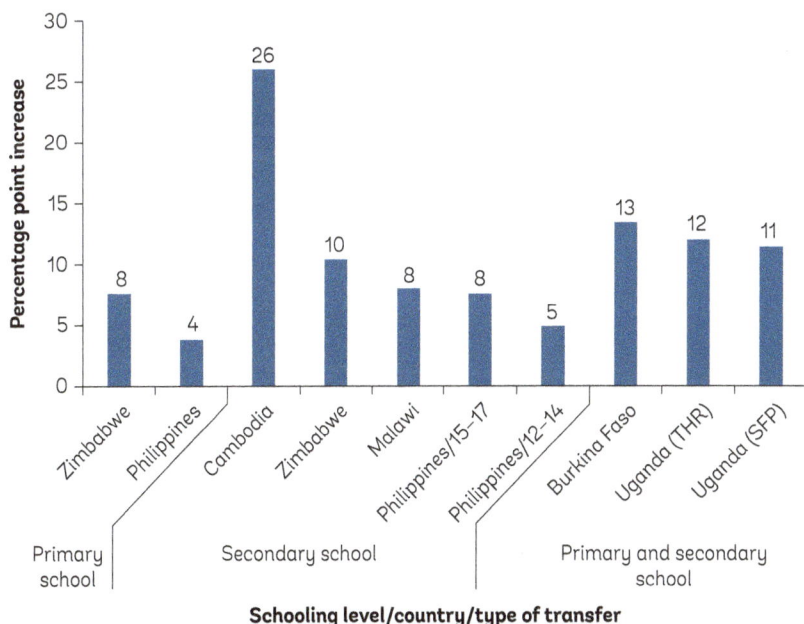

Source: World Bank, based on a review of selected impact evaluation studies.
Note: Percentage point increase in outcomes among program beneficiaries with respect to nonbeneficiaries (control group). SFP = school feeding program; THR = take-home ration.

nificant decrease in intimate partner violence in Ecuador and a reduction in street crime in Brazil.[17] With the enormous policy implications involved, and current studies limited to Latin

Figure 4.11 The proportion of social safety net beneficiary households owning a productive asset has grown

Percentage point increase compared to control group

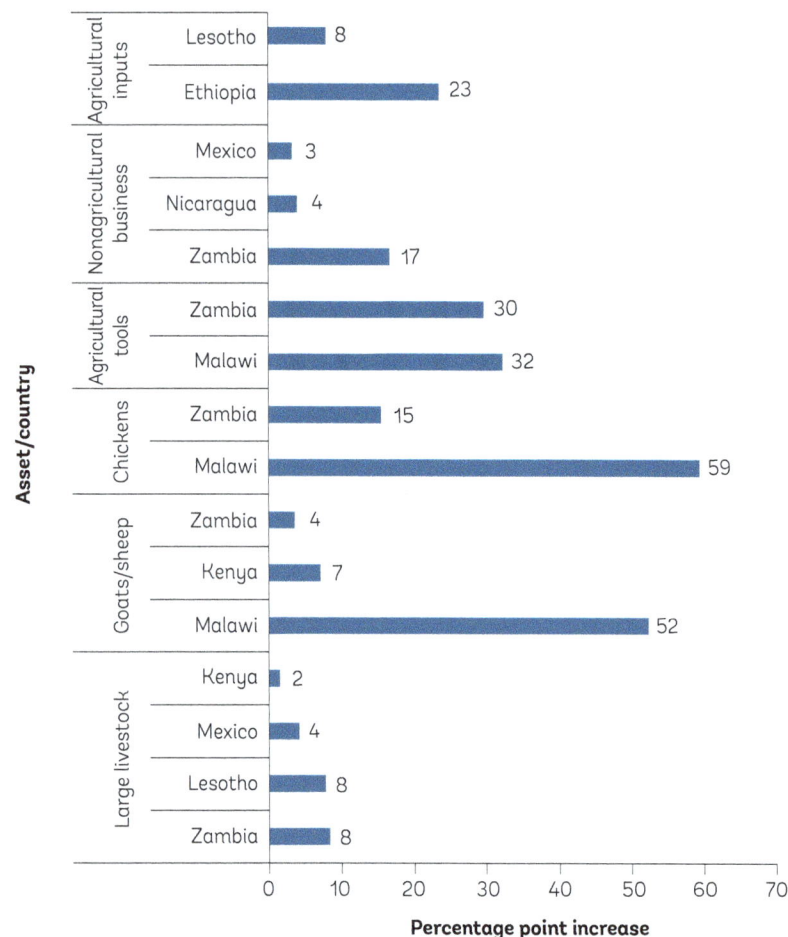

Source: World Bank, based on a review of selected impact evaluation studies.
Note: Percentage point increase in outcomes among program beneficiaries with respect to nonbeneficiaries (control group).

America, further evidence needs to be collected to supplement these findings. There is also growing interest in the "graduation" agenda: how to help social safety net beneficiaries move out of extreme poverty and into sustainable livelihoods and more productive jobs. Yet much remains to be explored on how best to link social safety nets with complementary programs and services—such as asset transfers, financial inclusion, skills training, and job search assistance—and the effects of such services on beneficiaries' job prospects and earnings. The adaptation of social safety nets to urban areas is an issue of growing relevance in a number of countries, and so is the customization of safety nets in fragile and disaster-prone contexts. Finally, a coherent evidence base of cost-benefit analysis of safety net programs is still scarce. Filling this knowledge gap would significantly add to the discussion on social safety net performance.

Notes

1. The 2012–2022 Social Protection and Labor Strategy, World Bank, http://www.worldbank.org/en/topic /social protectionlabor/publication/social-protection -labor-strategy-2012-2022.

2. Examples of such process indicators are the average duration of the application process, the percentage of payments on hold for more than a certain number of weeks and months, the percentage of beneficiaries recertified within the period established in the operations manual, the percentage of suspected cases of error and fraud that are investigated, and the percentage of conditionality compliance reports that

Figure 4.12 Social safety nets have high multiplier effects

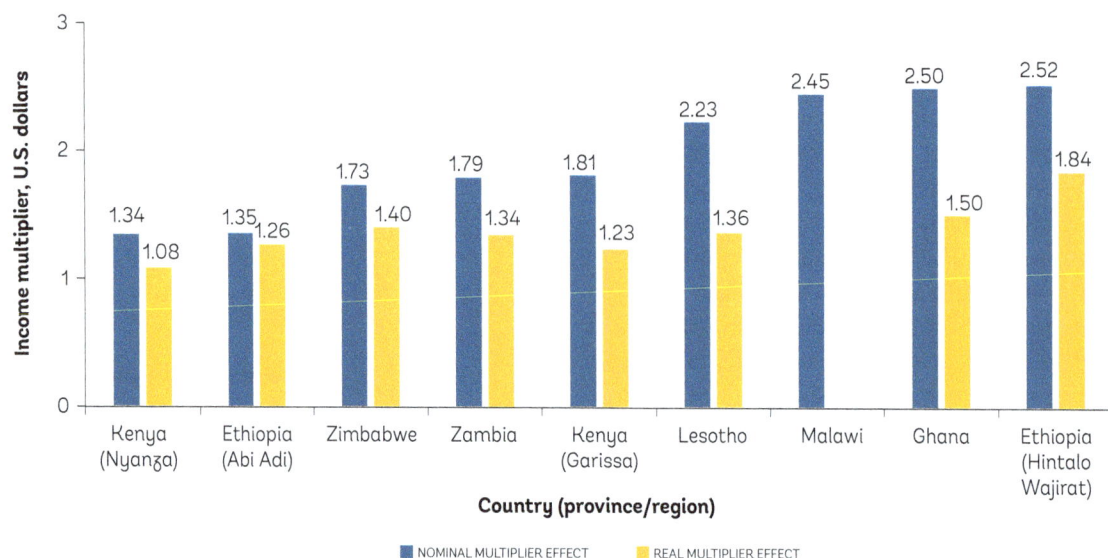

Sources: Tirivayi, Knowles, and Davis 2013. Data for Malawi from Davies and Davey 2008.
Note: Multiplier effects refer to increases in local income for each dollar spent on social safety nets. Real multiplier effects are adjusted for inflation.

are received on time, in the case of conditional cash transfer (CCT) programs (Rubio 2012).

3. The poor are defined as those belonging to the poorest quintile, relative to the national consumption/income distribution.

4. Categorical allowances and benefits use specific categories or population groups to define benefit eligibility, such as a particular age group, geographic location, gender, or demographic composition. Children allowances and universal social pensions for citizens above a certain age are examples of categorical benefits.

5. It is assumed that the welfare aggregate of a recipient household—in the absence of the program—falls by the value of the transfer. To establish the impact of a safety protection program(s) on poverty, one ought to compare poverty without the program(s) ("pre-transfer"), to poverty with it ("post-transfer"). Then the transfer received under the program would need to be subtracted from the welfare aggregate and the poverty measure would need to be recalculated to get a pre-transfer/program poverty measure. Comparing the two poverty measures gives an estimate of the program's poverty impact.

6. The search strategy focused on rigorous impact evaluation studies of social safety net interventions (cash, in-kind transfer, public works) published as journal articles, chapters in books, reports, or as working papers. The search relied on existing impact evaluation databases, including 3IE's Impact Evaluation Repository, DIME's IE Working Paper Series, and the World Bank's Development Impact Blog series, among other publicly available sources. The analysis offered here is not meant to provide a comprehensive review of the evidence; rather, it aims to summarize results from selected studies and illustrate the overall trend in the impact evaluation literature. Importantly, the analysis focuses only on positive and statistically significant impacts. The impact of safety nets can also be mixed, not statistically significant, or even negative, indicating the need for comprehensive reviews of the evidence.

7. Akresh, De Walque, and Kazianga 2013 (Burkina Faso); Martorano and Sanfilippo 2012 (Chile).

8. Haushofer and Shapiro 2013 (Kenya); Seidenfeld, Handa, and Tembo 2013 (Zambia); Braido, Olinto, and Perrone 2012 (Brazil); Hidrobo and others 2012 (Ecuador); Macours, Premand, and Vakis 2012 (Nicaragua); Dasso and Fernandez 2014 (Peru).

9. Merttens and others 2013 (Kenya); Daidone and others 2014 (Lesotho); Gertler, Martinez, and Rubio-Codina 2012 (Mexico); American Institutes for Research 2013 (Zambia).

10. Covarrubias, Davis, and Winters 2012 (Malawi); Seidenfeld and others 2014 (Zambia); Hoddinott and others 2012 (Ethiopia).

11. Macours, Premand, and Vakis 2012 (Nicaragua); Gertler, Martinez, and Rubio-Codina 2012 (Mexico); Seidenfeld and others 2014 (Zambia).

12. De Brauw and others 2012 (Brazil); Larranaga, Contreras, and Ruiz-Tagle 2012 (Chile); Alzúa, Cruces, and Ripani 2014 (Honduras, Mexico, and Nicaragua); Chaudhury, Friedman, and Onishi 2014 (Philippines).

13. The From Protection to Production (PtoP) project is a multicountry impact evaluation of cash transfers in Sub-Saharan Africa. The project is a collaborative effort between the FAO, the UNICEF Eastern and Southern Africa Regional Office, and the governments of Ethiopia, Ghana, Kenya, Lesotho, Malawi, Zambia, and Zimbabwe.

14. Taylor and others 2014 (Zimbabwe); Thome, Taylor, Kagin, and others 2014 (Ghana).

15. The Punjab Female School Stipend in Pakistan (Alam, Baez, and Del Carpio 2011); Familias en Acción in Colombia (Baez and Camacho 2011); Red de Protección Social in Nicaragua (Barham and others 2014); the INCAP Supplementation Programme in Guatemala (Hoddinott and others 2008); Juntos in Peru (Perova and Vakis 2012); Oportunidades in Mexico (Gertler, Martinez, and Rubio-Codina 2012); and the Jamaica Study in Jamaica (Walker and others 2011; Gertler and others 2013).

16. Measuring long-term impacts of social safety net programs is often difficult. Many programs that are evaluated using experimental and quasi-experimental methods make use of the fact that budget constraints force programs to be phased in over time, allowing for the creation of a valid counterfactual. However, the scale-up of the program results in the control group receiving treatment, therefore no longer becoming a valid counterfactual.

17. Chioda, De Mello, and Soares 2012; Hidrobo and others 2012; Walker and others 2011.

References

Abramovsky, L., O. Attanasio, K. Barron, P. Carneiro, and G. Stoye. 2014. "Challenges to Promoting Social Inclusion of the Extreme Poor: Evidence from a Large-Scale Experiment in Colombia." IFS Working Paper 14/33, Institute for Fiscal Studies, London.

Akresh, R., D. De Walque, and H. Kazianga. 2013. "Cash Transfers and Child Schooling: Evidence from a Randomized Evaluation of the Role of Conditionality." Policy Research Working Paper 6340, World Bank, Washington, DC.

Alam, Andaleeb, J. Baez, and X. Del Carpio. 2011. "Does Cash for School Influence Young Women's Behavior in the Longer Term? Evidence from Pakistan." IZA Discussion Papers 5703, Institute for the Study of Labor (IZA), Bonn.

Alzúa, M. L., G. Cruces, and L. Ripani. 2014. "Welfare Programs and Labor Supply in Developing Countries: Experimental Evidence from Latin America." Journal of Population Economics 26 (4): 1255–84.

American Institutes for Research. 2013. Zambia's Child Grant Program: 24-Month Impact Report. Washington, DC: American Institutes for Research.

Attanasio, O., S. Cattan, E. Fitzsimons, C. Meghir, and M. Rubio-Codina. 2015. "Estimating the Production Function for Human Capital: Results from a Randomized Control Trial in Colombia." IZA Discussion Paper 8856, Institute for the Study of Labor (IZA), Bonn.

Baez, J. E., and A. Camacho. 2011. "Assessing the Long-Term Effects of Conditional Cash Transfers on Human Capital: Evidence from Colombia." Policy Research Working Paper 5681, World Bank, Washington, DC.

Barham, T., K. Macours, J. A. Maluccio, F. Regalia, V. Aguilera, and M. E. Moncada. 2014. *Assessing Long-Term Impacts of Conditional Cash Transfers on Children and Young Adults in Rural Nicaragua*. Impact Evaluation Report 17. New Delhi: International Initiative for Impact Evaluation.

Barker, M., D. Filmer, and J. Rigolini. 2015. *Evaluating Food versus Cash Assistance in Rural Cambodia*. Washington, DC: World Bank.

Braido, L. H., P. Olinto, and H. Perrone. 2012. "Gender Bias in Intrahousehold Allocation: Evidence from an Unintentional Experiment." *Review of Economics and Statistics* 94 (2): 552–65.

Chaudhury, N., J. Friedman, and J. Onishi. 2014. *Philippines Conditional Cash Transfer Program: Impact Evaluation 2012*. Washington, DC: World Bank.

Chioda, L., J. M. De Mello, and R. R. Soares. 2012. *Spillovers from Conditional Cash Transfer Programs: Bolsa Família and Crime in Urban Brazil*. World Bank, Washington, DC.

Covarrubias, K., B. Davis, and P. Winters. 2012. "From Protection to Production: Productive Impacts of the Malawi Social Cash Transfer Scheme." *Journal of Development Effectiveness* 4 (1): 50–77.

Cunha, J. M. 2014. "Testing Paternalism: Cash versus In-kind Transfers." *American Economic Journal: Applied Economics* 6 (2): 195–230.

Daidone, S., B. Davis, J. Dewbre, and K. Covvarubias. 2014. *Lesotho's Child Grant Programme: 24-Month Impact Report on Productive Activities and Labour Allocation*. Rome: Food and Agriculture Organization.

Dasso, R., and F. Fernandez. 2014. *Temptation Goods and Conditional Cash Transfers in Peru*. Washington, DC: International Food and Policy Research Institute.

Davies, S., and J. Davey. 2008. "A Regional Multiplier Approach to Estimating the Impact of Cash Transfers on the Market: The Case of Cash Transfers in Rural Malawi." *Development Policy Review* 26 (1): 91–111.

De Brauw, A., D. Gilligan, J. Hoddinott, V. Moreira, and S. Roy. 2012. *The Impact of Bolsa Familia on Child, Maternal, and Household Welfare*. Washington, DC: International Food Policy Resarch Institute.

Evans, D., S. Hausladen, K. Kosec, and N. Reese. 2014. *Community-Based Conditional Cash Transfers in Tanzania: Results from a Randomized Trial*. Washington, DC: World Bank.

Evans, David K. and A. Popova. 2014. "Cash Transfers and Temptation Goods: A Review of Global Evidence." Policy Research Working Paper 6886, World Bank, Washington, DC.

Ferré, C., and I. Sharif. 2014. "Can Conditional Cash Transfers Improve Education and Nutrition Outcomes for Poor Children in Bangladesh? Evidence from a Pilot Project." Policy Research Working Paper 7077, World Bank, Washington, DC.

Gentilini, U. 2014. "Our Daily Bread: What Is the Evidence on Comparing Cash versus Food Transfers?" Social Protection and Labor Discussion Paper 1420, World Bank, Washington, DC.

Gertler, P. J., J. Heckman, R. Pinto, A. Zanolini, C. Vermeersch, and S. Walker. 2013. "Labor Market Returns to Early Childhood Stimulation: A 20-Year Follow-Up to an Experimental Intervention in Jamaica." NBER Working Paper 19185, National Bureau of Economic Research, Cambridge, MA.

Gertler, P. J., S. W. Martinez, and M. Rubio-Codina. 2012. "Investing Cash Transfers to Raise Long-Term Living Standards." *American Economic Journal: Applied Economics* 4 (1): 164–92.

Haushofer, J., and J. Shapiro. 2013. *Household Response to Income Changes: Evidence from an Unconditional Cash Transfer Program in Kenya*. Massachusetts Institute of Technology. http://www.princeton.edu /~joha/publications/Haushofer_Shapiro_UCT _2013.pdf.

Hidrobo, M., J. Hoddinott, A. Margolies, V. Moreira, and A. Peterman. 2012. *Impact Evaluation of Cash, Food Vouchers, and Food Transfers among Colombian Refugees and Poor Ecuadorians in Carchi and Sucumbíos*. Washington, DC: International Food Policy Research Institute.

Hoddinott, J., G. Berhane, D. O. Gilligan, N. Kumar, and A. S. Taffesse. 2012. "The Impact of Ethiopia's Productive Safety Net Programme and Related Transfers on Agricultural Productivity." *Journal of African Economies* 21 (5): 761–86.

Hoddinott, J., J. A. Maluccio, J. R. Behrman, R. Flores, and R. Martorell. 2008. "Effect of a Nutrition Intervention during Early Childhood on Economic Productivity in Guatemalan Adults." *The Lancet* 371 (9610): 411–16.

Jung, H., and A. Hasan. 2014. "The Impact of Early Childhood Education on Early Achievement Gaps: Evidence from the Indonesia Early Childhood Education and Development (ECED) Project." Policy Research Working Paper 6794, World Bank, Washington, DC.

Kagin, J., E. Taylor, F. Alfani, and B. Davis. 2014. *Local Economy-wide Impact Evaluation (LEWIE) of Ethiopia's Social Cash Transfer Pilot Programme*. Rome: Food and Agriculture Organization.

Larranaga O., D. Contreras, and J. Ruiz-Tagle. 2012. "Impact Evaluation of Chile Solidario: Lessons and

Policy Recommendations." *Journal of Latin American Studies* 44 (02): 347–72.

Macours, K., P. Premand, and R. Vakis. 2012. "Transfers, Diversification and Household Risk Strategies: Experimental Evidence with Lessons for Climate Change Adaptation." Policy Research Working Paper 6053, World Bank, Washington, DC.

Martorano, B., and M. Sanfilippo. 2012. "Innovative Features in Conditional Cash Transfers: An Impact Evaluation of Chile Solidario on Households and Children." Innocenti Working Paper 2012-03, UNICEF Innocenti Research Centre, Florence, Italy.

Meller, M., and S. Litschig. 2014. "Saving Lives: Evidence from a Conditional Food Supplementation Program." *Journal of Human Resources* 49 (4): 1014–52.

Merttens, F., A. Hurrell, M. Marzi, R. Attah, M. Farhat, A. Kardan, and I. MacAuslan. 2013. *Kenya Hunger Safety Net Programme Monitoring and Evaluation Component. Impact Evaluation Final Report: 2009 to 2012*. Oxford, U.K.: Oxford Policy Management Limited.

Orbeta Jr., A., A. Abdon, M. del Mundo, M. Tutor, M. T. Valera, and D. Yarcia. 2014. *Keeping Children Healthy and in School: Evaluating the Pantawid Pamilya Using Regression Discontinuity Design Second Wave Impact Evaluation Results*. Washington, DC: World Bank.

Osei-Akoto, I., S. Bawakyillenuo, G. Owusu, E. Larbi Offei, C. Yaw Okyere, and I. Komla Agbelie. 2014. *Short-Term Impact Evaluation Report: Labour-Intensive Public Works (LIPW) of Ghana Social Opportunities Project (GSOP)*. Institute of Statistical, Social and Economic Research (ISSER), University of Ghana.

Pellerano, L., M. Moratti, M. Jakobsen, M. Bajgar, and V. Barca. 2014. *Child Grants Programme Impact Evaluation. Follow-Up Report*. Oxford Policy Management for the European Union, UNICEF, and the Food and Agriculture Organization.

Perova, E., and R. Vakis. 2012. 5 Years in Juntos: New Evidence on the Program's Short- and Long-Term Impacts. *Economía* 35 (69): 53–82.

Rawat, R., E. Faust, J. A. Maluccio, and S. Kadiyala. 2014. "The Impact of a Food Assistance Program on Nutritional Status, Disease Progression, and Food Security among People Living with HIV in Uganda." *Journal of Acquired Immune Deficiency Syndromes* 66 (1): e15–22.

Rosas, N., and S. Sabarwal. 2014. *Opportunity and Resilience: Do Public Works Have It All? Evidence from a Randomized Evaluation in Sierra Leone*. Washington, DC: World Bank.

Rubio, G. M. 2012. "Building Results Frameworks for Safety Nets Projects." Social Protection and Labor Discussion Paper 73703, World Bank, Washington, DC.

Seidenfeld, D., S. Handa, and G. Tembo. 2013. *24-Month Impact Report for the Child Grant Programme*. Ministry of Community Development, Mother and Child Health, Government of Zambia.

Seidenfeld, D., S. Handa, G. Tembo, S. Michelo, C. Harland Scott, and L. Prencipe. 2014. *The Impact of an Unconditional Cash Transfer on Food Security and Nutrition: The Zambia Child Grant Programme*. Brighton, U.K.: Institute of Development Studies.

Taylor, E., K. Thome, B. Davis, D. Seidenfeld, and S. Handa. 2014. *Evaluating Local General Equilibrium Impacts of Zimbabwe's Harmonized Social Cash Transfer Programme*. Rome: Food and Agriculture Organization.

Thome, K., J. Taylor, B. Davis, S. Handa, D. Seidenfeld, and G. Tembo. 2014. *Local Economy-wide Impact Evaluation (LEWIE) of Zambia's Child Grant Programme*. PtoP Project Report. Food and Agriculture Organization, UNICEF, and the World Bank.

Thome, K., J. E. Taylor, J. Kagin, B. Davis, R. Osei Darko, and I. Osei-Akoto. 2014. *Local Economy-wide Impact Evaluation (LEWIE) of Ghana's Livelihood Empowerment against Poverty (LEAP) Programme*. Rome: Food and Agriculture Organization.

Tirivayi, N., M. Knowles, and B. Davis. 2013. *The Interaction between Social Protection and Agriculture: A Review of Evidence*. Rome: Food and Agriculture Organization.

Walker, S. P., S. M. Chang, M. Vera-Hernandez, and S. Grantham-McGregor. 2011. "Early Childhood Stimulation Benefits Adult Competence and Reduces Violent Behavior." *Pediatrics* 127 (5): 849–57.

World Bank. 2011. *Program Keluarga Harapan: Main Findings from the Impact Evaluation of Indonesia's Pilot Household Conditional Cash Transfer Program*. Washington, DC: World Bank.

Weblinks

ASPIRE (The Atlas of Social Protection: Indicators of Resilience and Equity), World Bank, www.worldbank.org/aspire/.

DIME's IE Working Paper Series, http://go.worldbank.org/69LQQAL850.

3IE's Impact Evaluation Repository, http://www.3ieimpact.org/evidence/impact-evaluations/.

World Bank's Development Impact Blog Series, http://blogs.worldbank.org/impactevaluations/.

Strengthening linkages between cash transfers and early childhood development (ECD) can be a win-win. Promoting early childhood development can help cash transfer programs achieve their core objectives of protecting the most vulnerable, fostering investments in human capital, and reducing the intergenerational transmission of poverty. At the same time, cash transfer programs can help scale up early childhood development services.

Cash transfer programs can serve as effective vehicles for promoting early childhood nutrition, health, and development, in addition to their more traditional role of providing income support to the poor and vulnerable. Where ECD services exist, cash transfer programs can help households overcome barriers to access, for instance, by making the transfers conditional on health visits, growth monitoring sessions, or attendance in preschool. Cash transfer programs can also help encourage changes in parenting practices to promote early childhood nutrition, psychosocial stimulation, or health. For instance, programs can package unconditional cash transfers with parenting information for caregivers. A growing number of safety net programs are using *accompanying measures* to achieve these objectives.

> *Cash transfer programs can serve as effective vehicles for promoting early childhood nutrition, health, and development.*

Cash transfer programs with strong accompanying measures can improve ECD outcomes by fostering behavioral changes among parents. This approach is particularly relevant for low-income countries, where existing ECD services are limited and where targeted cash transfers provide a primary (and often the only) vehicle for reaching poor and vulnerable households. Accompanying measures can include a range of social marketing, community-based, or home-visit activities to encourage psychosocial stimulation or growth-promotion practices by parents. In Bangladesh, for example, the Shombob pilot program significantly reduced the incidence of wasting among children who were 10–22 months old when the program started (Ferré and Sharif 2014). The program was a cash transfer intervention, conditional on regular growth monitoring of children aged 0–36 months. Participation in monthly nutrition-related sessions by mothers of young children was encouraged, although not mandatory. The pilot was also able to improve nutrition knowledge among mothers, including in relation to the importance of exclusive breastfeeding.

Other countries are testing similar approaches, including Burkina Faso, Djibouti, Mali, and Niger. In West Africa, many countries are delivering unconditional cash transfers with accompanying ECD measures. For instance, in Niger, the national safety net program is implementing an unconditional cash transfer with a range of accompanying measures aimed at encouraging parenting practices conducive to early childhood development. (World Bank 2013). The behavioral change component explicitly focuses on improving nutrition, psychosocial stimulation, health, and sanitation practices. Implementation is contracted out to nongovernmental organizations (NGOs), which deliver activities based on a curriculum and implementation strategy developed by the government. Each beneficiary household participates in up to three activities per month over 18 months: a village assembly delivered by a NGO operator; a small-group meeting delivered by a community educator; and a home-visit delivered by the community educator. Participation in the three activities is close to 95 percent. A large number of nonbeneficiaries also participate, creating strong social dynamics around the program.

Accompanying measures to promote ECD are also being implemented in middle-income countries. In Indonesia, the conditional cash transfer (CCT) program Keluarga Harapan (PKH) covers 3 million poor families nationwide. The program not only provides cash, but also provides beneficiary mothers with skills. Training modules seek to promote sustainable behavioral changes in relation to early childhood education and parenting practices, and extend to such topics as family finances or microenterprises. The training modules are given during monthly meetings that CCT beneficiaries have at the local level, over three years. Messages are harmonized through the use of videos that represent daily situations of a typical CCT family.

References

Ferré, C., and I. Sharif. 2014. "Can Conditional Cash Transfers Improve Education and Nutrition Outcomes for Poor Children in Bangladesh? Evidence from a Pilot Project." Policy Research Working Paper 7077, World Bank, Washington, DC.

World Bank. 2013. http://www.worldbank.org/en/news/feature/2013/11/05/niger-invests-in-early-childhood-through-social-safety-nets.

Section 5.

Social Safety Nets in Urban Areas: Emerging Issues and Practices

I n 2007, the world reached the tipping point whereby the urban population outstripped that of rural areas.[1] Currently, 3.9 billion people, or 54 percent of the global population, live in urban settings. The share is expected to increase to 66 percent by 2050, when an additional 2.4 billion people are projected to live in cities. Nearly 90 percent of them may be concentrated in Asia and Africa, with about half of such an increase occurring in just six countries: China, the Democratic Republic of Congo, India, Indonesia, Nigeria, and Pakistan.

The process of urbanization and the process of development are closely intertwined. Urbanization is the result of the spatial concentration of people, economic activities, and physical infrastructure. This concentration can spark various benefits because of the so-called agglomeration economies. Cities generate about 65 percent of global gross domestic product (GDP), with the world's 300 largest metropolitan economies accounting for nearly half of global growth in 2014. People tend to move to and live in urban areas to pursue economic upward mobility, access better services, and enhance their quality of life.

Yet urbanization does not automatically translate into development. For instance, an estimated 863 million people live in precarious settlements or slums, lacking access to basic water and sanitation services. In more than half of developing countries for which data are available, urban youth-to-adult unemployment ratios are higher than in rural areas. The number of urban poor living on less than US$1.25/day—or some 285 million people—has remained steady over the past quarter-century, while rural poverty numbers have declined sharply. Estimates based on national poverty lines show that in about one-third of developing countries, the number of urban poor is higher than those in rural settings. Residential patterns, social networks, occupational concentration, and social norms operate differently in urban areas, leading to new forms of social exclusion. To put it simply, poverty is urbanizing and it is doing so rapidly (see highlight 5, on understanding urban poverty).

Against this backdrop, countries are increasingly recognizing the need for more inclusive urbanization pathways. As systems to address urban poverty are reimagined, there is growing interest in the role that targeted social safety nets can play in urban areas. Preliminary estimates from household surveys in 98 countries show that, on average, 28 percent of the rural population is covered by a social safety net program, while 25 percent of the urban population benefits from these programs (figure 5.1). In contrast, the coverage of social insurance schemes and labor market programs is almost three times higher in urban settings than in rural areas. However, in either urban or rural areas, labor market programs cover less than 4 percent of the population.

There are variations in coverage of social safety nets, depending on country income status and region. The rate of coverage of the urban poorest quintile in upper-middle-income countries (57.3 percent) is three times higher than that in low-income countries (18.9 percent). While differences between urban and rural coverage of the bottom quintile exist across country groups, urban and rural coverage in lower-middle-income countries are almost identical (figure 5.2). However, the difference amounts to about 8.5 percentage points in low-income countries.

As a "first generation" of urban social safety net programs is emerging, countries are following different pathways in introducing and expanding programs. Evidence from those early experiences points to the different and complex nature of urban poverty, as well as a range of patterns in the introduction and scale-up of social safety nets in cities. These include variations in whether to start first in urban or rural areas, whether to adjust the design to urban contexts, and whether to use a national system that will span urban and rural settings.

In some contexts, national programs cover both urban and rural areas, with some design variants between those contexts. Within this group, some countries have gradually built on mature rural social safety net programs and transitioned them into urban areas. For exam-

Poverty is rapidly urbanizing. There is growing interest in the role that targeted social safety nets can play to reduce urban poverty and address emerging vulnerabilities.

■ Main Messages for Section 5

- Urban poverty is complex and dynamic, and presents specific features that require that social safety net interventions be tailored to specific local urban contexts.
- The coverage of the poor in urban areas is lower than in rural settings. The difference amounts to about 8.5 percentage points in low-income countries.
- Emerging urban social safety net programs are starting to adapt to urban contexts, although more practical learning, experimentation, and knowledge exchange are needed.

Figure 5.1 Coverage of social safety nets is lower in urban areas than in rural settings, but urban dwellers are better covered by social insurance and labor market programs

Percent of population covered by social protection and labor programs

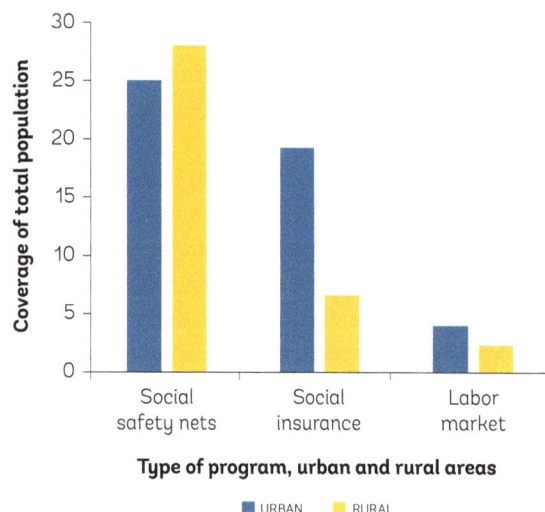

Type of program, urban and rural areas

■ URBAN ■ RURAL

Source: ASPIRE.
Note: Coverage rates refer to the percent of total population receiving social safety nets, social insurance, and labor market programs. Aggregate statistics are based on countries with information on social safety net programs and urban-rural area of residence (98 countries).

Figure 5.2 The urban poor are less covered by social safety nets than are the rural poor

Percent of households in the poorest quintile covered by social safety net programs

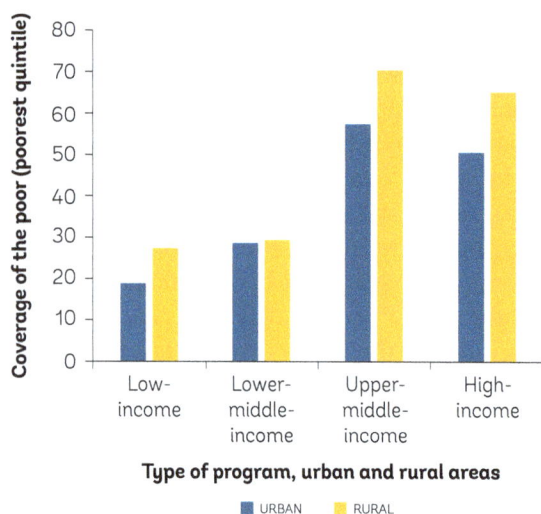

Type of program, urban and rural areas

■ URBAN ■ RURAL

Source: ASPIRE.
Note: Coverage rates refer to the percent of poor receiving any social safety net transfer. The poor are defined as those households in the poorest quintile of the national consumption/income distribution. Aggregate statistics are based on countries with information on social safety net programs and urban-rural area of residence (98 countries).

ple, in Mexico about 40 percent of the beneficiaries of the Prospera (formerly Oportunidades) program live in urban and peri-urban areas, up from 7 percent at the early stages of roll-out in 1997–98. Other countries have followed an opposite pattern, commencing programs in urban contexts and expanding them to rural areas. In China, for example, the unconditional cash transfer (UCT) Dibao was formally adopted in 1997–99 following several years of piloting at the local level. Urban Dibao beneficiaries rose from 0.85 million in 1996 to 21.4 in 2013. In 2007, the rural version was launched, making the program national and covering a total of 74.5 million people.

In other contexts, large-scale programs may cover both urban and rural areas, but they may not envision major design adjustments across rural to urban spaces. This is the case for most countries in Europe and Central Asia, for Brazil's Bolsa Família, and for the Public Food Distribution System in India. In some cases, however, urban areas may present a different set of linkages to complementary interventions (such as productive inclusion measures in urban Brazil) or offer the opportunity to test innovations (such as delivery of food entitlements in urban Raipur, India).

In most low-income countries, social safety nets tend to be mainly rural. Yet in some cases, programs have been launched in urban areas, such as the cash-based Programa Subsidio de Alimentos in Mozambique and the Food Subsidy Program in Kenya. Other countries, such as Ethiopia and Mali, have started or planned to implement urban social safety nets, leveraging their years of experience with rural interventions.

Yet as countries roll out their first generation of programs, the initial performance has tended to be lower than expected, including in terms of coverage. This result could stem from several factors. For example, while poverty is increasingly concentrated in urban areas, rural settings may still be prioritized in social safety net coverage, especially on the basis of higher prevalence of poverty in those areas (that is, urban areas may have larger numbers of poor people, but lower rates of poverty). In other cases, there might be a perception that social safety nets may not be needed or appropriate in urban areas, chiefly because of more vibrant labor markets. Yet the poorest individuals tend to have precarious, low-paying, and informal jobs. At the same time, active labor market programs to boost employability have often found it challenging to match labor market needs with the aspirations, capabilities, and profiles of the poorest. Moreover, a sizable share of the portfolio of interventions for urban poverty tends to fall under the remit of urban planning and development, such as slum upgrading programs. Those essential and critical interventions have focused on the engineering of urban infrastructure (including drainage, water supply, and public sanitation facilities), and arguably have yielded more limited direct impacts on the "people" side of the poverty equation. Furthermore, large-scale subsidy schemes, especially those that are food- and energy-based, have been popular in urban areas. In the East Asia and Pacific region, those interventions account for over 50 percent of total social assistance programs. Yet the distributional impact of such measures is considerably regressive, with limited benefits accruing to the poorest segments of the urban populace.

In most cases, however, it is the techncial design and implementation of programs that may pose special performance challenges. For instance, a range of technical hurdles, such as the fluid expansion and contraction of poor urban informal settlements over time, has stifled an effective identification of the urban poor. Even when prospective beneficiaries are identified "on paper," it is challenging to reach and communicate with them about available programs. And even when people are reached, programs may not be attractive enough to offset relatively high urban opportunity costs. The result may be limited program enrollment and take-up. The discussion that follows considers how some of those issues are emerging from recent country practices, drawing on experiences from a dozen countries that have experimented with social safety net programs of different size, form, and stage of maturity.

While policy makers tend to place a stronger emphasis on service delivery across sectors, skills transfer, and interventions that encourage beneficiaries to "graduate" from the service in urban areas, the institutional framework that could underpin these dimensions is generally fragmented. To be effective, approaches to urban poverty should work in many dimensions at many levels. This requires a significant degree of integration among institutions, government levels, and public-private partnerships. In practice, however, roles and responsibilities are often unclear and spread across multiple actors. In India, for example, urban health spans four ministries and nutrition spans six, with multiple levels involved within each. In particular, municipalities tend

to vary significantly in accounting practices and their capacity to deliver services. Cities, provinces, and municipalities may each have their own programs, which may not necessarily be consistent with national schemes. While this challenge may be compelling for rural areas as well, the spatial proximity and concentration of those administrative entities and functions in urban contexts amplifies the need for coordination among them. Limited analytical work has been conducted to document and appraise the nature and scale of urban social safety net interventions available at different governmental levels.

The issue of financing arrangements for urban social safety nets is closely related to institutional set-ups. For example, in China the urban Dibao program provides means-tested UCTs to over 20 million people. In the mid-1990s, the program envisioned mixed financing responsibilities between enterprises and local governments. The situation changed over time, with the share of central transfers increasing from 29 percent in 1999 to 65 percent in 2012, including supporting the poorest provinces. Central transfers also vary significantly between provinces. The richer coastal provinces—where many rural migrant workers flock—receive no central budgetary allocations. In contrast, both central and western provinces receive central budgetary allocations. As China is now experimenting with relaxing its *hukou* system,[2] those financing arrangements would become an important part of the debate around if and how to support poor rural migrants currently not eligible for Dibao in cities where they live and work. Governance and financing can become particularly complex as programs enter large metropolitan areas. For example, when Familias in Accion was expanded to cities throughout Colombia, local authorities in Bogotá did not introduce Familias; the program was not operated through the mayor's office, as in other cities, but was instead managed by the federal government. The limited coordination with the mayor's office became a key constraint of the program. Challenges in devising clear responsibilities between government lines in urban areas might be particularly difficult in contexts where such roles are blurred and capacities limited, as in a number of low-income countries.

The measurement of urban poverty is important for both fiscal allocations and program design. The assessment and identification of poor areas and poor people constitutes the central information base upon which programs are designed and fiscal allocation criteria are determined. Hence it is very important that poverty be appropriately conceptualized, defined, and measured. The assessment of urban poverty often includes metrics for employment status, education levels, and housing proxies, as in Romania. In El Salvador, such dimensions were integrated with security and crime-related variables. In particular, an Urban Poverty and Social Exclusion Map was devised through rigorous statistical and geospatial analysis based on the population and housing censuses. By producing geo-referenced data at the level of individual city blocks, the map could be used to identify precarious urban settlements (or AUPs, in their Spanish-language acronym) where the Programa de Apoyo Temporal al Ingreso (PATI) social safety net program could be implemented (map 5.1).

Generally, urban programs use multiple targeting methods to select and prioritize potential beneficiaries. In the case of PATI, the intervention provides temporary income support (US$100/month for 6 months) to vulnerable urban populations in exchange for their participation in both physical labor activities and skills training programs. The program combines geographical targeting (identifying AUPs) with self-selection, mechanisms to prioritize participants, and community validation of participation. Impact evaluations show that about 72

percent of PATI beneficiaries belong to the two poorest income quintiles. In a number of cases, the experience and local knowledge of nongovernmental organizations has been a precious asset for targeting beneficiaries and mobilizing communities. This was the case in an urban voucher program in two cities in Burkino Faso, Ouagadougou and Bobo Dioulasso, although the applicability of the approach for larger-scale programs could be limited. In other programs, adjustments have been made to targeting protocols to reach special profiles, such as street families in Manila. Considerations such as these have raised new challenges to targeting, such as the identification of urban "poverty hotspots" where people could be found only at night (to sleep) and places that may not be reported in administrative maps (such as streets lacking names).

A recurrent question is whether and how to adapt proxy-means test (PMT) approaches for targeting in urban contexts. Country case studies show that both PMT coefficients and their weights may need to be tailored to urban specificities. For example, in Mexico in the rural formula, remittances have twice the weight as in urban areas, and not having a refrigerator has three times the weight. In contrast, in the urban formula, renting a living space has twice the weight as in rural areas, likely reflecting the higher share of expenditure for urban housing. The treatment of housing conditions also varies,

Map 5.1 The Programa de Apoyo Temporal al Ingreso (PATI) in El Salvador is implemented in precarious urban settlements

a. Precarious urban settlements in San Salvador, El Salvador

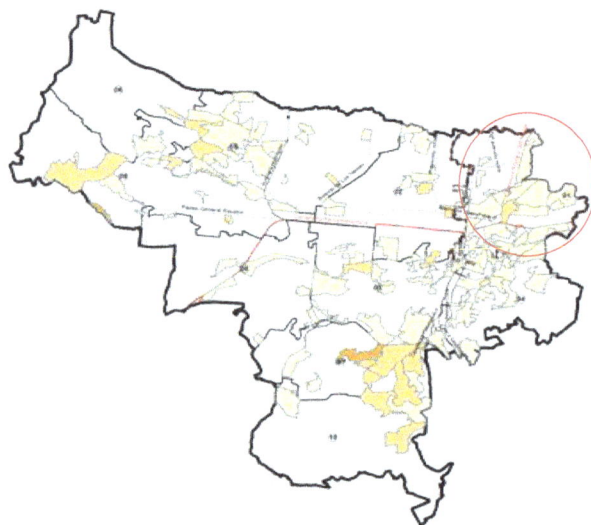

b. Enlarged view of zip code 01 area, San Salvador

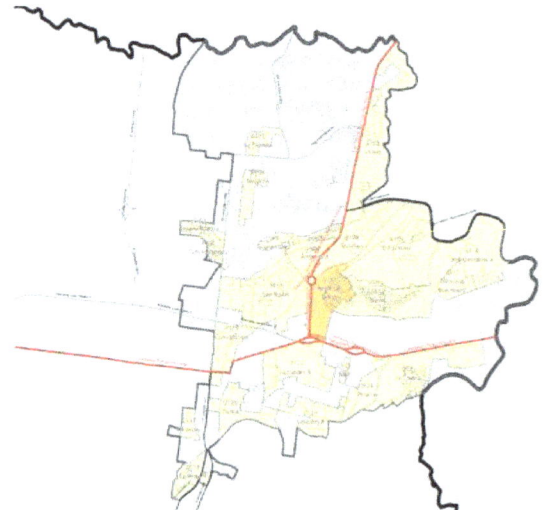

Source: Gentilini, forthcoming.
Note: Precarious urban settlements are shown in yellow and orange.

with the floor condition having nearly twice the weight in rural areas. In Mozambique, urban PMT formulas have a number of additional variables, such as having a computer or electricity, which are strong indicators of wealth, though less prevalent in rural areas, where electricity is a weaker predictor of welfare. Another frequently raised issue is reaching households with characteristics that are seldom captured in PMT models—not what kind of materials their house is made of, but whether they have a house at all (the homeless or street families). To capture such households, a modified version of the Philippines' conditional cash transfer (CCT) program Pantawid was devised to address the specific profile of homeless households. The pilot, now underway, is designed to integrate street families into the flagship CCT program, while providing a complementary package of interventions, including housing and livelihood measures.

After targeted populations have been identified, a number of conditions must be met to ensure program take-up by prospective beneficiaries. A key lesson is the need for extensive communications and outreach tailored to urban communities. Television and radio spots are useful—but not if the poor lack access to TVs or radios. For instance, Brazil included a range of informal information dissemination mechanisms, such as local associations, loudspeakers, and churches. Registration sites must also be accessible. If they cannot be reached easily because of distance, poor public transport, safety, or other reasons, prospective beneficiaries will not be able to apply. In other cases, illiterate individuals who are unable to complete forms may simply not apply for benefits to which they are entitled. For example, South Africa has addressed this concern for its Old Age and Child Support Grants through the use of local community committees that help prospective beneficiaries—such as elderly widows—with the application process. The United States has introduced similar mechanisms for its main social safety net, the Supplemental Nutrition Assistance Program (SNAP), including supporting the urban elderly, whose enrollment rates are up to 20 percentage points lower than average participation.

Early experiences underscore the importance of learning and ensuring operational flexibility to adjust design and processes. For example, the Mexican Oportunidades program was intro-

duced in 1997 in rural areas. Starting in 2001, it was gradually expanded in phases in urban areas of different sizes. Within selected urban communities, an extensive information campaign preceded the registration process. This was followed by a temporary establishment of a program office in each locality, where individual households could register for the program. Households that were deemed eligible were then visited at home to verify this information; they then had to visit the program's office to receive the results of their application. As a result, only 51 percent of eligible urban households enrolled in the program in the initial phase. Consequently, program officials revisited how to reach potential participants, such as full-day poor working mothers and those living in highly populated areas. Given beneficiaries' higher mobility and opportunity costs, processes were put in place to reduce the time needed to enroll in the program (for example, using a short prescreening interview called Cedula Urbana). A social intermediation service (Modelo de Atención Personalizada de Oportunidades) was introduced to reach out directly to potential beneficiaries, providing personalized service to navigate the social protection system, and establishing a relationship of trust and support—an approach pioneered and widely used in the Chile Solidario program.

Similarly, as Colombia's Familias en Acción CCT program was introduced in Bogotá, initial enrollment levels were significantly lower than expected. About two-thirds of surveyed households did not apply. Reasons included that prospective beneficiaries were unfamiliar with program benefits; did not know that they could register; and did not have time to register because they held multiple jobs. Among those who attempted to enroll, about half did not manage to do so because of insufficient knowledge of eligibility criteria (figure 5.3). To address low take-up rates, part of the strategy was a month-long, large-scale registration process that established new locations where individuals could learn more about the program and register.[3]

An interesting pattern emerging across countries is the tendency to combine social safety nets with complementary labor-related interventions. In urban areas, there is growing interest in leveraging social safety nets to enhance the employability of the poor, including through wage or self-employment. The PATI program

Figure 5.3 Problems with the initial enrollment process of the Familias Program in Bogotá prevented most people from enrolling

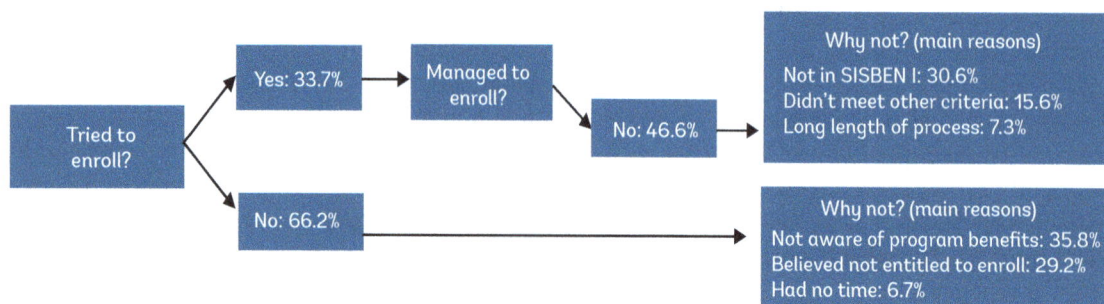

			Why not? (main reasons)
Tried to enroll?	Yes: 33.7% → Managed to enroll?	No: 46.6% →	Not in SISBEN I: 30.6% Didn't meet other criteria: 15.6% Long length of process: 7.3%
	No: 66.2% →		Not aware of program benefits: 35.8% Believed not entitled to enroll: 29.2% Had no time: 6.7%

Source: Gentilini, forthcoming.
Note: Data refer to 2011. SISBEN I = Sistema de Identificación de Beneficiarios de Subsidios Sociales (system of identification for social subsidies beneficiaries).

in El Salvador is one example, although similar approaches are being taken in Ghana, Latvia, and the Philippines, and are a key institutional innovation in more mature programs in Argentina, Brazil, and Mexico. Yet experience remains limited, especially in Africa and Asia. For example, a recent review of 106 small-scale self-employment interventions found only a handful of programs that are specifically targeted to urban areas. These show some promising results in Bangladesh, Ethiopia, Kenya, the Lao People's Democratic Republic, and Liberia, yet they also underscore the challenge of tailoring interventions to the specific skills, aptitudes, and social capital of informal, poor subsistence entrepreneurs, as opposed to more successful vocational ones.

Altogether, these preliminary considerations suggest that an agenda is only just emerging for using social safety nets to help tackle urban poverty. Interest and know-how about social safety nets are growing, but the role of social safety nets in urban areas—and within the urbanization process more widely—remains a complex, dynamic, and largely uncharted domain. As such, it is raising a range of strategic questions, including the following:

- What are the synergies and trade-offs between social protection, urban development, social services, and economic agendas in cities?
- How can social safety net programs be more closely integrated with compelling urban development activities, such as slum upgrading, housing policy, and urban resilience?
- How can the links between urban social protection and economic agendas be har-

nessed, including supporting unskilled urban migrants, assisting subsistence entrepreneurs, and providing childcare for full-day working mothers?
- What is the cross-country experience and evidence regarding social protection for temporary and long-term intra-country migrants?
- What is the role of social safety nets in supporting urban strategies to reduce violence, integrate service delivery, or assist people living in areas with unclear land tenure?
- What is the experience with institutional and financing arrangements of local and central governments involved with social protection in cities?
- How can civil society and communities strengthen voice and accountability of administrations involved in social safety nets in cities, as well as strengthen partnerships with the public and private sectors?

In many ways, approaches to urban social safety nets epitomize the science of delivery. While some countries are institutionalizing mature urban programs, most are undergoing an iterative process of experimentation, learning, and organic adaptation. The agenda of making social safety nets more "spatially sensitive" includes positioning social safety net programs within a broader framework for inclusive cities where infrastructure, economic, and social spheres all interact. This would include a better understanding not only of design and delivery choices, but also of how social protection can enhance the policy and institutional synergies with urban development, labor, and other social sector agendas as part of efforts to make cities more inclusive.

Notes

1. This section draws heavily on Gentilini (forthcoming) and the sources therein.

2. Hukou is the institutional mechanism that, among other functions, ties Dibao to place of origin rather than residency.

3. Low coverage in Bogotá could also be the result of the competition between national-level and district-level supply of social protection programs.

Reference

Gentilini, U. Forthcoming. "Safety Nets in Urban Areas: Emerging Issues, Evidence and Practices," World Bank, Washington, DC.

Urban poverty exhibits some peculiar characteristics that generate new sources of vulnerability and poverty profiles, such as higher physical and income mobility, even among the poorest households.[1] In Indonesia, for instance, about 20 percent of households that were initially surveyed in urban areas could not be found in the same residence six months later. These mobile urban groups often do not have permanent places of residence and tend to be migrant workers. In urban Mexico, only 7 percent of households that were extremely poor in 2002 remained so in 2007. Yet chronic poverty persists in urban contexts. For instance, in Latin America, a sizable number of urban people were living on less than US$4/day in 2004 and 2012, preliminary evidence indicates. In Brazil, for every one chronically poor person in rural areas, there are two who live in urban areas.

The wider availability of short-term employment means that the urban "working poor" face opportunity and transaction costs to participate in safety net programs. For instance, in Lima and Rio de Janeiro, most of the poor live 30–40 kilometers from employment hubs, and commute on average 3 hours a day. In Montevideo, residents living in slums outside the city cite the lack of access to public transport as a major constraint to accessing jobs. In Kampala, many motorized transport options are unaffordable for the poor, with transport fares absorbing 41 percent of incomes for the poorest 20 percent of the population (70 percent of urban workers in Kampala walk to work). In Mexico, children and youth may prefer to take public transport to school to avoid street violence, rather than to walk or take school buses, cutting into household income. Also for safety reasons, residents in low-income areas of Dar es Salaam spend between 10 percent and 30 percent of their income on transport.

The complex nature of urban poverty presents opportunities and challenges in designing and implementing social safety nets in urban areas.

Insecurity, crime, gender-based domestic violence, and intergenerational conflict tend to loom large in urban settings and generate social and economic costs. An estimated 30 percent of hospital admissions in Latin America are the result of urban violence, while the associated health costs account for up to 5 percent of GDP in Colombia. Living in informal settlements is reported as a key source of anxiety of the poor, including daily fears of violence and abuse. The overcrowding of poor-quality housing in marginal areas, including clustering in risky locations (such as along river banks and railway yards), often perpetuates marginalization, vulnerability to climate hazards, discrimination, and neighborhood stigma. For example, a unique 30-year longitudinal study from Brazil shows that living in a favela is the most widely perceived stigmatizing factor among 96 percent of the interviewed households. As a favela dweller in Sao Paulo put it in the *Voices of the Poor* report, ". . . one day a company called me for a job, but when they realized I lived in Bode [a favela] they changed their minds, thinking that I was one of those *marginais* they couldn't trust."

The cost of living in urban areas, including for food and housing, can be considerably higher than in rural settings. For example, simulations of Mexico show that the transfer amount needed to fully compensate for the labor market income of 16-year-olds would mean quadrupling the size paid by most conditional cash transfers. In urban Nepal, dwellers spend about 28 percent of their income on housing, while rural households spend about four times less. The poorest are more likely to rent than the better off. For example, in Kampala 78 percent of households in the poorest quintile rent, compared with 63 percent in the richest quintile. Although poor urban and rural households generally devote a similar share of income on food, often in the range of 60–75 percent of the household budget, the urban poor obtain food almost entirely through market-based transactions. While urban dwellers are more likely to be shielded from seasonal fluctuations in domestic commodity prices, they tend to be more exposed to global food price volatility. Moreover, the nutrition transition in urban diets toward higher calories, fats, and prepared foods introduces new forms of health and nutrition risks, including obesity and cardiovascular diseases.

Unlike rural areas, cities tend to generate more limited community arrangements, social networks, and support mechanisms. Especially in new settlements and slums, barriers such as different languages, lack of family connections, and the dynamic in-and-out flow of temporary migrants, for example, can create substantial pockets of social exclusion and marginalization. This does not mean that informal networks are nonexistent; they are often strong, though they may take on specific characteristics. In Ethiopia, for the example, the *idir* system, a way for people to provide help and mutual support, is widely present in urban contexts, alongside mechanisms of mutual support among clusters of migrants. These informal urban mechanisms are seldom considered for social protection programming.

The rapid expansion of cities, as well as the management of densities within them, requires institutions that manage land effectively and strategically. These include a transparent system to convert land use, a clear definition of property rights, a robust mechanism to value land and property, and a strong judicial system. However, the capacity to formulate, oversee, and enforce standards is generally limited in developing countries, often leading to haphazard urbanization patterns. For example, in Colombia about 1,100 municipal governments are responsible for delivery of infrastructure and social services, land use, and economic development planning. Their accounting practices and their capacity to deliver services tend to vary greatly. An outcome of such diversity is the uneven capacity to coordinate interventions and assign clear responsibilities among government levels in highly populated areas—a particular challenge in low-income countries.

Access to basic services such as water, electricity, and sanitation is often hindered because capacity is overwhelmed and services are not affordable. The density of cities makes it more affordable to expand services; evidence from 78 countries shows that it costs significantly less to provide piped water in urban areas as opposed to in sparsely populated settings. However, when the supply of land, housing, and services do not keep up with the rising demand from growing populations moving into the cities, low-income households often resort to slums. More than 70 percent of Africa's urban population live in slums. For example, there is one toilet for every 500 people in Nairobi's slums. In Dhaka, only 9 percent of households in the poorest quintile benefit from a sewage line, and less than one-third of them access piped water. An implication of those inequities is that the poor tend to bear the cost for basic service provision: a review of 47 countries showed that the average water prices charged by private vendors compared with the public network were 4.5 times higher in peri-urban or unplanned settlements with unclear tenure. In Accra's slums, the cost of water from private vendors can amount to up to 10 percent of households' monthly income.

Note

1. This highlight is based on a World Bank compilation of studies, including those cited in Gentilini (forthcoming).

Reference

Gentilini, U. Forthcoming. "Safety Nets in Urban Areas: Emerging Issues, Evidence and Practices," World Bank, Washington, DC.

Appendixes

Definitions, Methodology, and Data Sources

Definitions and Methodology

This appendix presents the concepts, programs, indicators, and data sources used in this report and the associated World Bank database, the Atlas of Social Protection: Indicators of Resilience and Equity (ASPIRE).

Concepts

Social safety nets (SSNs) are measures designed to provide regular and predictable support to poor and vulnerable people. A distinctive feature of social safety nets is their *noncontributory* character: that is, beneficiaries do not have to pay or contribute financially to receive the benefits.[1]

Social safety nets are also referred to as *social assistance* or *social transfers* and fall within broader *social protection systems.* In general, *social protection* also includes *social insurance,* such as health insurance and contributory pensions,[2] as well as *labor market programs,* such as services to facilitate access to jobs (including skills training and job search support) (*social protection and labor, SPL*). While social safety net programs are often specifically targeted to people in need (such as poor, vulnerable, food insecure, or malnourished people), in a number of cases programs are designed for particular groups in the population (such as children, the elderly, and indigenous people). In other cases, rights-based approaches may provide transfers to the entire population, independently of need or demographic characteristics.

Poverty has many dimensions, and this report underscores the importance of understanding the multiple factors that cause and stem from poverty. However, for measurement purposes, the most robust and comparable indicator is material poverty. This is defined here as an unacceptably low level of welfare measured in terms of income or consumption. For this report, two definitions of poverty are used. On the one hand,

relative poverty is defined as a level of welfare in the bottom 20 percent of the national distribution: that is, the poverty rate is set at 20 percent in each country. On the other hand, *absolute poverty* is defined using the *international standard* of US$1.25/day per capita in purchasing power parity terms. In both cases, the concept of poverty can be applied only to survey data, and uses the definition of welfare that is either the definition used by national statistical offices or developed by the World Bank in its work with the national statistical agencies. The absolute poverty rate defined using the international standard for most developing countries is below 20 percent, so sometimes it is also referred to as *extreme poverty*—even though there are exceptions in which the bottom 20 percent is just a subset of the absolute poor.

Urban areas in this report are as defined and reported in country surveys. However, this report recognizes that such country-specific definitions vary by context, including being based on administrative and/or density metrics. For instance, the literature often distinguishes between megacities (more than 10 million inhabitants), large cities (5–10 million people), medium-sized cities (1–5 million dwellers), cities of 500,000–1 million people, and small cities (less than 500,000 people).

Programs

The definition of social safety nets used in this report includes cash transfers (conditional and unconditional);[3] in-kind transfers such as school feeding[4] and targeted food assistance; fee waivers to support access to education, health, and housing; and social care services. Although vouchers or near-cash transfers have a number of commonalities with both cash and in-kind modalities, vouchers are considered in this report as part of a broader set of in-kind transfers. *Social pensions,* including old-age benefits and pensions, disability pensions and benefits, and veteran benefits, are included in the unconditional cash transfer category.

General price subsidies—such as subsidies for energy, electricity, food, housing, and transport—are not classified as a part of the social safety net in this report, even though some studies include those measures in definitions of social safety nets.[5] General price subsidies are measures that keep prices for consumers below market levels, and thus benefit households through lower prices. As such, people need to pay part of the price to access the transfer. General price subsidies are universal in the sense that all consumers have access to the same commodities at the same price. The amount received by a beneficiary is a function of the quantity purchased, and market access. Section 2 of this report compares spending on social safety nets with spending on energy, electricity, and food subsidies.

Energy subsidies include government interventions and subsidized sales of petroleum products, including gasoline and diesel used for transport. *Subsidies for electricity* lower prices for generating electricity for agricultural use, kerosene used for lighting and heating, and liquefied petroleum gas used for cooking. *Universal food subsidies* are government interventions to lower the price the general population pays for staple foods. Governments may also provide universal access to food or other commodities through subsidized sales at public distribution centers or designated private outlets on a first-come, first-served basis.

The social safety net program types captured in the ASPIRE database are grouped in seven categories in this report (table A.1).

Table A.1 Classification of Social Safety Net Programs

Program category	Program subcategory
Conditional cash transfers (CCTs)	Poverty-targeted cash transfers[a]
	Family and child allowance (including orphan and vulnerable children benefits)[a]
	Scholarship benefits[a]
Unconditional cash transfers (UCTs)	Poverty-targeted cash transfers
	Family and child allowances (including orphan and vulnerable children benefits)
	Scholarship benefits in cash
	Housing and utility allowance benefits in cash
	Emergency support in cash
	Old-age social pensions
	Disability social pensions and benefits
	Veterans pensions
	Funeral grants, burial allowances
	Public-private charity, including zakat
	Other cash transfers
Unconditional in-kind transfers (UITs)	Food stamps and vouchers
	Food distribution programs
	Nutritional programs (therapeutic, supplementary, and PLHIV[b])
	In-kind emergency support
	Other food/in-kind program
School feeding	School feeding
Public works (PW)	Cash for work
	Food for work
	Workfare
Fee waivers	Reduced medical and health fees
	Educational fee waivers
	Housing/utility fee waivers
Other SSN	Other social assistance transfers
	Social care services: Care for children/youth
	Social care services: Care for family
	Social care services: Care for the disabled
	Social care services: Care for older persons
	Other social safety nets

a. This report includes under the category of conditional cash transfers any cash transfer program that has a conditionality component in its operation manual, even if it is weakly conditioned or weakly enforced (it has *soft conditionalities*). Box 1.2 in section 1 discusses variations in the enforcement of conditionalities across programs.
b. PLHIV = People Living with HIV/AIDS.

Various social safety net programs are run by different agencies and ministries, and thus outlays are dispersed throughout the budget.[6] Because official publications rarely contain consolidated data on social safety net budgets, this report provides a unique attempt to piece together such data from different sources around the world.

Since countries usually have multiple social safety net programs (on average, 20 programs), the same beneficiary can in principle benefit from several interventions as long as he or she meets the eligibility criteria. This feature is called *overlap*. It can be the result of conscious effort (in cases in which different programs are seen as complementary), or can reflect inefficiencies and lack of coordination between social safety net programs.

Indicators

Enrollment rates in this report are defined as the sum of individual beneficiaries on the rolls of all social safety net programs in a country,[7] as a percent of the population in that country. This is a new metric at the country level—not used in the 2014 edition—that builds on program-level data on the number of beneficiaries for all existing social safety net programs in the country.[8]

Beneficiary rolls are the lists of names of people participating in safety net programs. Enrollment rates should not be interpreted as coverage rates because some individuals may receive multiple benefits and thus may be on the rolls of more than one program. A *social registry* is the list of individuals or households potentially eligible to participate in social safety net programs. The actual list of beneficiaries of social safety nets is called the *beneficiary registry*.

Program enrollment rates are based on administrative data in ASPIRE (see appendix C for the primary sources of largest programs only); they are aggregated by social safety net program categories according to the ASPIRE classification (table A.1) by all social safety net programs by summing up the number of individual beneficiaries in the rolls of all social safety net programs in the country for which data are available in ASPIRE. Given the nature of the data source (program administrative records), it is not possible to avoid double-counting of beneficiaries when aggregating program-level data into the seven categories and total SSN category.[9]

When the data reporting unit in administrative records is "households," the enrollment rate is derived by multiplying the number of beneficiary households by the average household size obtained by official estimates (from the national statistical offices) and divided by the total population—thus accounting for indirect beneficiaries (see discussion on coverage). When an official estimate of the average household size is not available, it is approximated to the global average of 5.[10]

Coverage rates in this report refer to the percentage of the population participating in social safety net programs (including both direct and indirect beneficiaries), based on household surveys. The *coverage of the poor rate* refers to the percentage of the poor participating in social safety net programs (including both direct and indirect beneficiaries), based on household surveys.[11] The poor can be defined either as those households in the poorest quintile of the consumption or income distribution (after receiving social safety net transfers) or those households living below $1.25/day (in terms of 2005 U.S. dollars adjusted for purchasing power parity), after receiving social safety net transfers. Programs are aggregated in eight social safety net categories and according to the ASPIRE classification (the seven categories described above plus *social pensions*, including old-age social pensions, disability social pensions and benefits, and war veteran benefits).[12]

Often multiple programs or transfers are aggregated in one of the eight social safety net categories. A detailed description of which program or original variables in the surveys have been aggregated into each harmonized social safety net category is available at www.world bank.org/aspire/documentation. The nature of the data source prevents double-counting of beneficiaries when households receive more than one benefit in the same category. For example, if a household receives a family allowance as well as emergency cash support, it is counted only once in the coverage indicator of unconditional cash transfer programs. Similarly, the coverage of social safety net programs is derived by summing up individuals receiving any type of social safety net benefits, correcting for double-counting. The household size recorded in the survey is used to estimate direct and indirect individual beneficiaries (see discussion of household size in the discussion on the enrollment rate). Global, regional, and income group aggregates are obtained as weighted averages of country indicators using household survey expansion factors for the sample of 105 countries for which indicators are available.

Adequacy is defined as the total transfer amount received by all beneficiaries in a quintile as a share of the total welfare of beneficiaries in that quintile. It is based on household survey data. The indicator is estimated by program type, for the entire population and by quintiles of the welfare distribution after the transfer. Programs are aggregated into social safety nets categories according to the ASPIRE classification. Specifically, adequacy of benefits is calculated as the amount of transfers received by a quintile divided by the total income or consumption of beneficiaries in that quintile.[13]

Benefit incidence is defined as the percentage of benefits going to each group/quintile of the post-transfer welfare distribution relative to the total benefits going to the population. It is based on household survey data. The indicator is estimated by program type and by quintiles of the post-transfer welfare distribution. Programs are aggregated into social safety net categories according to the ASPIRE classification. Specifically, benefit incidence is equal to the sum of all transfers received by all individuals in the quintile divided by the sum of all transfers received by all individuals in the population. Indicators for all social safety net programs provide the totals summing up social safety net program categories as per the ASPIRE classification.

Beneficiary incidence for a population group (such as the poorest quintile) is defined as the percentage of program beneficiaries in that particular group or quintile relative to the total number of beneficiaries in the population. It is based on household survey data. Specifically, beneficiary incidence is the number of individuals in each quintile living in a household where at least one member participates in a social safety net program divided by the number of individuals participating in social protection and labor programs in the population.

Spending as percent of GDP refers to total program spending, including spending on benefits and on administrative costs. This measure captures both the recurrent and capital program budget. It is based on administrative program records. Program spending is analyzed as a percent of GDP of the respective year.

Spending on each of the seven categories and for all social safety net programs in the country is aggregated by summing up the most recent program-level spending as a percent of GDP of the respective year for all social safety net programs, according to the ASPIRE classification (the seven categories described earlier). The aggregation methodology relies on the most recent data on program spending available in ASPIRE. The latest available year may vary by program for some countries. In those cases, the total spending by social safety net categories and for all social safety net programs is estimated for an indicated time frame (for example, 2010–14, as shown in appendix D) and is analyzed with the assumption that program spending does not vary much within that time frame. For 21 countries of the 120 included in the analysis of spending as percent of GDP, only aggregate data on safety net spending are available; for those 21 countries, data are not disaggregated by program (respective data sources are reported in appendix D).

The *poverty headcount reduction* is the simulated change on poverty headcount due to social safety net programs. The *poverty headcount ratio* is the percentage of the population below the relative poverty line (the poorest quintile of national consumption distribution). It is measured assuming the absence of the programs (pre-transfer welfare). Specifically, the poverty headcount reduction is computed as (the poverty headcount pre-transfer minus the poverty headcount post-transfer) divided by the poverty headcount pre-transfer. Indicators for all social safety net programs provide the totals summing up social safety net program categories as per the ASPIRE classification. Regional and income group aggregates are obtained as simple averages of country indicators.

The *poverty gap reduction* is the simulated change in the poverty gap due to social safety net programs. The *poverty gap index* is the average percentage shortfall in income of poor people from the relative poverty line (the poorest quintile of national consumption distribution). It is measured assuming the absence of the programs. Specifically, the poverty gap reduction is computed as (the poverty gap pre-transfer minus the poverty gap post-transfer) divided by the poverty gap pre-transfer. Indicators for all social safety net programs provide the totals summing up social safety net program categories as per the ASPIRE classification. Regional and income group aggregates are obtained as simple averages of country indicators.

Unlike poverty, *vulnerability* does not have a strict definition. It is typically determined by assessing the risks of deprivation or exposure to shocks for different social or demographic groups. Since these risks and exposures/shocks may differ across countries and there are no international standards to define them, this report does not use any separate grouping. The poor are the ones who are typically considered as most "vulnerable." Their level of consumption is already below a standard that is deemed a minimum, and any shocks can send them into a spiral of losses leading to destitution.

Different Definitions of "Coverage Rates"

Since the data collection for administrative data and household surveys entails very different processes that may rely on very different concepts and definitions, the coverage rates of social safety net programs derived from either administrative data or household survey data may differ substantially. However, both sources are important and complement each other. Obviously, possible double-counting combining numbers of beneficiaries of different social safety net programs from the administrative data overstates the actual coverage. In the ASPIRE data platform, there are 105 countries, economies, and territories with indicators of coverage based on household survey data, as well as enrollment rates in social safety net programs based on administrative data. Despite some outliers with large discrepancies between these two sources (administrative data and household surveys), the majority of countries present rather consistent outcomes. This is reassuring, and suggests that survey-based indicators can be relied upon to assess how many people—and in particular, how many poor people—are covered by social safety net programs.

The use of the term "coverage" as it applies to social safety nets, is somewhat confusing. It comes from a literature that emphasizes the insurance aspects of the social protection. From that point of view, "coverage" means protection against a specific risk. Coverage in this sense refers to persons protected for a given risk/contingency or persons benefiting from specific social protection benefits. There are various dimensions of coverage from this insurance or actuarial perspective, which are discussed extensively in the literature (see note 6 and box A.1). While in some way social safety nets can be viewed as covering the risk of poverty and destitution, they do not address contingent or future risk; they represent an action to address the condition that the poor are already in.

One important aspect that has bearing on measuring the scale of social safety nets is who is the beneficiary or *unit of assistance*. It is often an individual who is receiving support (a direct beneficiary), but it can also be a family (including indirect beneficiaries). The distinction between *direct beneficiaries* and *indirect beneficiaries* is important because alternative definitions of the beneficiary unit may significantly affect the results (table A.2). Depending on the type of program and the target group, the direct beneficiary of a safety net program may be an individual, a family, or a household. However, in a broader sense, all household members benefit from the additional resources provided by the program, even when it is targeted to a particular individual within a household.

There is a strong economic rationale for assigning benefits to the entire household when assessing the incidence of a program. Consider a child allowance program in a country where children account for 25 percent of the population and families with children account for 60 percent of the population. If only direct beneficiaries are taken into account, the coverage of the program will be 25 percent of the population; however, if all beneficiaries—direct and indirect—are counted, coverage will be 60 percent. Given the negative correlation between household size and welfare level, using households as beneficiary units for safety net programs where the assistance unit is an individual will improve statistics measuring both coverage and targeting accuracy. Whenever possible, the analyst should report both results. If only one set of results is to be reported, the set based on indirect beneficiaries is preferred, as these results are the only way to compare programs that serve different types of assistance units.

Conceptually, program coverage is a necessary, but not sufficient, condition for a program to be effective in improving living conditions of its target group. The program can be considered effective only if it reaches its intended beneficiaries and provides them with adequate benefits (cash, in-kind goods, services) to ameliorate the condition for which the program was initially designed.

Data Sources

The analysis in this report draws heavily on the ASPIRE database, which includes a set of indicators based on household surveys (discussed in sections 4 and 5 of this report) and indicators of program size (number of beneficiaries) and

Box A.1 Coverage Considered from an Insurance or Actuarial Perspective

Assessing coverage from an insurance or *actuarial perspective* requires analyzing different life risks and social protection needs as stipulated in the national legislation. In addition, the assessment must look at effective coverage, or the extent to which persons are actually covered. In other words, the analysis should ascertain whether the legal provisions are being implemented in practice and whether schemes provide certain protections in practice, even if that protection is not prescribed by law.

The assessment therefore should distinguish between:

- *Legal (statutory) coverage* (groups covered by statutory schemes for a given social protection function or branch in national legislation), and
- *Effective coverage* (the proportion of persons covered within the entire population or target group by social security measures in each specific function). Effective coverage is assessed in terms of both:
  - *Protected persons* (the number of persons who are eligible for benefits, and whose benefits are guaranteed, but who are not necessarily currently receiving those benefits—such as those who are actually contributing to or affiliated with a contributory scheme); and

- *Actual beneficiaries* (the proportion of the population affected by a certain contingency who actually receive the respective benefit).

Social safety nets from this perspective have a "filler" function: they pick up the risks that are left uncovered by other parts of social protection. This "residual" approach to social safety nets is reflected in the standard classification of social protection in terms of "functions" to protect against the social risks and needs that can arise throughout the life cycle. In particular, these include:

- Lack of or insufficient work-related income (caused by sickness, disability, maternity, employment injury, unemployment, or death of a family member)
- Lack of access to health care
- Insufficient family support
- Insufficient support in old age
- General poverty and social exclusion.

Poverty in this view is regarded as separate, "life-cycle" risk. In fact it is not. In most cases, poverty is a condition that is determined by structural factors beyond the control or "risk management" of an individual or a group. It affects people in different stages of the life cycle. It may or may not stem from insufficient protection against the life-cycle risks.

Source: International Labour Office 2014.

spending based on administrative data (discussed in sections 1 and 2).

Administrative Data

Program-level administrative data on spending and number of beneficiaries in ASPIRE include both primary and secondary sources: official government reports and the official website; data provided directly by government officials through country dialogue with the World Bank; published World Bank country reports; and other international databases (from the Asian Development Bank, Economic Commission for Latin America and the Caribbean of the United Nations, and World Food Programme). When official program-level administrative data are not available, data have been collected and compiled

by the World Bank local consultants working closely with government agencies implementing social safety net programs.[14] The sample of countries for which data are available on the program number of beneficiaries includes 136 countries (see appendix C). The sample of countries for which data on program spending are available includes 120 countries (see appendix D).

Household Survey Data

Sources of ASPIRE indicators based on nationally representative household surveys include: household income expenditure/budget surveys, Living Standard Measurement Surveys (LSMS), Multiple Indicator Cluster Surveys (MICs), Surveys on Income and Living Conditions (SILCs), and Welfare Monitoring Surveys.

Table A.2 Alternative Definitions of Coverage

Measure	Numerator	Denominator
Coverage of direct beneficiaries	The total number of individuals who report receiving program benefits (that is, only those individuals who directly receive the benefit)	The national population
Coverage of households	The number of households that report having at least one direct beneficiary	The total number of households in the country
Coverage of individuals within households	All individuals who live in houses where there is at least one beneficiary	The national population
Coverage of target individuals	The number of individuals who meet program criteria (such as age or income) and receive the benefit	The total population that meets the program's criteria
Coverage of target households	The number of households where at least one individual who meets program criteria (such as age or income) and receives the benefit resides	The total number of households where at least one person who meets the program's criteria resides
Coverage of target individuals within households	The total number of people living in households where at least one individual who meets program criteria (such as age or income) and receives the benefit resides	The total number of people living in households where at least one person who meets the program's criteria resides

While ASPIRE indicators based on household surveys are available for 112 countries, economies, and territories,[15] the analysis in this report focuses on only the 105 where national household surveys collect information on participation and transfer amounts received from social safety net programs.[16] Compared to the 2014 edition of this report, the analysis in the 2015 edition extends to new household surveys in 44 new countries (table A.3).[17]

Nationally representative household surveys are a valuable tool to analyze the performance of SPL programs in two unique ways. First, given the availability of a welfare aggregate (total household income or consumption), surveys measure not only the global coverage of SPL programs, but also the coverage of the poor. Second, they also allow estimations of the population that is not covered by SPL programs, but that may be in a great need of government interventions due to their vulnerability (the poor, the unemployed, the disabled, and so on). Moreover, such surveys are the only source of data to enable estimates of the impact of existing[18] (or simulated) social protection benefits on reductions in household poverty or inequality.

However, important caveats need to be considered because household surveys have their own limitations.[19] The extent to which information on specific transfers and programs is captured in household surveys can vary across

Table A.3 New Countries Included in the 2015 Edition (Household Surveys for 44 Countries)

Country	Survey year	Country	Survey year	Country	Survey year	Country	Survey year
Belize	2009	Djibouti	2002	Kiribati	2006	Namibia	2003
Benin	2003	Dominica	2002	Lebanon	2004	Niger	2011
Botswana	2009	Ethiopia	2004	Lesotho	2010	Palau	2006
Burkina Faso	2003	Fiji	2008	Liberia	2007	Papua New Guinea	2009
Cabo Verde	2007	Gabon	2005	Lithuania	2008	Senegal	2011
Cameroon	2007	Gambia, The	1998	Madagascar	2010	Sierra Leone	2011
Colombia	2012	Haiti	2001	Maldives	2004	Solomon Islands	2005
Comoros	2004	Honduras	2011	Marshall Islands	1999	South Africa	2005
Congo, Dem. Rep.	2005	Hungary	2007	Mauritania	2008	Swaziland	2000
Congo, Rep.	2005	Jamaica	2002	Micronesia, Fed. Sts.	2000	Syrian Arab Republic	2003
Côte d'Ivoire	2002	Jordan	2006	Morocco	2009	Togo	2006

countries. Very often household surveys do not capture the universe of social protection and labor programs in the country—only the largest programs. Many household surveys have limited information on social protection and labor programs. Some surveys collect information only on participation without including the transfer amounts; others mix information on public programs with private transfers, making it difficult to isolate individual SPL programs.

Therefore, information on country social protection and labor programs reflected in the ASPIRE indicators based on household surveys is limited to what is captured in the respective national household surveys and does not necessarily represent the universe of programs existing in the country. In addition, the availability of ASPIRE indicators depends on the type of questions included in the survey. If transfer amounts are available, for example, indicators on adequacy and the impact on poverty can be generated. If only program participation ques-

tions are included in the survey, only nonmonetary indicators can be generated, such as coverage or beneficiary incidence.[20]

In this sense, household surveys are a powerful complement to the information provided by administrative data. When properly planned and executed, the administrative and household survey data should be broadly consistent. There are of course specific issues related to the accuracy of reporting and possible sampling issues that may prevent broad matching of data. This is why some applications—such as the tax-benefit micro-simulation model for the European Union (EUROMOD)—use imputed data or a combination of reported and imputed information. However, in practice, the main issue is not ensuring the accuracy of responses, but rather establishing the appropriate correspondence of survey questions to existing social safety net programs and schemes.[21] Table A.4 lists the household surveys used in the analysis.

Table A.4 Household Surveys Used in the Report (105 Countries, Economies, and Territories)

Country/economy/territory	Survey year	Survey name
Afghanistan	2007	National Risk and Vulnerability Assessment (NRVA)
Albania	2008	Living Standards Measurement Survey
Argentina	2010	Encuesta Permanente de Hogares Continua
Armenia	2009	Integrated Living Conditions Survey 2009 (ILCS)
Azerbaijan	2008	Household Survey on Monitoring Targeted Social Assistance Programme 2008
Bangladesh	2010	Household Income and Expenditure Survey 2010
Belarus	2010	Household Sample Survey
Belize	2009	Living Standards Measurement Survey (LSMS)
Bhutan	2007	Living Standards Survey 2007—South Asia Labor Flagship Dataset
Bolivia	2007	Encuesta de Hogares
Bosnia and Herzegovina	2007	Household Budget Survey
Botswana	2009	Core Welfare Indicators Survey
Brazil	2009	Pesquisa Nacional por Amostra de Domicilios
Bulgaria	2007	Multi-Topic Household Survey
Burkina Faso	2003	Enquête sur les Conditions de Vie des Ménages 2003, Questionnaire Unifié sur les Indicateurs de Base du Bien-être
Cabo Verde	2007	Questionário Unificado de Indicadores Básicos de Bem-Estar (QUIBB)
Cambodia	2008	Socio-Economic Survey 2008
Cameroon	2007	Troisième Enquête Camerounaise Auprès des Ménages 2007
Chile	2009	Encuesta de Caracterización Socio-Económica Nacional (CASEN)
Colombia	2012	Encuesta Nacional de Calidad de Vida (ENCV)
Congo, Dem. Rep.	2004	Enquête 1-2-3 sur l'Emploi, le Secteur Informel et les Conditions de Vie des Ménages
Congo, Rep.	2005	Enquête Congolaise auprès des Ménages pour l'Evaluation de la Pauvreté 2005
Costa Rica	2009	Encuesta de Hogares de Propósitos Múltiples
Côte d'Ivoire	2002	Enquête sur le Niveau de Vie des Ménages de Côte d'Ivoire 2002
Croatia	2008	Household Budget Survey
Djibouti	2012	Enquete Djiboutienne Aupres des Menages (EDAM 3-IS)

(Table continues next page)

Table A.4 Household Surveys Used in the Report (105 Countries, Economies, and Territories) *(Continued)*

Country/economy/territory	Survey year	Survey name
Dominica	2002	Survey of Living Conditions (SLC)
Dominican Republic	2009	Encuesta Nacional de Fuerza de Trabajo
Ecuador	2010	Encuesta Nacional de Empleo Desempleo y Subempleo
Egypt, Arab Rep.	2008	Pan Survey
El Salvador	2009	Encuesta de Hogares de Propósitos Múltiples
Ethiopia	2010	Household Income, Consumption and Expenditures
Fiji	2008	Household Income and Expenditure Survey
Gabon	2005	Enquête Gabonaise pour l'Evaluation et le Suivi de la Pauvreté 2005
Gambia, The	1998	Household Poverty Survey
Georgia	2011	Welfare Monitoring Survey
Ghana	2013	Living Standards Survey V 2012–13
Guatemala	2006	Encuesta Nacional de Condiciones de Vida
Haiti	2001	Enquête sur les Conditions de Vie en Haïti 2001
Honduras	2011	Encuesta Permanente de Hogares de Propósitos Múltiples
Hungary	2007	Household Budget Survey
India	2009	National Sample Survey 2009–10 (66th round)—Schedule 10-Employment and Unemployment
Indonesia	2009	Survei Sosial Ekonomi Nasional 2009, Maret
Iraq	2006	Household Socio-Economic Survey 2006–07
Jamaica	2010	Survey of Living Conditions
Jordan	2010	Household Income and Expenditure Survey 2010
Kazakhstan	2007	Household Budget Survey
Kenya	2005	Integrated Household Budget Survey 2005–06
Kiribati	2006	Household Income and Expenditure Survey
Kosovo	2006	Household Budget Survey
Kyrgyz Republic	2006	Kyrgyz Integrated Household Survey 2006
Latvia	2008	Household Budget Survey
Lebanon	2004	National Survey of Household Living Conditions 2004, Multipurpose Survey
Lesotho	2014	CMS Quarter III 2013/2014
Liberia	2007	Core Welfare Indicators Questionnaire 2007
Lithuania	2008	Household Budget Survey
Madagascar	2010	Enquete Periodique Aupres Des Menages 2010 (EPM 2010)
Malawi	2010	Third Integrated Household Survey 2010–11
Malaysia	2008	Household Income Survey
Maldives	2004	Vulnerability and Poverty Assessment Survey II 2004
Mauritania	2008	Enquete Permanente Sur Les Conditions De Vie Des Menages
Mauritius	2006	Household Budget Survey 2006–07
Mexico	2010	Encuesta Nacional de Ingresos y Gastos de los Hogares
Micronesia, Fed. Sts.	2000	Population and Housing Census 2000
Moldova	2010	Household Budget Survey
Mongolia	2007	Household Socio-Economic Survey 2007–08
Morocco	2009	Household and Youth Survey
Mozambique	2008	Inquérito Sobre Orçamento Familiar 2008–09
Namibia	2003	National Household Income and Expenditure Survey 2003/2004
Nepal	2010	Living Standards Survey 2010–11, Third Round
Nicaragua	2005	Encuesta Nacional de Hogares sobre Medición de Nivel de Vida
Niger	2011	Enquête Nationale sur les Conditions de Vie des Ménages 2010–11
Nigeria	2010	General Household Survey, Panel 2010
Pakistan	2009	Social and Living Standards Measurement Survey 2009–10—Panel Component
Palau	2006	Household Income and Expenditure Survey

(Table continues next page)

Table A.4 Household Surveys Used in the Report (105 Countries, Economies, and Territories) *(Continued)*

Country/economy/territory	Survey year	Survey name
Panama	2008	Encuesta de Niveles de Vida
Papua New Guinea	2009	Household Income and Expenditure Survey 2009–10
Paraguay	2009	Encuesta Permanente de Hogares
Peru	2009	Encuesta Nacional de Hogares-Condiciones de Vida y Pobreza
Philippines	2013	Annual Poverty Indicators Survey
Poland	2005	Household Budget Survey
Romania	2008	Household Budget Survey
Russian Federation	2007	Household Budget Survey
Rwanda	2005	Enquête Intégrale sur les Conditions de Vie des ménages (EICV)
Senegal	2011	Enquête de Suivi de la Pauvreté au Sénégal 2011
Serbia	2007	Household Budget Survey
Sierra Leone	2011	Integrated Household Survey (SLIHS)—Main Survey
Slovak Republic	2009	Household Income and Living Conditions Survey
Solomon Islands	2005	Household Income and Expenditure Survey
South Africa	2010	Income and Expenditure Survey
Sri Lanka	2006	Household Income and Expenditure Survey 2006–07
Swaziland	2010	Household Income and Expenditure Survey
Tajikistan	2011	Panorama
Tanzania	2008	National Panel Survey
Thailand	2009	Household Socio-Economic Survey
Timor-Leste	2007	Survey of Living Standards 2007 and Extension 2008
Turkey	2012	Household Income and Consumption Expenditures Survey 2012
Uganda	2009	Uganda National Panel Survey 2009–10
Ukraine	2006	Household Living Conditions Survey 2006
Uruguay	2009	Encuesta Continua de Hogares
Venezuela, RB	2006	Encuesta de Hogares por Muestreo 2006—SEDLAC-Base de Datos Armonizada
Vietnam	2006	Household Living Standard Survey
West Bank and Gaza	2007	Expenditure and Consumption Survey
Yemen, Rep.	2005	Household Budget Survey
Zambia	2010	Living Conditions Monitoring Survey VI (LCMS VI)

Notes

1. This differentiates social safety nets from contributory forms of social protection, where prior contributions (and participation in the labor market) determine eligibility for benefits. The noncontributory nature also means that social safety net programs cannot be self-financed (as are most social insurance programs) and must rely on support from public budgets.

2. Social insurance programs minimize the negative impact of economic shocks on individuals and families. They include publicly provided or mandated insurance schemes against old age, disability, death of the main household provider, maternity leave, sickness cash benefits, and entitlement to health insurance. Social insurance programs are contributory. Beneficiaries receive benefits or services in recognition of contributions to an insurance scheme.

3. *Conditional cash transfers (CCTs)* are periodic monetary benefits to poor households that require beneficiaries to comply with specific behavioral requirements to encourage investments in human capital (such as school attendance, immunizations, and health check-ups).

4. School feeding programs were named "conditional food transfers" in the 2014 edition of this report.

5. See, for example, Grosh and others 2008.

6. Indeed, social safety nets are not considered to be a part of standard budget classifications, such as the main international framework to report budgetary data, the Classification of the Functions of Governments (COFOG). Developed by the International Monetary Fund (IMF), COFOG breaks down government expenditures according to their purpose independently from the nature of the administrative unit in charge of this expenditure. "Social protection" as a whole is one of the functions used in COGOF. Under COFOG, the term is used to cover the following subfunctions: "sickness and disability," "old age," "survivors," "family and children," "unemployment," "housing," "social exclusion

not elsewhere classified," and some other related categories. No "social safety net" category exists in this framework. See http://www.imf.org/external/pubs/ft/gfs/manual/pdf/all.pdf. See also International Labour Organization (ILO) 1957, "Resolution concerning the development of social security statistics," http://www.ilo.org/public/english/bureau/stat/download/res/socsec.pdf.

7. The sum of individual beneficiaries refers to the annual average stock or end-year number of direct beneficiaries. The beneficiary reporting unit may be either households or individuals.

8. ASPIRE includes programs that are implemented by the central/federal government and have more than 1,000 individual beneficiaries. For some countries, the inventory of programs included may not be exhaustive; thus country enrollment rates may be underestimated.

9. Avoiding double-counting would require perfectly interoperable program management information systems with common beneficiary identifications (IDs).

10. While five might be an overestimation of the household size in some Eastern Europe and Latin American countries, it might be an underestimation in some African and Asian countries. The assumption is that five is close to the average *global* household size.

11. Specifically, the coverage rate is equal to the number of individuals in the poorest quintile who live in a household where at least one member receives the transfer divided by the number of individuals in the poorest quintile.

12. Social pensions in this report and ASPIRE are aggregated within the unconditional cash transfers category.

13. See http://datatopics.worldbank.org/aspire/documentation.

14. In Bolivia, Costa Rica, the Dominican Republic, Ethiopia, Guatemala, Namibia, Nicaragua, Nigeria, Panama, South Africa, St. Lucia, Sudan, Uganda, West Bank and Gaza, and Zimbabwe.

15. ASPIRE indicators based on household surveys are publicly available at www.worldbank.org/aspire.

16. For 7 of the 112 countries, economies, and territories, the survey instrument collects information only on contributory pensions and other social insurance. These 7 jurisdictions are not considered in the analysis.

17. Data on the new countries were uploaded to the ASPIRE portal in July 2014 and updated in March 2015. Please visit www.worldbank.org/aspire/documentation for detailed information on survey names, links to the micro-data catalog to download the micro-data, the methodology used, and program documentation.

18. Benefits existing at the time of the survey; they may no longer be active.

19. See www.worldbank.org/aspire/indicator_caveats.

20. Another caveat is related to the fact that the sample design of household surveys does not take beneficiary incidence of social protection into account; thus final outcomes are biased down. For example, estimates from the Europe and Central Asia region show that the share of total social assistance captured in household surveys ranges from 30 percent to 90 percent when compared to administrative data on budgets for social assistance transfers. This is because many such programs are targeted to narrow groups, which are underrepresented in nationwide surveys. Moreover, statistical estimates for these small subsamples are characterized by large sampling errors. There are ways to address such problems. For example, in Mexico, an oversample of rural areas was needed to provide the correct coverage of the Oportunidades program in the household survey data. In Armenia, targeted program beneficiaries are oversampled in the national survey. However, this report did not adopt these methods across all countries.

21. Often questions on the amount and receipt of social protection and labor benefits in survey instruments are not specific enough to infer the nature of the benefit (contributory versus noncontributory); the specific program the benefit is part of (if the program name is not specified in the question); or the type of benefit (for example, old-age, disability, and survivorship pensions may be lumped in one general question).

References

Grosh, M., C. Del Ninno, E. Tesliuc, and A. Ouerghi. 2008. *For Protection and Promotion: The Design and Implementation of Effective Social Safety Nets*. Washington, DC: World Bank.

International Labour Office (ILO). 2014. *World Social Protection Report 2014/15: Building Economic Recovery, Inclusive Development, and Social Justice*. Washington, DC: Brookings Institution Press.

Weblinks

ASPIRE (Atlas of Social Protection: Indicators of Resilience and Equity), World Bank, www.worldbank.org/aspire/.

COFOG (Classification of the Functions of Government), United Nations Statistics, http://unstats.un.org/unsd/cr/registry/regcst.asp?Cl=4.

EUROMOD (Tax-Benefit Microsimulation Model for the European Union), Institute for Social and Economic Research (ISER), https://www.iser.essex.ac.uk/euromod.

Appendix B. Countries, Economies, and Territories Included in the Report

	Country/economy/territory	Code	Region	Income classification	Population (millions)
1	Afghanistan	AFG	South Asia	Low-income	30.6
2	Albania	ALB	Europe and Central Asia	Upper-middle-income	2.8
3	Algeria	DZA	Middle East and North Africa	Upper-middle-income	39.2
4	Angola	AGO	Africa (Sub-Saharan)	Upper-middle-income	21.5
5	Antigua and Barbuda	ATG	Latin America and the Caribbean	High-income	0.1
6	Argentina	ARG	Latin America and the Caribbean	Upper-middle-income	41.4
7	Armenia	ARM	Europe and Central Asia	Lower-middle-income	3.0
8	Azerbaijan	AZE	Europe and Central Asia	Upper-middle-income	9.4
9	Bahrain	BHR	Middle East and North Africa	High-income	1.3
10	Bangladesh	BGD	South Asia	Low-income	156.6
11	Belarus	BLR	Europe and Central Asia	Upper-middle-income	9.5
12	Belize	BLZ	Latin America and the Caribbean	Upper-middle-income	0.3
13	Benin	BEN	Africa (Sub-Saharan)	Low-income	10.3
14	Bhutan	BTN	South Asia	Lower-middle-income	0.8
15	Bolivia	BOL	Latin America and the Caribbean	Lower-middle-income	10.7
16	Bosnia and Herzegovina	BIH	Europe and Central Asia	Upper-middle-income	3.8
17	Botswana	BWA	Africa (Sub-Saharan)	Upper-middle-income	2.0
18	Brazil	BRA	Latin America and the Caribbean	Upper-middle- income	200.4
19	Bulgaria	BGR	Europe and Central Asia	Upper-middle-income	7.3
20	Burkina Faso	BFA	Africa (Sub-Saharan)	Low-income	16.9
21	Burundi	BDI	Africa (Sub-Saharan)	Low-income	10.2
22	Cabo Verde	CPV	Africa (Sub-Saharan)	Lower-middle-income	0.5
23	Cambodia	KHM	East Asia & Pacific	Low-income	15.1
24	Cameroon	CMR	Africa (Sub-Saharan)	Lower-middle-income	22.3
25	Central African Republic	CAF	Africa (Sub-Saharan)	Low-income	4.6
26	Chad	TCD	Africa (Sub-Saharan)	Low-income	12.8
27	Chile	CHL	Latin America and the Caribbean	High-income	17.6
28	China	CHN	East Asia & Pacific	Upper-middle-income	1,357.4
29	Colombia	COL	Latin America and the Caribbean	Upper-middle-income	48.3
30	Comoros	COM	Africa (Sub-Saharan)	Low-income	0.7
31	Congo, Dem. Rep.	ZAR	Africa (Sub-Saharan)	Low-income	67.5
32	Congo, Rep.	COG	Africa (Sub-Saharan)	Lower-middle-income	4.4
33	Costa Rica	CRI	Latin America and the Caribbean	Upper-middle-income	4.9
34	Côte d'Ivoire	CIV	Africa (Sub-Saharan)	Lower-middle-income	20.3
35	Croatia	HRV	Europe and Central Asia	High-income	4.3
36	Czech Republic	CZE	Europe and Central Asia	High-income	10.5
37	Djibouti	DJI	Middle East and North Africa	Lower-middle-income	0.9
38	Dominica	DMA	Latin America and the Caribbean	Upper-middle-income	0.1
39	Dominican Republic	DOM	Latin America and the Caribbean	Upper-middle-income	10.4
40	Ecuador	ECU	Latin America and the Caribbean	Upper-middle-income	15.7
41	Egypt, Arab Rep.	EGY	Middle East and North Africa	Lower-middle-income	82.1
42	El Salvador	SLV	Latin America and the Caribbean	Lower-middle-income	6.3
43	Equatorial Guinea	GNQ	Africa (Sub-Saharan)	High-income	0.8

(Table continues next page)

Appendix B. Countries, Economies, and Territories Included in the Report (Continued)

Country/economy/territory	Code	Region	Income classification	Population (millions)
44 Eritrea	ERI	Africa (Sub-Saharan)	Low-income	6.3
45 Estonia	EST	Europe and Central Asia	High-income	1.3
46 Ethiopia	ETH	Africa (Sub-Saharan)	Low-income	94.1
47 Fiji	FJI	East Asia & Pacific	Upper-middle-income	0.9
48 Gabon	GAB	Africa (Sub-Saharan)	Upper-middle-income	1.7
49 Gambia, The	GMB	Africa (Sub-Saharan)	Low-income	1.8
50 Georgia	GEO	Europe and Central Asia	Lower-middle-income	4.5
51 Ghana	GHA	Africa (Sub-Saharan)	Lower-middle-income	25.9
52 Grenada	GRD	Latin America and the Caribbean	Upper-middle-income	0.1
53 Guatemala	GTM	Latin America and the Caribbean	Lower-middle-income	15.5
54 Guinea	GIN	Africa (Sub-Saharan)	Low-income	11.7
55 Guinea-Bissau	GNB	Africa (Sub-Saharan)	Low-income	1.7
56 Guyana	GUY	Latin America and the Caribbean	Lower-middle-income	0.8
57 Haiti	HTI	Latin America and the Caribbean	Low-income	10.3
58 Honduras	HND	Latin America and the Caribbean	Lower-middle-income	8.1
59 Hungary	HUN	Europe and Central Asia	Upper-middle-income	9.9
60 India	IND	South Asia	Lower-middle-income	1,252.1
61 Indonesia	IDN	East Asia & Pacific	Lower-middle-income	249.9
62 Iran, Islamic Rep.	IRN	Middle East and North Africa	Upper-middle-income	77.4
63 Iraq	IRQ	Middle East and North Africa	Upper-middle-income	33.4
64 Jamaica	JAM	Latin America and the Caribbean	Upper-middle-income	2.7
65 Jordan	JOR	Middle East and North Africa	Upper-middle-income	6.5
66 Kazakhstan	KAZ	Europe and Central Asia	Upper-middle-income	17.0
67 Kenya	KEN	Africa (Sub-Saharan)	Low-income	44.4
68 Kiribati	KIR	East Asia & Pacific	Lower-middle-income	0.1
69 Kosovo	KSV	Europe and Central Asia	Lower-middle-income	1.8
70 Kuwait	KWT	Middle East and North Africa	High-income	3.4
71 Kyrgyz Republic	KGZ	Europe and Central Asia	Lower-middle-income	5.7
72 Lao PDR	LAO	East Asia & Pacific	Lower-middle-income	6.8
73 Latvia	LVA	Europe and Central Asia	High-income	2.0
74 Lebanon	LBN	Middle East and North Africa	Upper-middle-income	4.5
75 Lesotho	LSO	Africa (Sub-Saharan)	Lower-middle-income	2.1
76 Liberia	LBR	Africa (Sub-Saharan)	Low-income	4.3
77 Libya	LBY	Middle East and North Africa	Upper-middle-income	6.2
78 Lithuania	LTU	Europe and Central Asia	High-income	3.0
79 Macedonia, FYR	MKD	Europe and Central Asia	Upper-middle-income	2.1
80 Madagascar	MDG	Africa (Sub-Saharan)	Low-income	22.9
81 Malawi	MWI	Africa (Sub-Saharan)	Low-income	16.4
82 Malaysia	MYS	East Asia & Pacific	Upper-middle-income	29.7
83 Maldives	MDV	South Asia	Upper-middle-income	0.3
84 Mali	MLI	Africa (Sub-Saharan)	Low-income	15.3
85 Marshall Islands	MHL	East Asia & Pacific	Upper-middle-income	0.1

(Table continues next page)

Country/economy/territory		Code	Region	Income classification	Population (millions)
86	Mauritania	MRT	Africa (Sub-Saharan)	Lower-middle-income	3.9
87	Mauritius	MUS	Africa (Sub-Saharan)	Upper-middle-income	1.3
88	Mexico	MEX	Latin America and the Caribbean	Upper-middle-income	122.3
89	Micronesia, Fed. Sts.	FSM	East Asia & Pacific	Lower-middle-income	0.1
90	Moldova	MDA	Europe and Central Asia	Lower-middle-income	3.6
91	Mongolia	MNG	East Asia & Pacific	Lower-middle-income	2.8
92	Montenegro	MNE	Europe and Central Asia	Upper-middle-income	0.6
93	Morocco	MAR	Middle East and North Africa	Lower-middle-income	33.0
94	Mozambique	MOZ	Africa (Sub-Saharan)	Low-income	25.8
95	Myanmar	MMR	East Asia & Pacific	Low-income	53.3
96	Namibia	NAM	Africa (Sub-Saharan)	Upper-middle-income	2.3
97	Nepal	NPL	South Asia	Low-income	27.8
98	Nicaragua	NIC	Latin America and the Caribbean	Lower-middle-income	6.1
99	Niger	NER	Africa (Sub-Saharan)	Low-income	17.8
100	Nigeria	NGA	Africa (Sub-Saharan)	Lower-middle-income	173.6
101	Oman	OMN	Middle East and North Africa	High-income	3.6
102	Pakistan	PAK	South Asia	Lower-middle-income	182.1
103	Palau	PLW	East Asia & Pacific	Upper-middle-income	0[a]
104	Panama	PAN	Latin America and the Caribbean	Upper-middle-income	3.9
105	Papua New Guinea	PNG	East Asia & Pacific	Lower-middle-income	7.3
106	Paraguay	PRY	Latin America and the Caribbean	Lower-middle-income	6.8
107	Peru	PER	Latin America and the Caribbean	Upper-middle-income	30.4
108	Philippines	PHL	East Asia & Pacific	Lower-middle-income	98.4
109	Poland	POL	Europe and Central Asia	High-income	38.5
110	Qatar	QAT	Middle East and North Africa	High-income	2.2
111	Romania	ROM	Europe and Central Asia	Upper-middle-income	20.0
112	Russian Federation	RUS	Europe and Central Asia	High-income	143.5
113	Rwanda	RWA	Africa (Sub-Saharan)	Low-income	11.8
114	Samoa	WSM	East Asia & Pacific	Lower-middle-income	0.2
115	São Tomé and Príncipe	STP	Africa (Sub-Saharan)	Lower-middle-income	0.2
116	Saudi Arabia	SAU	Middle East and North Africa	High-income	28.8
117	Senegal	SEN	Africa (Sub-Saharan)	Lower-middle-income	14.1
118	Serbia	SRB	Europe and Central Asia	Upper-middle-income	7.2
119	Seychelles	SYC	Africa (Sub-Saharan)	Upper-middle-income	0.1
120	Sierra Leone	SLE	Africa (Sub-Saharan)	Low-income	6.1
121	Slovak Republic	SVK	Europe and Central Asia	High-income	5.4
122	Slovenia	SVN	Europe and Central Asia	High-income	2.1
123	Solomon Islands	SLB	East Asia & Pacific	Lower-middle-income	0.6
124	Somalia	SOM	Africa (Sub-Saharan)	Low-income	10.5
125	South Africa	ZAF	Africa (Sub-Saharan)	Upper-middle-income	53.0
126	South Sudan	SSD	Africa (Sub-Saharan)	Lower-middle-income	11.3
127	Sri Lanka	LKA	South Asia	Lower-middle-income	20.5

(Table continues next page)

Appendix B. Countries, Economies, and Territories Included in the Report (Continued)

	Country/economy/ territory	Code	Region	Income classification	Population (millions)
128	St. Kitts and Nevis	KNA	Latin America and the Caribbean	High-income	0.1
129	St. Lucia	LCA	Latin America and the Caribbean	Upper-middle-income	0.2
130	St. Vincent and the Grenadines	VCT	Latin America and the Caribbean	Upper-middle-income	0.1
131	Sudan	SDN	Africa (Sub-Saharan)	Lower-middle-income	38.0
132	Suriname	SUR	Latin America and the Caribbean	Upper-middle-income	0.5
133	Swaziland	SWZ	Africa (Sub-Saharan)	Lower-middle-income	1.2
134	Syrian Arab Republic	SYR	Middle East and North Africa	Lower-middle-income	22.8
135	Tajikistan	TJK	Europe and Central Asia	Low-income	8.2
136	Tanzania	TZA	Africa (Sub-Saharan)	Low-income	49.3
137	Thailand	THA	East Asia & Pacific	Upper-middle-income	67.0
138	Timor-Leste	TMP	East Asia & Pacific	Lower-middle-income	1.2
139	Togo	TGO	Africa (Sub-Saharan)	Low-income	6.8
140	Tonga	TON	East Asia & Pacific	Upper-middle-income	0.1
141	Trinidad and Tobago	TTO	Latin America and the Caribbean	High-income	1.3
142	Tunisia	TUN	Middle East and North Africa	Upper-middle-income	10.9
143	Turkey	TUR	Europe and Central Asia	Upper-middle-income	74.9
144	Turkmenistan	TKM	Europe and Central Asia	Upper-middle-income	5.2
145	Tuvalu	TUV	East Asia & Pacific	Upper-middle-income	0[a]
146	Uganda	UGA	Africa (Sub-Saharan)	Low-income	37.6
147	Ukraine	UKR	Europe and Central Asia	Lower-middle-income	45.5
148	United Arab Emirates	ARE	Middle East and North Africa	High-income	9.3
149	Uruguay	URY	Latin America and the Caribbean	High-income	3.4
150	Uzbekistan	UZB	Europe and Central Asia	Lower-middle-income	30.2
151	Vanuatu	VUT	East Asia & Pacific	Lower-middle-income	0.3
152	Venezuela, RB	VEN	Latin America and the Caribbean	Upper-middle-income	30.4
153	Vietnam	VNM	East Asia & Pacific	Lower-middle-income	89.7
154	West Bank and Gaza	WBG	Middle East and North Africa	Lower-middle-income	4.2
155	Yemen, Rep.	YEM	Middle East and North Africa	Lower-middle-income	24.4
156	Zambia	ZMB	Africa (Sub-Saharan)	Lower-middle-income	14.5
157	Zimbabwe	ZWE	Africa (Sub-Saharan)	Low-income	14.1

Source: Population data from World Development Indicators 2013. The regional and income classifications are based on a World Bank list of economies, July 2014.

Note: The following were not included in the report and may be added in future issues of *The State of Social Safety Nets*: Andorra; Aruba; Australia; Austria; The Bahamas; Barbados; Belgium; Bermuda; Brunei Darussalam; Canada; Cayman Islands; Channel Islands; Cuba; Curaçao; Cyprus; Denmark; Faeroe Islands; Finland; France; French Polynesia; Germany; Greece; Greenland; Guam; Hong Kong SAR, China; Iceland; Ireland; Isle of Man; Israel; Italy; Japan; the Democratic People's Republic of Korea; the Republic of Korea; Liechtenstein; Luxembourg; Macao SAR, China; Malta; Monaco; Nauru; the Netherlands; New Caledonia; New Zealand; Northern Mariana Islands; Norway; Poland; Portugal; Puerto Rico; Samoa; San Marino; Sint Maarten (Dutch part); Spain; Sweden; Switzerland; United Kingdom; United States; Virgin Islands (U.S.).

a. The population in Palau and in Tuvalu is greater than 0 but less than 50,000 individuals.

Appendix C. (Part 1) Program Inventory

Country/ economy/ territory	Conditional cash transfer				Unconditional cash transfer			
	Program name	Number of beneficiaries	Year	Data source	Program name	Number of beneficiaries	Year	Data source
Afghanistan	—	—	—	—	Martyrs and Disabled Benefit Program	265,000	2014	World Bank 2014d
Albania	—	—	—	—	Ndihme Ekonomike	106,635[a]	2014	SPeeD
Algeria	—	—	—	—	—	—	—	—
Angola	Angola CCT School Program	900,000	2012	World Bank 2012a	Angola Social Pension Program	1,000,000	2012	World Bank 2012a
Antigua and Barbuda	—	—	—	—	—	—	—	—
Argentina	Asignación Universal por Hijo para la Protección Social	3,540,717	2012	Government of Argentina	Pensión no contributiva por discapacidad	716,058	2011	LAC database
Armenia	—	—	—	—	Family Poverty Benefit (PMT)	96,309[a]	2012	SPeeD
Azerbaijan	—	—	—	—	Targeted Social Assistance	548,663	2012	SPeeD
Bahrain	—	—	—	—	Large-scale Temporary Cash Transfer Program (CTP)	—	—	—
Bangladesh	Stipend for primary students	7,800,000	2009	UNICEF 2013	Old-age allowance	2,475,000	2011	Helpage
Belarus	—	—	—	—	Child care benefit, for children up to 3 years old	315,867	2012	SPeeD
Belize	Building Opportunities for Our Social Transformation (BOOST)	8,600	2011	ECLAC	Social pension	3,711	2011	Helpage
Benin	Program for girls education	100	2008	World Bank 2011h	Projet de services décentralisés conduits par les communautés (PSDCC)	13,000	2015	Government of Benin
Bhutan	—	—	—	—	—	—	—	—
Bolivia	Bono Juancito Pinto	1,887,625	2013	Government of Bolivia	Renta Dignidad	838,866	2014	Helpage
Bosnia and Herzegovina	—	—	—	—	Child Protection Allowance	105,844	2010	SPeeD
Botswana	—	—	—	—	Old-Age Pension (OAP)	91,446	2010	World Bank 2011a
Brazil	Bolsa Familia	14,014,252[a]	2015	MDS	Old-age social pensions	5,852,000	2012	Government of Brazil
Bulgaria	—	—	—	—	Family or child allowance	797,903	2013	SPeeD
Burkina Faso	Burkin-Nong-Saya (CT with complementary activities)	—	—	—	Cash Transfers to Orphans and Vulnerable Children	6,500	2010	World Bank 2011b
Burundi	—	—	—	—	Take a Step Forward (Terintambwe)	2,000[a]	2012	World Bank 2014b
Cabo Verde	—	—	—	—	Social pensions	23,000	2011	Helpage

Unconditional food and in-kind				Country/economy/territory
Program name	Number of beneficiaries	Year	Data source	
Emergency Food Assistance	1,800,000	2013	WFP 2015a	Afghanistan
—	—	—	—	Albania
—	—	—	—	Algeria
Angola Nutrition Program	800,000	2012	World Bank 2012a	Angola
—	—	—	—	Antigua and Barbuda
Plan Nacional de Seguridad Alimentaria	1,954,000	2006	ECLAC	Argentina
—	—	—	—	Armenia
—	—	—	—	Azerbaijan
—	—	—	—	Bahrain
Public Food Distribution System	2,100,000	2009	World Bank 2010a	Bangladesh
—	—	—	—	Belarus
Women's Iron and Folic Acid Distribution Program	9,000	2009	World Bank 2010b	Belize
Various food distribution programs in response to crises	50,991	2008	World Bank 2011h	Benin
—	—	—	—	Bhutan
Assistance to drought-affected populations in Bolivia	50,000	2013	WFP 2015c	Bolivia
—	—	—	—	Bosnia and Herzegovina
Vulnerable Group Feeding Program	231,000	2010	World Bank 2011a	Botswana
Segurança Alimentar e Nutricional dos Povos Indígenas	—	—	—	Brazil
Assistance for pupils and students	48,845	2013	SPeeD	Bulgaria
Urban voucher program (EMOP)	338,915	2009	World Bank 2011b	Burkina Faso
WFP food distribution (all programs)	743,377	2012	World Bank 2014b	Burundi
Nutritional support to vulnerable groups and persons living with the human immunodeficiency virus (HIV) (CP10399.0 component 2)	—	—	—	Cabo Verde

(Table continues next page)

Country/ economy/ territory	Conditional cash transfer				Unconditional cash transfer			
	Program name	Number of beneficiaries	Year	Data source	Program name	Number of beneficiaries	Year	Data source
Cambodia	CESSP Scholarship Program (Cambodia Education Sector Support Project)	—	—	—	—	—	—	—
Cameroon	Pilot CCT with Productive Aspects	2,000[a]	2014	Government of Cameroon	—	—	—	—
Central African Republic	—	—	—	—	—	—	—	—
Chad	Conditional cash grants in refugee camps and Households Resilience Programs	988,624	2014	CARE International	Programs for food security	305,480	2014	Oxfam
Chile	Subsidio unico familiar	2,066,618	2012	Government of Chile	Old-age solidarity pensions	1,000,806	2014	Helpage
China	Educational subsidies and free education	—	—	—	Dibao	74,500,000	2013	Government of China
Colombia	Familias en Accion	12,300,000	2013	ECLAC	Programa Colombia Mayor	1,258,000	2014	Helpage
Comoros	—	—	—	—	—	—	—	—
Congo, Dem. Rep.	—	—	—	—	World Food Programme (cash and voucher program)	234,000	2013	WFP 2015e
Congo, Rep.	Lisungi	—	—	—	Cash transfer program in Brazzaville and Point-Noire	—	—	—
Costa Rica	Avancemos	171,534	2013	Government of Costa Rica	Social pension	70,536	2013	Government of Costa Rica
Côte d'Ivoire	—	—	—	—	Cash transfer project in Abidjan	54,000	2013	WFP 2015g
Croatia	—	—	—	—	Child and family benefits	216,013	2011	SPeeD
Czech Republic	—	—	—	—	Benefit in material need	71,153[a]	2008	Tesliuc and others
Djibouti	Cantine and transport subsidy for university students	900	2014	Government of Djibouti	Food voucher (July–September)	3,500[a]	2014	WFP 2015h
Dominica	—	—	—	—	—	—	—	—
Dominican Republic	Solidaridad/PROSOLI	2,355,615	2014	ECLAC	Suplemento Alimenticio del Programa de Protección a la Vejez en Extrema Pobreza	99,802[a]	2013	Government of Dominican Republic
Ecuador	Bono de Desarollo Humano	444,562[a]	2014	Government of Ecuador	Bono matrícula para la eliminación del aporte voluntario	3,015,199	2010	LAC database
Egypt, Arab Rep.	—	—	—	—	Social solidarity pension	7,000,000	2014	Government of Egypt
El Salvador	Comunidades Solidarias Rurales	75,385[a]	2013	Government of El Salvador	Universal basic pension for the elderly	28,200	2013	Government of El Salvador

| Unconditional food and in-kind | | | | Country/ economy/ territory |
Program name	Number of beneficiaries	Year	Data source	
Mother and Child Health Program	114,000	2008	Government of Cambodia, WFP, and World Bank 2009	Cambodia
Nutrition program by CARE	20,000	2010	World Bank 2011c	Cameroon
General food distribution to IDPs and returnees	333,000	2013	WFP 2015d	Central African Republic
General food distribution to IDPs and returnees	104,440	2014	Oxfam	Chad
Programa nacional de alimentación complementaria	685,510	2012	Government of Chile	Chile
Wubao	5,500,000	2008	World Bank 2010e	China
Programa de Alimentación al Adulto Mayor—Juan Luis Londoňo de la Cuesta	417,230	2010	LAC database	Colombia
—	—	—	—	Comoros
World Food Programme food distribution program	714,900	2013	WFP 2015e	Congo, Dem. Rep.
Food assistance to refugees	70,000	2013	WFP 2015f	Congo, Rep.
Cen-cinai	157,249	2010	Government of Costa Rica	Costa Rica
General food distribution to IDPs	379,000	2013	WFP 2015g	Côte d'Ivoire
Child care (both cash and in-kind)	391,836	2011	SPeeD	Croatia
—	—	—	—	Czech Republic
WFP food distribution	28,255	2014	WFP 2015h	Djibouti
—	—	—	—	Dominica
Provisión Alimentaria-Comedores Económicos	—	—	—	Dominican Republic
Alimentate Ecuador	935,061	2010	LAC database	Ecuador
Support to nutrition	15,000	2011	WFP 2013b	Egypt, Arab Rep.
Programa de Agricultura Familiar	536,137[a]	2013	Government of El Salvador	El Salvador

(Table continues next page)

Country/ economy/ territory	Conditional cash transfer				Unconditional cash transfer			
	Program name	Number of beneficiaries	Year	Data source	Program name	Number of beneficiaries	Year	Data source
Equatorial Guinea	—	—	—	—	—	—	—	—
Eritrea	CCT	—	—	—	—	—	—	—
Estonia	—	—	—	—	Subsistence benefit (means-tested benefit)	136,376[a]	2009	SPeeD
Ethiopia	—	—	—	—	Pilot social cash transfer, Tigray	3,367[a]	2013	UNICEF-REPOM
Fiji	Care and Protection Allowance (C&P)	8,000	2008	ADB 2009b	Poverty Benefit Scheme (PBS)	25,000	2009	ADB 2009b
Gabon	—	—	—	—	—	—	—	—
Gambia, The	Family Strengthening Program	130,000	2011	COMCEC	Emergency Food Security Response	20,000	2013	WFP 2015j
Georgia	—	—	—	—	Targeted social assistance	428,492	2013	SPeeD
Ghana	—	—	—	—	Livelihood Empowerment Against Poverty (LEAP)	85,000[a]	2014	Government of Ghana
Grenada	Support for Education, Empowerment & Development (SEED)	—	—	—	Public assistance	4,000	2008	UN Women
Guatemala	Mi Bono Seguro— Bono Seguro Escolar	588,400[a]	2013	Government of Guatemala	Atencion al Adulto Mayor (MINTRA)	108,664	2013	Government of Guatemala
Guinea	—	—	—	—	Cash transfer for nutrition and for girls' education	—	—	—
Guinea-Bissau	—	—	—	—	Social pension	2,000	2006	Government of Guinea-Bissau 2007
Guyana	—	—	—	—	Social pension	42,500	2014	Helpage
Haiti	Ti Manman Cheri	86,234	2014	Haiti Economic and Social Assistance Fund (FAES)	Scholarship program (Kore etidyan)	31,409	2014	Haiti Economic and Social Assistance Fund (FAES)
Honduras	Bono 10,000	2,347,505	2011	ECLAC	Matrícula gratis	1,750,000	2010	LAC database
Hungary	For the Road	26,000	2008	Friedman and others 2009	Regular social assistance	269,000	2009	Tesliuc and others
India	Janani Suraksha Yojana	77,820,610	2014	Government of India	Indira Gandhi National Old Age Pension Scheme (IGNOAPS)	20,885,795	2014	India, Ministry of Health and Family Welfare 2015
Indonesia	Program Keluarga Harapan	2,400,000	2013	ADB 2013	Bangtuan Langsung Tui (BLT)	15,530,897	2013	ADB 2013
Iran, Islamic Rep.	—	—	—	—	Compensatory cash transfer	6,100,000	2009	World Bank 2010c
Iraq	—	—	—	—	Social Protection Network	877,520	2013	Government of Iraq
Jamaica	Programme of Advancement through Health and Education (PATH)	375,242	2014	Government of Jamaica	Old-age social pensions	56,989	2014	Government of Jamaica

Unconditional food and in-kind				Country/ economy/ territory
Program name	Number of beneficiaries	Year	Data source	
—	—	—	—	Equatorial Guinea
Blanket feeding for children under 5	187,000	2011	UNICEF 2012	Eritrea
—	—	—	—	Estonia
Food assistance under Joint Emergency Operation Programme	2,500,000	2013	UNOCHA 2015	Ethiopia
Food Voucher Program (FVP)	—	—	—	Fiji
—	—	—	—	Gabon
Blanket supplementary feeding for children under 5	200,000	2013	WFP 2015j	Gambia, The
—	—	—	—	Georgia
Free exercise books	4,768,806	2013	Government of Ghana	Ghana
Food Security Program	1,000	2008	UN Women	Grenada
Mi Bolsa Segura (MIDES)	196,341	2013	Government of Guatemala	Guatemala
Food and nutritional assistance to Ivoirian refugees	6,000	2013	WFP 2015k	Guinea
—	—	—	—	Guinea-Bissau
National School Uniform Programme	—		Internal World Bank monitoring tool	Guyana
Unconditional food transfer relief assistance	300,000	2014	WFP 2015l	Haiti
Comedores Solidarios	39,000	2011	LAC database	Honduras
—	—	—	—	Hungary
Integrated Child Development Services	—	—	—	India
—	—	—	—	Indonesia
—	—	—	—	Iran, Islamic Rep.
Food rations from Public Distribution System (PDS)	—	—	—	Iraq
Rural Feeding Programme	4,000	2010	World Bank 2011f	Jamaica

(Table continues next page)

Country/ economy/ territory	Conditional cash transfer				Unconditional cash transfer			
	Program name	Number of beneficiaries	Year	Data source	Program name	Number of beneficiaries	Year	Data source
Jordan	—	—	—	—	National Aid Fund	250,000	2011	WFP 2013a
Kazakhstan	Bota CCT	135,000	2010	World Bank 2011g	Targeted social assistance	104,100[a]	2012	SPeeD
Kenya	—	—	—	—	Cash transfer for OVC (CT-OVC)	1,265,000	2015	Internal World Bank documentation
Kiribati	—	—	—	—	Elderly pension	2,090	2010	Helpage
Kosovo	—	—	—	—	Social Assistance Scheme (Ndihma I and II)	30,741	2013	SPeeD
Kuwait	Families with Students grant	—	—	—	Physical Disability Grant	—	—	—
Kyrgyz Republic	—	—	—	—	Monthly Benefit for Poor Families with Children (MBPF)	361,500	2012	World Bank 2014c
Lao PDR	—	—	—	—	—	—	—	—
Latvia	—	—	—	—	Guaranteed minimum income	121,833[a]	2011	SPeeD
Lebanon	—	—	—	—	Family and education allowance	—	—	—
Lesotho	Child Grants Program (CGP)	30,000	2012	World Bank 2012b	Old-age social pensions	83,000	2012	World Bank 2012b
Liberia	—	—	—	—	E-FED (Ebola Food & Economic Development Program)	125,000	2014	Mercy Corps
Libya	—	—	—	—	—	—	—	—
Lithuania	—	—	—	—	Social benefit	50,000	2009	SPeeD
Macedonia, FYR	CCT increased child allowance	7,122	2014	SPeeD	Social financial assistance	44,852	2011	SPeeD
Madagascar	CCT	—	—	—	Family allowance	—	—	—
Malawi	—	—	—	—	Social Cash Transfer Scheme (SCTS)	143,741[a]	2014	Government of Malawi
Malaysia	—	—	—	—	Bantuan Rakyat 1 Malaysia (BR1M) scheme	15,300,000	2014	World Bank 2015
Maldives	—	—	—	—	Old-age pension scheme	15,248	2012	Helpage
Mali	Maternal Grants for Education (Bourses Maman)	5,427	2007	World Bank 2011i	JIGISEMEJIRI cash transfer program	5,000	2014	Government of Mali
Marshall Islands	—	—	—	—	—	—	—	—
Mauritania	—	—	—	—	WFP/Food Security Commission cash transfer program	30,000[a]	2011	World Bank 2014a
Mauritius	—	—	—	—	Noncontributory pension	180,770	2012	Helpage
Mexico	Prospera	25,631,340	2013	Government of Mexico	65 y mas	5,100,000	2013	Helpage

Unconditional food and in-kind				Country/economy/territory
Program name	Number of beneficiaries	Year	Data source	
Urban Targeted Food Assistance	115,000	2011	WFP 2013a	Jordan
—	—	—	—	Kazakhstan
General relief food distribution (GFD)	635,000	2015	WFP 2015n	Kenya
—	—	—	—	Kiribati
—	—	—	—	Kosovo
—	—	—	—	Kuwait
Wheelchairs, assistive appliances for persons with disabilities	800	2012	World Bank 2014c	Kyrgyz Republic
—	—	—	—	Lao, PDR
—	—	—	—	Latvia
—	—	—	—	Lebanon
Nutrition Support for Malnourished Children and Other Vulnerable Groups	134,000	2011	World Bank 2012b	Lesotho
Nutrition intervention (WFP)	31,500	2011	WFP 2015o	Liberia
—	—	—	—	Libya
—	—	—	—	Lithuania
—	—	—	—	Macedonia, FYR
Nutrition-related transfers in kind	52,000	2010	World Bank 2012c	Madagascar
Food stamps and vouchers	1,709,000	2011	WFP 2013c	Malawi
Milk program	—	—	—	Malaysia
—	—	—	—	Maldives
Government nutrition program	450,000	2010	World Bank 2011i	Mali
—	—	—	—	Marshall Islands
Emergency food distribution program	585,000	2012	World Bank 2014a	Mauritania
Food stamps and vouchers	—	—	—	Mauritius
Milk grant benefit	6,070,993	2009	LAC database	Mexico

(Table continues next page)

Country/ economy/ territory	Conditional cash transfer				Unconditional cash transfer			
	Program name	Number of beneficiaries	Year	Data source	Program name	Number of beneficiaries	Year	Data source
Micronesia, Fed. Sts.	—	—	—	—	—	—	—	—
Moldova	—	—	—	—	Ajutor Social	27,152[a]	2010	SPeeD
Mongolia	—	—	—	—	Cash assistance to elderly women	125,600	2010	ADB 2012a
Montenegro	—	—	—	—	Family material support and benefits based on social care	12,830[a]	2008	SPeeD
Morocco	Tayssir	80,000	2008	World Bank 2011d	Family allowances	538,000	2008	World Bank 2011d
Mozambique	—	—	—	—	Food Subsidy Program (Programa de Subsidio de Alimentos, PSA)	291,604	2013	Instituto Nacional de Acção Social (INAS)
Myanmar	—	—	—	—	—	—	—	—
Namibia	Namibia Students Financial Assistance	20,909	2013	Government of Namibia	Provision of Social Assistance (funeral grants)	175,659	2013	Government of Namibia
Nepal	—	—	—	—	Old-age pension scheme	922,741	2014	Government of Nepal
Nicaragua	Mi Beca familiar	—	—	—	Defensa Civil	403,016	2013	Government of Nicaragua
Niger	Projet de Filets Sociaux	—	—	—	Family allowance	—	—	—
Nigeria	Kano CCT for Girls' Education	16,271	2014	Government of Nigeria	Eradication of Extreme Poverty and Hunger/ Cash transfer	47,746	2013	Government of Nigeria
Oman	—	—	—	—	—	—	—	—
Pakistan	Benazir Income Support Program (BISP), CCT component	51,000	2014	Government of Pakistan	Benazir Income Support Program (BISP)	4,800,000	2014	Government of Pakistan
Palau	—	—	—	—	—	—	—	—
Panama	Red de Oportunidades	72,773[a]	2014	Government of Panama	Social pension	91,856	2014	Government of Panama
Papua New Guinea	—	—	—	—	—	—	—	—
Paraguay	Tekoporâ	554,484	2010	ECLAC	Old-age social pensions	100,272	2014	Helpage
Peru	Juntos	3,881,875	2013	LAC database	Pension 65	317,298	2014	Helpage
Philippines	Pantawid Pamilyang Pilipino Program (4Ps)	4,100,000[a]	2014	Government of the Philippines	Tulong Para Kay Lolo at Lola	1,000,000	2013	Government of the Philippines
Poland	—	—	—	—	Family allowance	2,337,668	2013	SPeeD
Qatar	—	—	—	—	—	—	—	—
Romania	Money for High School	79,810	2014	Government of Romania	Universal Child Allowance (UCA)	3,886,850	2011	SPeeD

Unconditional food and in-kind				Country/ economy/ territory
Program name	Number of beneficiaries	Year	Data source	
—	—	—	—	Micronesia, Fed. Sts.
—	—	—	—	Moldova
Food stamp program	96,600	2010	ADB 2012a	Mongolia
—	—	—	—	Montenegro
Un million de cartables	1,304,100	2008	Government of Morocco	Morocco
Programa de Apoio Social Directo	125,000[a]	2013	Instituto Nacional de Acção Social (INAS)	Mozambique
—	—	—	—	Myanmar
—	—	—	—	Namibia
—	—	—	—	Nepal
Programa de Seguridad Alimentaria Nutricional	54,217	2013	Government of Nicaragua	Nicaragua
Saving Lives, Reducing Malnutrition and Protecting Livelihoods of Vulnerable Populations	820,738[a]	2013	WFP 2015p	Niger
Save the Children	7,000	2012	UNICEF 2012	Nigeria
—	—	—	—	Oman
				Pakistan
—	—	—	—	Palau
Bono Familiar para la compra de alimentos	9,200[a]	2009	LAC database	Panama
—	—	—	—	Papua New Guinea
Programme to Progressively Decrease Child Work in the Streets: Food and Health Services	1,904	2009	ECLAC	Paraguay
Vaso de Leche	1,768,049	2010	LAC database	Peru
—	—	—	—	Philippines
Food benefit (in-kind and cash)	856,315	2013	SPeeD	Poland
—	—	—	—	Qatar
Food allowance (milk and bread)	2,060,061	2010	SPeeD	Romania

(Table continues next page)

Country/ economy/ territory	Conditional cash transfer				Unconditional cash transfer			
	Program name	Number of beneficiaries	Year	Data source	Program name	Number of beneficiaries	Year	Data source
Russian Federation	—	—	—	—	Child allowances	10,500,000	2009	Russian Federal State Statistics Service 2010
Rwanda	—	—	—	—	Fond d'Assistance aux Rescapees du Genocide (FARG)	21,039	2014	Government of Rwanda
Samoa	—	—	—	—	Senior citizens benefit	8,700	2010	Helpage
São Tomé and Príncipe	Maes Carenciadas	6,120[a]	2014	Government of São Tomé and Príncipe	Old-age social pension	3,000	2014	Government of São Tomé and Príncipe
Saudi Arabia	Support assistance for school bags and uniforms	428,028	2011	World Bank 2012f	Regular assistance: divorced/widowed women	370,846	2011	World Bank 2012f
Senegal	CCT–Educational support for vulnerable children	5,000	2010	World Bank 2013e	Child nutrition program (NETS)	26,300	2010	Garcia and Moore 2011
Serbia	—	—	—	—	Child allowances	394,557	2013	SPeeD
Seychelles	—	—	—	—	Retirement pension	6,751	2013	Government of Seychelles
Sierra Leone	—	—	—	—	Orphans and Vulnerable Children (OVC) benefits	—	—	—
Slovak Republic	Motivation allowance	31,000	2011	Sundaram, Strokova, and Gotcheva 2012	Material need benefit	111,000	2011	Sundaram, Strokova, and Gotcheva 2012
Slovenia	—	—	—	—	Child benefits	371,000	2007	Government of Slovenia
Solomon Islands	—	—	—	—	—	—	—	—
Somalia	—	—	—	—	Cash and Voucher Monitoring Group (CVMG) Program	96,700	2011	Dunn and others 2013
South Africa	—	—	—	—	Child Support Grant	11,341,988	2013	Government of South Africa
South Sudan	—	—	—	—	—	—	—	—
Sri Lanka	Grade C scholarship and bursaries program for school children	85,000	2012	Government of Sri Lanka	Monthly assistance for disabled	16,600[a]	2013	Government of Sri Lanka
St. Kitts and Nevis	—	—	—	—	Assistance pensions	1,000	2008	World Bank 2009b
St. Lucia	—	—	—	—	Public assistance program	3,133[a]	2014	Government of St. Lucia
St. Vincent and the Grenadines	—	—	—	—	Public assistance relief	6,000	2009	World Bank 2010f
Sudan	—	—	—	—	Zakat	6,844,703	2013	Government of Sudan
Suriname	—	—	—	—	Old-age social pensions	44,739	2003	Helpage
Swaziland	—	—	—	—	Education Grant Scheme for OVCs (also known as the Bursary Scheme and Capitation Grant Scheme)	118,219	2010	World Bank 2012g
Syrian Arab Republic	—	—	—	—	Social Welfare Fund	—	—	—

Unconditional food and in-kind				Country/ economy/ territory
Program name	Number of beneficiaries	Year	Data source	
—	—	—	—	Russian Federation
Food stamps and vouchers	—	—	—	Rwanda
—	—	—	—	Samoa
Cantine for elderly poor	280	2014	Government of São Tomé and Príncipe	São Tomé and Príncipe
—	—	—	—	Saudi Arabia
Commissariat à la Sécurité Alimentaire	3,000,000	2010	World Bank 2013e	Senegal
—	—	—	—	Serbia
—	—	—	—	Seychelles
Food assistance for people living with HIV/ TB (MOHS/WFP)	—	—	—	Sierra Leone
—	—	—	—	Slovak Republic
—	—	—	—	Slovenia
—	—	—	—	Solomon Islands
Targeted Supplementary Feeding Program	718,000	2011	WFP 2012c	Somalia
Social Relief of Distress	—	—	—	South Africa
Supplementary Feeding Program	692,000	2011	World Bank 2013b	South Sudan
Samurdhi[a]	1,500,000	2011	World Bank 2012d	Sri Lanka
Uniforms and shoes	2,000	2008	World Bank 2009b	St. Kitts and Nevis
—	—	—	—	St. Lucia
Nutrition Support Program	1,000	2009	World Bank 2010f	St. Vincent and the Grenadines
General food distribution program	5,127,000	2011	WFP 2012b	Sudan
—	—	—	—	Suriname
Food distribution	88,511	2010	World Bank 2012g	Swaziland
—	—	—	—	Syrian Arab Republic

(Table continues next page)

Country/ economy/ territory	Conditional cash transfer				Unconditional cash transfer			
	Program name	Number of beneficiaries	Year	Data source	Program name	Number of beneficiaries	Year	Data source
Tajikistan	Conditional cash payments; allowances to large families and children	—	—	—	Targeted social assistance (pilot)	11,184[a]	2012	SPeeD
Tanzania	CCT part of Tanzania Social Action Fund (TASAF)	400,000[a]	2010	World Bank 2011l	TASAF	—	—	—
Thailand		—	—	—	Old-age allowance	5,698,414	2011	Helpage
Timor-Leste	Bolsa da Mae	15,150[a]	2012	Government of Timor-Leste	Transfers for the elderly	84,569	2012	Helpage
Togo	CT for vulnerable children in Togo (government and [Projet de Développement Communautaire] PDCplus)	12,079[a]	2015	Government of Togo	CT to children (from 2 NGOs)	300	2010	World Bank 2012h
Tonga	—	—	—	—	—	—	—	—
Trinidad and Tobago	Targeted CCTs: Cash transfer component	35,906	2011	ECLAC	Old-age social pensions	79,942	2011	Helpage
Tunisia	—	—	—	—	Programme National d'Aide aux Familles Nécessiteuses (PNAFN) Cash transfers	235,000[a]	2011	World Bank 2013a
Turkey	Şartlı Eğitim Yardımı	1,965,633[a]	2013	SPeeD	2022 Sayili Kanun Kapsaminda Yapilan (old-age social pension)	632,407	2013	SPeeD
Turkmenistan	—	—	—	—	—	—	—	—
Tuvalu	—	—	—	—	—	—	—	—
Uganda	—	—	—	—	Senior citizens grant	91,843[a]	2013	Government of Uganda
Ukraine	—	—	—	—	Child care benefit	1,515,600	2012	SPeeD
United Arab Emirates	—	—	—	—	—	—	—	—
Uruguay	Asignaciones Familiares	527,704	2012	ECLAC	Noncontributory pensions for old age and disability	33,400	2013	Helpage
Uzbekistan		—	—	—	Social assistance to poor families	600,000	2011	CER 2014
Vanuatu	—	—	—	—	—	—	—	—
Venezuela, RB	—	—	—	—	Old-age social pensions	531,546	2013	Helpage
Vietnam	Decree 49 and its revision, Decree 74/2013/ND-CP	—	—	—	Social pensions	1,100,000	2011	Helpage

	Unconditional food and in-kind			Country/ economy/ territory
Program name	Number of beneficiaries	Year	Data source	
Food for tuberculosis patients	45,000	2011	WFP 2015q	Tajikistan
Most Vulnerable Children (MVC) Program	570,000	2010	World Bank 2011l	Tanzania
—	—	—	—	Thailand
Ad hoc in-kind support	—	—	—	Timor-Leste
Nutrition program by UNICEF	25,914	2010	World Bank 2012h	Togo
—	—	—	—	Tonga
—	—	—	—	Trinidad and Tobago
—	—	—	—	Tunisia
GIDA YARDIMI (food assistance)	2,442,599[a]	2013	SPeeD	Turkey
—	—	—	—	Turkmenistan
—	—	—	—	Tuvalu
Protracted Relief and Recovery Operations (PRRO) Uganda 200429–Stabilizing Food Consumption and Reducing Acute Malnutrition among Refugees and Extremely Vulnerable Households: Extremely Vulnerable Households component	352,495	2013	USAID	Uganda
—	—	—	—	Ukraine
—	—	—	—	United Arab Emirates
Tarjeta Uruguay social	265,392	2013	ECLAC	Uruguay
Support for breastfeeding (YICF)	475,000	2008	UNICEF 2009	Uzbekistan
—	—	—	—	Vanuatu
—	—	—	—	Venezuela, RB
Housing support for the poor	500,000[a]	2009	Castel 2010	Vietnam

(Table continues next page)

Appendix C. (Part 1) Program Inventory *(Continued)*

Country/ economy/ territory	Conditional cash transfer				Unconditional cash transfer			
	Program name	Number of beneficiaries	Year	Data source	Program name	Number of beneficiaries	Year	Data source
West Bank and Gaza	—	—	—	—	Cash Transfer Program (CTP)	115,951[a]	2014	MOSA
Yemen, Rep.	Basic Education Support for Girls CCT	39,791	2014	Progress report	Social Welfare Fund (SWF)	1,504,663[a]	2014	Progress report
Zambia	—	—	—	—	Social Cash Transfer Scheme	114,500	2012	World Bank 2012i
Zimbabwe	—	—	—	—	Harmonized cash transfer	37,297	2013	Government of Zimbabwe

Source: World Bank, based on sources noted.

Note: CCT = conditional cash transfer; COMCEC = Standing Committee for Economic and Commercial Cooperation of the Organization of the Islamic Cooperation; CT = cash transfer; ECLAC = Economic Commission for Latin America and the Caribbean of the United Nations; IDPs = internally displaced persons; LAC = Latin America and the Caribbean; MDS = Ministry of Social Development and Fight Against Hunger; NGO = nongovernmental organization; OVC = Orphans and Vulnerable Children; SPeeD = Social Protection Expenditure and Evaluation Database for Europe and Central Asia; USAID = U.S. Agency for International Development; WFP = World Food Programme; — = not available.

a. Data refer to a total number of households; all other beneficiary data refer to the number of individual beneficiaries.

	Unconditional food and in-kind			Country/economy/territory
Program name	Number of beneficiaries	Year	Data source	
Food rations, in-kind assistance	45,000[a]	2014	WFP 2015r	West Bank and Gaza
Emergency Food and Nutrition Support to Food Insecure and Conflict-Affected People	4,313,631	2013	WFP 2015s	Yemen, Rep.
STEPS/OVC	204,251	2012	World Bank 2012i	Zambia
Assistance to Food Insecure Vulnerable Groups	204,255[a]	2013	WFP 2015t	Zimbabwe

Appendix C. (Part 2) Program Inventory

Country/ economy/ territory	School feeding				Public works			
	Program name	Number of beneficiaries	Year	Data source	Program name	Number of beneficiaries	Year	Data source
Afghanistan	School feeding	740,000	2013	WFP 2015a	Assets Creation Programme	250,000	2014	WFP 2015a
Albania	School feeding	—	—	—	Employment program	834	2013	SPeeD
Algeria	School feeding	31,000	2011	WFP 2013d	—	—	—	—
Angola	School feeding	221,000	2011	WFP 2013d	—	—	—	—
Antigua and Barbuda	—	—	—	—	—	—	—	—
Argentina	Comedores Escolares	1,715,737	2010	LAC database	Plan de Empleo Comunitario (PEC)	399,860	2010	LAC database
Armenia	School feeding	38,000	2011	WFP 2013d	Work practice for unemployed and disabled	4,161	2014	SPeeD
Azerbaijan	—	—	—	—	—	—	—	—
Bahrain	School feeding	—	—	—	—	—	—	—
Bangladesh	School Feeding Programme in poverty-prone areas	1,930,000	2011	WFP 2013d	Employment Generation Program for the Poorest (EGPP)	1,400,000	2014	Government of Bangladesh
Belarus	School feeding	—	—	—	Public works	80,700	2012	SPeeD
Belize	School feeding	—	—	—	—	—	—	—
Benin	School feeding program	324,000	2011	WFP 2013d	Le Projet de services décentralisés conduits par les communautés (PSDCC)	12,000	2015	Government of Benin 2015
Bhutan	School feeding	30,345	2011	WFP 2015b	—	—	—	—
Bolivia	School feeding	1,906,000	2011	WFP 2013d	Empleo Digno e Intensivo de Mano de Obra	—	—	—
Bosnia and Herzegovina	School feeding	—	—	—	—	—	—	—
Botswana	School feeding	330,000	2011	WFP 2013d	Ipelegeng (self-reliance) Labor-Intensive Public Works (LIPW) program	19,431	2010	World Bank 2011a
Brazil	National School Feeding Program	47,271,000	2011	LAC database	Economia Solidaria—Programa Economia Solidaria em Desemvolvimento	534,053	2012	Government of Brazil
Bulgaria	School feeding	—	—	—	Direct job creation	17,892	2010	SPeeD
Burkina Faso	School feeding (various programs)	2,209,000	2011	WFP 2013d	WFP public works	—	—	—
Burundi	School feeding	190,000	2011	WFP 2013d	WFP Public Works (excluding the ones through IFAD)	32,405	2012	World Bank 2014b
Cabo Verde	School feeding	86,000	2011	WFP 2013d	Frentes de Alta Intensidade de Mão de Obra (FAIMOs)	—	—	—
Cambodia	School feeding	756,000	2011	WFP 2013d	Emergency Food Assistance Project	1,300[a]	2009	Subbarao and others 2013
Cameroon	School feeding	55,366	2010	WFP 2013d	—	—	—	—
Central African Republic	School feeding	284,000	2011	WFP 2013d	Food for assets	89,000	2011	WFP 2015d

Fee waivers				Country/economy/territory
Program name	Number of beneficiaries	Year	Data source	
—	—	—	—	Afghanistan
Energy benefit	45,833[a]	2014	SPeeD	Albania
—	—	—	—	Algeria
—	—	—	—	Angola
—	—	—	—	Antigua and Barbuda
—	—	—	—	Argentina
—	—	—	—	Armenia
—	—	—	—	Azerbaijan
—	—	—	—	Bahrain
n.a.	n.a.	n.a.	n.a.	Bangladesh
Subsidies for housing and utilities	1,490,000	2011	World Bank 2011e	Belarus
—	—	—	—	Belize
—	—	—	—	Benin
—	—	—	—	Bhutan
—	—	—	—	Bolivia
—	—	—	—	Bosnia and Herzegovina
—	—	—	—	Botswana
—	—	—	—	Brazil
Energy benefit	251,876	2013	SPeeD	Bulgaria
—	—	—	—	Burkina Faso
Abolition of primary school fee	471,274	2012	World Bank 2014b	Burundi
—	—	—	—	Cabo Verde
—	—	—	—	Cambodia
—	—	—	—	Cameroon
				Central African Republic

(Table continues next page)

Country/ economy/ territory	School feeding				Public works			
	Program name	Number of beneficiaries	Year	Data source	Program name	Number of beneficiaries	Year	Data source
Chad	School feeding	265,072	2014	WFP 2012a	Food for assets	325,000	2011	WFP 2012a
Chile	National board of student aid and scholarships	2,263,000	2011	WFP 2013d	Employment creation program (PROEMPLEO)	19,900	2012	Government of Chile 2013
China	School feeding	26,000,000	2011	WFP 2013d	—	—	—	—
Colombia	Programa de Alimentación Escolar	4,032,237	2010	LAC database	Programa de Empleo de Emergencia	14,300	2012	Government of Colombia
Comoros	School feeding	—	—		Community Development Support Fund (FADC, in French)	3,800	2009	Subbarao and others 2013
Congo, Dem. Rep.	School feeding	854,546	2013	WFP 2013d	WFP Public Works	3,145	2013	WFP 2015e
Congo, Rep.	School feeding	223,000	2011	WFP 2013d	Public works project	—	—	
Costa Rica	School feeding	623,000	2013	Government of Costa Rica	National employment	5,147	2011	LAC database
Côte d'Ivoire	School feeding	374,000	2011	WFP 2013d	Post-Conflict Assistance Project	3,000	2009	Subbarao and others 2013
Croatia	School feeding	152,000	2011	WFP 2013d	—	—	—	—
Czech Republic	—	—	—	—	—	—	—	—
Djibouti	School feeding	16,814	2014	WFP 2015h	Social Safety Net Project	5,129	2014	National Initiative for Social Development (INDS)
Dominica	School feeding	—	—	—	—	—	—	—
Dominican Republic	School feeding	1,320,116	2012	Government of Dominican Republic	—	—	—	—
Ecuador	Programa de Alimentación Escolar	1,789,000	2011	WFP 2013d	My First Job Program	2,150	2010	LAC database
Egypt, Arab Rep.	School feeding	7,002,000	2011	WFP 2013d	Labor Intensive Investment Project for Egypt	38,308	2014	WFP 2013d
El Salvador	Programa de Alimentacion Escolar	1,453,118	2013	Government of El Salvador	Temporary Income Support Program— Urban	23,456	2013	Government of El Salvador
Equatorial Guinea	—	—	—	—	—	—	—	—
Eritrea	—	—	—	—	Public works	—	—	Subbarao and others 2013
Estonia	School feeding	—	—	—	—	—	—	—
Ethiopia	School feeding	669,394	2013	WFP 2015i	Productive Safety Net Program[a]	6,889,910	2013	Government of Ethiopia
Fiji	—	—	—	—	—	—	—	—
Gabon	—	—	—	—	—	—	—	—
Gambia, The	School feeding	159,000	2011	WFP 2013d	—	—	—	—
Georgia	—	—	—	—	—	—	—	—

| Program name | Fee waivers | | | Country/ economy/ territory |
	Number of beneficiaries	Year	Data source	
—	—	—	—	Chad
—	—	—	—	Chile
Medical assistance	41,900,000	2008	Umapathi, Wang, and O'Keefe 2013	China
—	—	—	—	Colombia
—	—	—	—	Comoros
Indigent cards	6,000	2014	Government of Congo	Congo, Dem. Rep.
—	—	—	—	Congo, Rep.
Education scholarships	113,202	2013	LAC database	Costa Rica
—	—	—	—	Côte d'Ivoire
—	—	—	—	Croatia
—	—	—	—	Czech Republic
—	—	—	—	Djibouti
—	—	—	—	Dominica
Seguro Familiar de Salud—Regimen Subsidiado	—	—	—	Dominican Republic
Programa Textos Escolares	2,350,622	2010	LAC database	Ecuador
—	—	—	—	Egypt, Arab Rep.
Uniforms	1,386,767	2013	Government of El Salvador	El Salvador
—	—	—	—	Equatorial Guinea
—	—	—	—	Eritrea
Subsistence benefit to cover expenses for standard allotted living space	82,276[a]	2012	SPeeD	Estonia
—	—	—	—	Ethiopia
Free Bus Fare Program (FBFP)	—	—	—	Fiji
—	—	—	—	Gabon
—	—	—	—	Gambia, The
Domestic subsidies (household allowance)	59,741	2013	SPeeD	Georgia

(Table continues next page)

Appendix C. (Part 2) Program Inventory (Continued)

Country/ economy/ territory	School feeding				Public works			
	Program name	Number of beneficiaries	Year	Data source	Program name	Number of beneficiaries	Year	Data source
Ghana	Ghana School Feeding Programme	1,740,000	2013	Government of Ghana	Labour Intensive Public Works program (LIPW)	26,718	2014	Government of Ghana
Grenada	School feeding	—	—	—	Debushing Program	400	2009	Subbarao and others 2013
Guatemala	School feeding	3,052,000	2011	WFP 2013d	—	—	—	—
Guinea	School feeding	553,000	2011	WFP 2013d	Productive Social Safety Net Program			
Guinea-Bissau	School feeding	126,000	2011	WFP 2013d	—	—	—	—
Guyana	School feeding	17,000	2011	WFP 2013d	—	—	—	—
Haiti	School feeding (cantines scolaire)— nombre d'élève	818,828	2013	Haiti Economic and Social Assistance Fund (FAES)	National Project of Community Participation Development (PRODEP, in French)	450,000	2009	Subbarao and others 2013
Honduras	Programa Escuela Saludables	1,460,000	2011	WFP 2013d	Public works	13,000	2011	WFP 2015m
Hungary	School feeding	—	—	—	—	—	—	—
India	School feeding	104,500,000	2014	India, Ministry of Health and Family Welfare 2015	Mahatma Gandhi National Rural Employment Guarantee (MGNREG)	36,421,138[a]	2014	India, Ministry of Health and Family 2015
Indonesia	School feeding	125,000	2011	WFP 2013d	National Community Empowerment Program (PNPM Mandiri)	—	—	—
Iran, Islamic Rep.	School feeding	3,000	2011	WFP 2013d				
Iraq	School feeding	555,000	2011	WFP 2013d	—	—	—	—
Jamaica	School feeding	311,000	2011	WFP 2013d	—	—	—	—
Jordan	School nutrition	115,000	2011	WFP 2013d	Rural Food for Assets	42,000	2011	WFP 2013a
Kazakhstan	School feeding	—	—	—	"Road Map" program	247,000	2009	World Bank 2011g
Kenya	Regular school meals program	791,000	2015	WFP 2015n	Food-for-assets/cash-for-assets Protracted Relief and Recovery Operation (PRRO)	702,000	2015	WFP 2015n
Kiribati	—	—	—	—	—	—	—	—
Kosovo	—	—	—	—	—	—	—	—
Kuwait	School feeding	—	—	—	—			
Kyrgyz Republic	School feeding	400,000	2012	World Bank 2014c	Public works	—	—	—
Lao PDR	School feeding	177,000	2011	WFP 2013d	Poverty Reduction Fund	118,000	2009	Subbarao and others 2013
Latvia	School feeding	—	—	—	Public works	15,406	2011	SPeeD
Lebanon	School feeding	—	—	—	—	—	—	—
Lesotho	School feeding	445,000	2011	WFP 2013d	Integrated Watershed Management Public Works Program	96,000	2012	World Bank 2012b

| | Fee waivers | | | Country/ |
Program name	Number of beneficiaries	Year	Data source	economy/ territory
Capitation Grant Programme	5,741,198	2013	Government of Ghana	Ghana
—	—	—	—	Grenada
—	—	—	—	Guatemala
—	—	—	—	Guinea
—	—	—	—	Guinea-Bissau
—	—	—	—	Guyana
Fee waiver for primary education	1,399,173	2013	Haiti Economic and Social Assistance Fund (FAES)	Haiti
—	—	—	—	Honduras
—	—	—	—	Hungary
—	—	—	—	India
Social Health Insurance (Jamkesmas, including Jampersal)	86,400,000	2013	ADB 2013	Indonesia
—	—	—	—	Iran, Islamic Rep.
—	—	—	—	Iraq
Programme of Advancement through Health and Education (PATH): Health grant	—	—	—	Jamaica
—	—	—	—	Jordan
—	—	—	—	Kazakhstan
—	—	—	—	Kenya
—	—	—	—	Kiribati
—	—	—	—	Kosovo
Housing Conditions Grant (permanent to temporary)	—	—	—	Kuwait
Electricity compensation	532,300	2012	SPeeD	Kyrgyz Republic
—	—	—	—	Lao, PDR
Housing benefit	185,146[a]	2012	SPeeD	Latvia
—	—	—	—	Lebanon
—	—	—	—	Lesotho

(Table continues next page)

Country/ economy/ territory	School feeding				Public works			
	Program name	Number of beneficiaries	Year	Data source	Program name	Number of beneficiaries	Year	Data source
Liberia	WFP school feeding	648,000	2011	WFP 2013d	Economic recovery for Ebola-affected households	20,000	2014	Mercy Corps
Libya	—	—	—	—	—	—	—	—
Lithuania	School meal	198,440	2009	SPeeD	Temporary employment promotion	6,000	2008	Government of Lithuania, United Nations Development Programme, and European Commission 2009
Macedonia, FYR	—	—	—	—	—	—	—	—
Madagascar	School feeding	237,000	2011	WFP 2013d	Cash-for-work component of the Emergency Food Security and Reconstruction Project	222,995	2010	World Bank 2012c
Malawi	School feeding	1,800,000	2014	Government of Malawi	Public works program	259,540[a]	2014	Government of Malawi
Malaysia	School feeding	—	—	—	—	—	—	—
Maldives		—	—	—	—	—	—	—
Mali	School feeding (various programs)	354,000	2011	WFP 2013d	WFP food-for-work	180,000	2011	World Bank 2011i
Marshall Islands	School feeding	—	—	—	—	—	—	—
Mauritania	School feeding	150,000	2013	World Bank 2014a	Food-for-work	50,000	2013	World Bank 2014a
Mauritius	School Feeding Programme	—	—	—	Community infrastructure	—	—	—
Mexico	School feeding	5,164,000	2011	WFP 2013d	Programa de Empleo Temporal Ampliado	582,044	2010	LAC database
Micronesia, Fed. Sts.	—	—	—	—	—	—	—	—
Moldova	School feeding	—	—	—	Moldova Social Investment Fund	112,000	2009	Subbarao and others 2013
Mongolia	School feeding	280,400	2009	ADB 2012a	—	—	—	—
Montenegro	—	—	—	—	—	—	—	—
Morocco	School Feeding Program (various programs)	1,423,000	2011	WFP 2013d	National Initiative for Human Development Support Project (INDH)	4,000,000	2009	World Bank 2011d
Mozambique	School Feeding (Alimentação Escolar)	427,000	2011	WFP 2013d	Programa de Accao Social Produtiva	10,000	2014	Instituto Nacional de Acção Social (INAS)
Myanmar	—	—	—	—	—	—	—	—
Namibia	National School Feeding Programme to Orphans and Vulnerable Children	300,000	2013	Government of Namibia	—	—	—	—
Nepal	School feeding (various programs)	666,378	2014	Government of Nepal	Karnali Employment Program	323,600	2014	Government of Nepal

Fee waivers				Country/economy/territory
Program name	Number of beneficiaries	Year	Data source	
—	—	—	—	Liberia
—	—	—	—	Libya
Utility allowance (compensation for heating expenses)	111,000	2009	SPeeD	Lithuania
—	—	—	—	Macedonia, FYR
—	—	—	—	Madagascar
—	—	—	—	Malawi
—	—	—	—	Malaysia
Welfare assistance for medical services within Maldives and abroad	1,294	2010	ADB 2012b	Maldives
Cereal banks	1,800,000	2008	World Bank 2011i	Mali
—	—	—	—	Marshall Islands
—	—	—	—	Mauritania
School supplies	11,000	2008	World Bank 2011j	Mauritius
Education scholarships	—	—	—	Mexico
—	—	—	—	Micronesia, Fed. Sts.
Heating allowance	547,844[a]	2010	SPeeD	Moldova
Social Security for elderly	108,200	2010	ADB 2012a	Mongolia
Electricity bill subsidy	20,829[a]	2007	SPeeD	Montenegro
Villes Sans Bidonvilles	324,000[a]	2010	World Bank 2011d	Morocco
School fee waiver for secondary schools	5,900,000	2010	World Bank 2011k	Mozambique
—	—	—	—	Myanmar
Disease control (ART)	120,029	2013	Government of Namibia	Namibia
—	—	—	—	Nepal

(Table continues next page)

Country/ economy/ territory	School feeding				Public works			
	Program name	Number of beneficiaries	Year	Data source	Program name	Number of beneficiaries	Year	Data source
Nicaragua	School feeding	1,050,000	2013	Government of Nicaragua	—	—	—	—
Niger	School feeding (various programs)	168,000	2011	WFP 2013d	Public works	—	—	—
Nigeria	School feeding	155,000	2011	WFP 2013d	Community Service, Women & Youth Employment Programme (including graduate internship scheme) SURE-P	35,000	2012	World Bank 2013d
Oman	—	—	—	—	—	—	—	—
Pakistan	Tawana Pakistan initiative	2,078,000	2011	WFP 2013d				
Palau	—	—	—	—	—	—	—	—
Panama	School feeding	461,000	2011	WFP 2013d	Public works, training programs	110,095	2011	LAC database
Papua New Guinea	—	—	—	—	Public works program			
Paraguay	School feeding	10,000	2011	WFP 2013d	—	—	—	—
Peru	Qali Warma	2,700,705	2013	LAC database	Programa para la Generación de Empleo Social Inclusivo "Trabaja Perú"	65,433	2013	LAC database
Philippines	Breakfast feeding program	562,000	2013	Government of the Philippines	Food-for-Work for the Internally Displaced	—	—	—
Poland	School feeding	730,000	2011	WFP 2013d	Direct job creation	6,775	2011	SPeeD
Qatar	School feeding	—	—	—	—	—	—	—
Romania	School feeding	—	—	—	Direct job creation	7,447	2010	SPeeD
Russian Federation	School feeding	2,647,000	2011	WFP 2013d	Regional public works program	1,521,000	2009	World Bank 2010d
Rwanda	School feeding	25,000	2014	Government of Rwanda	Assistance to Refugees and Recovery Operations for the Most Vulnerable Household (Food for Work)	19,234	2014	Government of Rwanda
Samoa	—	—	—	—	—	—	—	—
São Tomé and Príncipe	School feeding	41,000	2014	Government of São Tomé and Príncipe	Grupo de Interesse de Manutenção de Estradas (GIME)	1,700[a]	2014	Government of São Tomé and Príncipe
Saudi Arabia	School feeding	—	—	—	—	—	—	—
Senegal	WFP School Lunch Program	764,000	2011	WFP 2013d	—	—	—	—
Serbia	School feeding	—	—	—	Public works	6,127	2012	SPeeD
Seychelles	School feeding	—	—	—	—	—	—	—
Sierra Leone	School feeding (MEST/ WFP/DFID/others)	530,000	2011	WFP 2013d	Rural Public Works and Shelter Programme, National Social Action Project (NS)	813,538	2011	World Bank 2012e
Slovak Republic	School feeding	—	—	—	—	—	—	—
Slovenia	School feeding	—	—	—	—	—	—	—

| | Fee waivers | | | Country/ economy/ territory |
Program name	Number of beneficiaries	Year	Data source	
Paquetes educativos soldarios	300,000	2013	Government of Nicaragua	Nicaragua
—	—	—	—	Niger
—	—	—	—	Nigeria
—	—	—	—	Oman
Social services (medical) centers/ projects	54,211	2008	World Bank 2013c	Pakistan
—	—	—	—	Palau
Beca universal	478,574	2013	Government of Panama	Panama
—	—	—	—	Papua New Guinea
—	—	—	—	Paraguay
—	—	—	—	Peru
PhilHealth-sponsored program	8,400,000[a]	2013	Government of the Philippines	Philippines
—	—	—	—	Poland
—	—	—	—	Qatar
Heating allowance	3,592,213	2009	SPeeD	Romania
Housing and heating subsidies	9,076,000	2009	Government of Russia	Russian Federation
—	—	—	—	Rwanda
—	—	—	—	Samoa
Scholarships	841[a]	2014	Government of São Tomé and Príncipe	São Tomé and Príncipe
—	—	—	—	Saudi Arabia
—	—	—	—	Senegal
—	—	—	—	Serbia
—	—	—	—	Seychelles
—	—	—	—	Sierra Leone
—	—	—	—	Slovak Republic
—	—	—	—	Slovenia

(Table continues next page)

Country/ economy/ territory	School feeding				Public works			
	Program name	Number of beneficiaries	Year	Data source	Program name	Number of beneficiaries	Year	Data source
Solomon Islands	—	—	—	—	Rapid Employment Program	—	—	—
Somalia	School feeding	76,000	2011	WFP 2013d	Cash-for-work Programme	780,000	2011	FAO 2013
South Africa	National School Nutrition Programme	9,159,773	2013	Government of South Africa	Extended Public Works Programme (EPWP)	350,068	2013	Government of South Africa
South Sudan	School feeding	400,000	2011	WFP 2013d	Food for assets	942,000	2011	World Bank 2013b
Sri Lanka	School Meal Program—Mid-day Meal Program	890,404	2013	Government of Sri Lanka	Food for work	—	—	—
St. Kitts and Nevis	School feeding	—	—	—		—	—	—
St. Lucia	School feeding	7,466	2012	Government of St. Lucia	Short-Term Employment Programme	9,487	2013	St. Lucia Social Development Fund (SSDF)
St. Vincent and the Grenadines	School feeding	—	—	—	Road Cleaning Program	3,000	2009	World Bank 2010f
Sudan	School Feeding Programme	2,015,675	2013	Government of Sudan	Food for assets	952,000	2011	WFP 2012b
Suriname	—	—	—	—	—	—	—	—
Swaziland	National School Meal Program	328,000	2011	WFP 2013d	Pilot food for work	—	—	—
Syrian Arab Republic	School feeding	46,000	2011	WFP 2013d	Public works program	—	—	—
Tajikistan	School feeding	330,000	2011	WFP 2013d	Direct job creation	—	—	—
Tanzania	Food for education	1,275,000	2011	WFP 2013d	Food-for-Assets Creation Program (WFP)	58,202	2010	World Bank 2011l
Thailand	School feeding	1,677,000	2011	WFP 2013d	Income generation activities	—	—	—
Timor-Leste	School feeding program	288,000	2011	WFP 2013d	Cash-for-Work	55,000	2008	ADB 2009a
Togo	School feeding (government and PDCplus)	30,937	2014	Government of Togo	Public works (PDCplus)	9,679	2014	Government of Togo
Tonga	School feeding	—	—	—	—	—	—	—
Trinidad and Tobago	School feeding	—	—	—	—	—	—	—
Tunisia	School feeding	240,000	2011	WFP 2013d	—	—	—	—
Turkey	School Milk Project	6,182,368	2013	SPeeD	Toplum Yararina Calisma Programlari (TYCP)	197,182	2013	SPeeD
Turkmenistan	—	—	—	—	—	—	—	—
Tuvalu	—	—	—	—	—	—	—	—
Uganda	WFP School Feeding Programme in Karamoja	112,511	2013	WFP (Country Programme 2009–2014 Document)	Northern Uganda Social Action Fund II Karamoja/Karamoja Productive Assets Programme (KPAP)	69,080[a]	2013	WFP (Country Programme 2009–2014 Document)
Ukraine	School feeding	—	—	—	Direct job creation	45,500	2012	SPeeD

Fee waivers				Country/economy/territory
Program name	Number of beneficiaries	Year	Data source	
—	—	—	—	Solomon Islands
—	—	—	—	Somalia
—	—	—	—	South Africa
—	—	—	—	South Sudan
Free school uniform material program	3,973,909	2013	Government of Sri Lanka	Sri Lanka
—	—	—	—	St. Kitts and Nevis
Education assistance	3,000	2008	World Bank 2009a	St. Lucia
—	—	—	—	St. Vincent and the Grenadines
—	—	—	—	Sudan
—	—	—	—	Suriname
Fee waivers for health care	—	—	—	Swaziland
—	—	—	—	Syrian Arab Republic
—	—	—	—	Tajikistan
National Agricultural Input Voucher Scheme (NAIVS)	1,800,000	2012	World Bank 2011l	Tanzania
Government scholarship program	—	—	—	Thailand
Food Security Fund	—	—	—	Timor-Leste
Free tuition for primary and "préscolaire" public and community schools	1,286,653	2009	World Bank 2012h	Togo
—	—	—	—	Tonga
—	—	—	—	Trinidad and Tobago
—	—	—	—	Tunisia
Genel Sağlik Sigortasi Prim Ödemeleri (green card project)	9,403,251[a]	2013	SPeeD	Turkey
—	—	—	—	Turkmenistan
—	—	—	—	Tuvalu
Inclusive Education for Girls Project—girls education component	1,182	2013	Program report	Uganda
Housing and utility allowances	1,845,300[a]	2012	SPeeD	Ukraine

(Table continues next page)

Appendix C. (Part 2) Program Inventory *(Continued)*

Country/ economy/ territory	School feeding				Public works			
	Program name	Number of beneficiaries	Year	Data source	Program name	Number of beneficiaries	Year	Data source
United Arab Emirates	—	—	—	—	—	—	—	—
Uruguay	School Feeding Programme	256,000	2011	WFP 2013d	Uruguay Trabaja	3,000	2012	ECLAC
Uzbekistan	School feeding	—	—	—	Public Works Employment Program	100[a]	2009	Subbarao and others 2013
Vanuatu	—	—	—	—	—	—	—	—
Venezuela, RB	School feeding	4,031,000	2011	WFP 2013d	—	—	—	—
Vietnam	School feeding	—	—	—	Public Works Program for Poor Unemployed or Underemployed Labourers	—	—	—
West Bank and Gaza	School feeding	65,000	2014	WFP 2015r	Cash for Work Program	—	—	—
Yemen, Rep.	School feeding	65,000	2011	WFP 2013d	Labor-intensive works by Social Fund for Development (SFD)	361,514	2014	SFD reports
Zambia	School Feeding Program	850,000	2012	World Bank 2012i	C-SAFE Zambia Project	22,412	2012	World Bank 2012i
Zimbabwe	SPLASH voucher program	7,200[a]	2010	CaLP 2011	Food mitigation program	140,500[a]	2013	Government of Zimbabwe

Source: World Bank, based on sources noted.

Note: ADB = Asian Development Bank; DFID = Department for International Development (United Kingdom); ECLAC = Economic Commission for Latin America and the Caribbean of the United Nations; IFAD = International Fund for Agricultural Development; LAC = Latin America and the Caribbean; MEST = Ministry of Education, Science and Technology; MOSA = Ministry of Social Affairs; SPeeD = Social Protection Expenditure and Evaluation Database for Europe and Central Asia; WFP = World Food Programme; — = not available.

[a] Data for beneficiaries marked with "a" refer to a total number of households; otherwise, data refer to the number of individual beneficiaries.

Fee waivers				Country/economy/territory
Program name	Number of beneficiaries	Year	Data source	
—	—	—	—	United Arab Emirates
—	—	—	—	Uruguay
—	—	—	—	Uzbekistan
—	—	—	—	Vanuatu
—	—	—	—	Venezuela, RB
—	—	—	—	Vietnam
Subsidized health insurance	75,000[a]	2014	MOSA	West Bank and Gaza
—	—	—	—	Yemen, Rep.
—	—	—	—	Zambia
—	—	—	—	Zimbabwe

References

ADB (Asian Development Bank). 2009a. *Democratic Republic of Timor-Leste: Updating and Improving the Social Protection Index*. Manila: Asian Development Bank.

———. 2009b. *Republic of Fiji: Updating and Improving the Social Protection Index*. Manila: Asian Development Bank.

———. 2012a. *Mongolia: Updating and Improving the Social Protection Index*. Manila: Asian Development Bank.

———. 2012b. *Republic of Maldives: Updating and Improving the Social Protection Index*. Manila: Asian Development Bank.

———. 2013. *The Social Protection Index*. Mandaluyong City, Philippines: Asian Development Bank.

CaLP (Cash Learning Partnership). 2011. *3W Review of Cash and Voucher Programs in Zimbabwe: 2011 Update Report*. Harare, Zimbabwe: CaLP.

Castel, P. 2010. "Fiscal Space Social Protection Policies in Vietnam." Paper for the 3rd China-ASEAN Forum on Social Development and Poverty Reduction, 4th ASEAN+3 High-Level Seminar. http://www.socialsecurityextension.org/gimi/gess/RessourcePDF.do;jsessionid=56e7bdd0fa0f77aee4f7c8e4d623514118bf8a88f4c58166e4942de8939a61d1.e3aTbhuLbNmSe34MchaRahaLc3j0?ressource.ressourceId=20142.

CER (Center for Economic Research). 2014. "Transformative Social Protection in a Transforming Economy and Society." Development Dialogue. Center for Economic Research, Tashkent, Ukbekistan.

Dunn, S., M. Brewin, and A. Scek. 2013. *Final Monitoring Report of the Somalia Cash and Voucher Transfer Programme, Phase 2: April 2012–March 2013*. London: Overseas Development Institute.

FAO (Food and Agriculture Organization). 2013. "Cash-Based Transfers in FAO's Humanitarian and Transition Programming." Guidance Note, Food and Agriculture Organization of the United Nations, Rome.

Friedman, E., E. Gallova, M. Herczog, and L. Surdu. 2009. "Assessing Conditional Cash Transfers as a Tool for Reducing the Gap in Educational Outcomes between Roma and non-Roma." REF Working Paper 4, Roma Education Fund, Budapest.

Garcia, M., and C. M. T. Moore. 2011. *The Cash Dividend: The Rise of Cash Transfer Programs in Sub-Saharan Africa*. Directions in Development Series. Washington, DC: World Bank.

Government of Benin, Ministry of Decentralization, Local Governance, Public Administration and Regional Development. 2015. Decentralized Community Driven Services Secretariat. http://www.psdcc.org.

Government of Cambodia, World Food Programme, and World Bank. 2009. "Safety Nets in Cambodia: Concept Note and Inventory." Policy Note, World Bank, Washington, DC.

Government of Chile. 2013. "Logros y Cifras." Subsecretaria del Trabajo. http://www.subtrab.trabajo.gob.cl/?page_id=121.

Government of India, Ministry of Health and Family Welfare. 2015. https://nrhm-mis.nic.in/SitePages/Home.aspx.

Government of Lithuania, United Nations Development Programme (UNDP), and European Commission. 2009. *Inclusive Lithuania: Thought Analysis-Based Policy Dialogue Towards Effective Decision Making*. Assessment Report. Vilnius, Lithuania: UNDP.

Government of Romania, Ministry of Education. 2015. Money for High School, Program webpage. http://baniliceu.edu.ro/Rapoarte2010/jfile/Judete/index.html.

Russian Federal State Statistics Service. 2010. "Social Status and Standard of Living of the Russian Population." http://www.gks.ru/bgd/regl/b11_44/IssWWW.exe/Stg/d02/09-21.htm.

Subbarao, K., C. del Ninno, C. Andrews, and C. Rodríguez-Alas. 2013. *Public Works as a Safety Net: Design, Evidence, and Implementation*. Washington, DC: World Bank.

Sundaram, R., V. Strokova, and B. Gotcheva. 2012. "Protecting the Poor and Promoting Employability: An Assessment of the Social Assistance System in the Slovak Republic." World Bank, Washington, DC.

Tesliuc, E., L. Pop, M. Grosh, and R. Yemtsov. 2014. *Last-Resort Income Support for the Poorest: A Review of Experience in Eastern Europe and Central Asia*. Directions in Development Series. Washington, DC: World Bank.

Umapathi, N., D. Wang, and P. O'Keefe. 2013. "Eligibility Thresholds for Minimum Living Guarantee Programs: International Practices and Implications for China." Social Protection and Labor Discussion Paper 1307, World Bank, Washington, DC.

UNICEF (United Nations Children's Fund). 2009. *Infant and Young Child Feeding Programme Review—Case Study: Uzbekistan*. New York: UNICEF.

———. 2012. *Integrated Social Protection Systems: Enhancing Equity for Children*. New York: UNICEF.

———. 2013. *Bangladesh Primary Education Stipends: A Qualitative Assessment*. Directorate of Primary Education (DPE), and Power and Participation Research Centre. New York: UNICEF.

UNOCHA (United Nations Office for Coordination and Humanitarian Affairs). 2015. "Humanitarian Response–Ethiopia." https://www.humanitarianresponse.info/en/operations/ethiopia.

WFP (World Food Programme). 2012a. "Budget Increase to PRRO Operation Chad 200289: Targeted Food Assistance for Refugees and Vulnerable People Affected by Malnutrition and Recurrent Food Crises." World Food Programme, Rome.

———. 2012b. "Food Assistance to Vulnerable Populations Affected by Conflict and Natural Disasters." Operation Document, EMOP 200151, World Food Programme, Rome.

———. 2012c. "Strengthening Food and Nutrition Security and Enhancing Resilience." Operation Document, Protracted Relief and Recovery Operation (PRRO)—Somalia 200443, World Food Programme, Rome.

———. 2013a. "Assistance to Food-Insecure and Vulnerable Jordanians Affected by the Protracted Economic Crisis Aggravated by the Syrian Conflict." Operation Document, PRRO 200537, World Food Programme, Rome.

———. 2013b. "Country Programme Egypt 2013–2017." World Food Programme, Rome.

———. 2013c. "Malawi, Emergency Operation 200608: Budget Revision No.3." World Food Programme, Rome.

———. 2013d. *The State of School Feeding Worldwide*. Rome: World Food Programme.

———. 2015a. "Afghanistan: WFP Activities." World Food Programme, Rome. http://www.wfp.org/countries/afghanistan/operations.

———. 2015b. "Bhutan: WFP Activities." World Food Programme, Rome. http://www.wfp.org/countries/bhutan/operations.

———. 2015c. "Bolivia: WFP Activities." World Food Programme, Rome. http://www.wfp.org/countries/bolivia/operations/current-operations.

———. 2015d. "Central African Republic: WFP Activities." World Food Programme, Rome. http://www.wfp.org/countries/operations.

———. 2015e. "Congo, Democratic Republic of: WFP Activities." World Food Programme, Rome. https://www.wfp.org/countries/congo-democratic-republic-of/operations.

———. 2015f. "Congo, Rep. of: WFP Activities." World Food Programme, Rome. http://www.wfp.org/countries/congo-republic-of/operations.

———. 2015g. "Côte D'Ivoire: WFP Activities." World Food Programme, Rome. http://www.wfp.org/countries/c%c3%b4te-d-ivoire/operations.

———. 2015h. "Djibouti: WFP Activities." World Food Programme, Rome. http://www.wfp.org/countries/djibouti/operations/current-operations.

———. 2015i. "Ethiopia: WFP Activities." World Food Programme, Rome. https://www.wfp.org/countries/ethiopia/operations.

———. 2015j. "The Gambia: WFP Activities." World Food Programme, Rome. http://www.wfp.org/countries/the-gambia/operations.

———. 2015k. "Guinea: WFP Activities." World Food Programme, Rome. http://www.wfp.org/countries/guinea/operations.

———. 2015l. "Haiti: WFP Activities." World Food Programme, Rome. http://www.wfp.org/countries/haiti/operations.

———. 2015m. "Honduras: WFP Activities." World Food Programme, Rome. https://www.wfp.org/countries/honduras/operations.

———. 2015n. "Kenya: WFP Activities." World Food Programme, Rome. http://www.wfp.org/countries/kenya/operations.

———. 2015o. "Liberia: WFP Activities." World Food Programme, Rome. http://www.wfp.org/countries/liberia/operations.

———. 2015p. "Niger: WFP Activities. " World Food Programme, Rome. http://www.wfp.org/countries/niger/operations.

———. 2015q. "Tajikistan: WFP Activities." World Food Programme, Rome. http://www.wfp.org/countries/tajikistan/operations.

———. 2015r. "West Bank and Gaza: WFP Activities." World Food Programme, Rome. http://www.wfp.org/countries/state-of-palestine/operations.

———. 2015s. "Yemen: WFP Activities. " World Food Programme, Rome. http://www.wfp.org/countries/yemen/operations.

———. 2015t. "Zimbabwe: WFP Activities." World Food Programme, Rome. http://www.wfp.org/countries/zimbabwe/operations.

World Bank. 2009a. "Saint Lucia: Social Safety Net Assessment." Policy Note, World Bank, Washington, DC.

———. 2009b. "St. Kitts and Nevis: Social Safety Net Assessment." Policy Note, World Bank, Washington, DC.

———. 2010a. *Bangladesh Poverty Assessment: Assessing a Decade of Progress in Reducing Poverty 2000–2010*. Bangladesh Development Series, Paper No. 31. Washington, DC: World Bank.

———. 2010b. *Belize: Issues and Options to Strengthen the Social Protection System*. Washington, DC: World Bank.

———. 2010c. "Iran's Subsidy Reform Program." Internal document, World Bank, Washington, DC.

———. 2010d. *Russian Labor Market: Monitoring Trends, Results 2010*. Washington, DC: World Bank.

———. 2010e. *Social Assistance in Rural China: Tackling Poverty through Rural DIBAO*. Washington, DC: World Bank.

———. 2010f. "St. Vincent and the Grenadines: Social Safety Net Assessment." Policy Note, World Bank, Washington, DC.

———. 2011a. *Botswana: Challenges to the Safety Net*. Washington, DC: World Bank.

———. 2011b. *Burkina Faso Social Safety Nets*. Washington, DC: World Bank.

———. 2011c. *Cameroun: Filets sociaux*. Washington, DC: World Bank.

———. 2011d. *Ciblage et protection sociale. Note d'orientation stratégique*. Report No. AAA65—MA, Washington, DC: World Bank.

———. 2011e. *Improving Targeting Accuracy of Social Assistance Programs in Belarus*. Social Assistance Policy Note 68791. Washington, DC: World Bank.

———. 2011f. *Jamaica Social Protection Assessment*. Washington, DC: World Bank.

———. 2011g. *Kazakhstan: Reforming the Last Resort Safety Net Program in an Upper-Middle-Income Country*. Washington, DC: World Bank.

———. 2011h. "Les filets sociaux au Bénin outil de réduction de la pauvreté." Working Paper. World Bank, Washington, DC.

———. 2011i. *Mali: Social Safety Nets*. Washington, DC: World Bank.

———. 2011j. *Mauritius: Social Protection Review and Strategy*. Washington, DC: World Bank.

———. 2011k. *Mozambique: Social Protection Assessment—Review of Social Assistance Programs and Social Protection Expenditures*. Washington, DC: World Bank.

———. 2011l. *Tanzania: Poverty, Growth, and Public Transfers*. Washington, DC: World Bank.

———. 2012a. *Angola: Social Protection Review*. Washington, DC: World Bank.

———. 2012b. *Lesotho: Inequality, Transfers and Safety Nets* (draft). Washington, DC: World Bank.

———. 2012c. *Madagascar—Three Years into the Crisis: An Assessment of Vulnerability and Social Policies and Prospects for the Future*. Washington, DC: World Bank.

———. 2012d. *Safety Nets in Sri Lanka: An Overview*. Washington, DC: World Bank.

———. 2012e. *Sierra Leone: Social Protection Assessment*. Washington, DC: World Bank.

———. 2012f. "Social Assistance Cash Transfer Programs in the Kingdom of Saudi Arabia: A Review in Light of International (Benchmarking) Experience." Internal document, World Bank, Washington, DC.

———. 2012g. *Swaziland: Public Transfers and the Social Safety Net*. Washington, DC: World Bank.

———. 2012h. *Togo: Towards a National Social Protection Policy and Strategy*. Report No. 71936-TG. Washington, DC: World Bank.

———. 2012i. *Zambia: Using Productive Transfers to Accelerate Poverty Reduction*. Washington, DC: World Bank.

———. 2013a. *Consolidation and Transparency: Transforming Tunisia's Health Care for the Poor*. UNICO Studies Series No. 4. Washington, DC: World Bank.

———. 2013b. Diagnostic Report of Social Safety Net Interventions in South Sudan. Washington, DC: World Bank.

———. 2013c. *Pakistan—Towards an Integrated National Safety Net System*. Washington DC : World Bank.

———. 2013d. "Project Appraisal Document on a Proposed Credit in the Amount of SDR194.7 Million to the Federal Republic of Nigeria for a Youth Employment and Social Support Operation." World Bank, Washington, DC.

———. 2013e. *Republic of Senegal: Social Safety Net Assessment*. Washington, DC: World Bank.

———. 2014a. *Building on Crisis Response to Promote Long-term Development. A Review of Social Safety Net Programs in the Islamic Republic of Mauritania*. Washington, DC: World Bank.

———. 2014b. *Burundi: Assessment of Social Safety Nets*. World Bank, Washington, DC.

———. 2014c. *Kyrgyz Republic Public Expenditure Review Policy Notes: Social Assistance*. Washington, DC: World Bank.

———. 2014d. *Social Protection Sector Review of Afghanistan*. Washington DC: World Bank.

———. 2015. *Social Protection for a Productive Malaysia*. Washington, DC: World Bank.

Appendix D. Spending on Social Safety Net Programs

Percent of GDP

Country/economy/territory	Year	Source	Conditional cash transfer	Unconditional cash transfer	Unconditional food and in kind	School feeding	Public works	Fee waivers	Other social safety nets	Total social safety nets
Afghanistan	—	—	—	—	—	—	—	—	—	—
Albania	2014	SPeeD	—	1.53	—	—	0.01	0.03	0.04	1.60
Algeria	—	—	—	—	—	—	—	—	—	—
Angola	—	—	—	—	—	—	—	—	—	—
Antigua and Barbuda	—	—	—	—	—	—	—	—	—	—
Argentina	2010–11	LAC database	0.41	0.79	0.11	0.02	0.26	—	—	1.58
Armenia	2012	SPeeD	—	1.38	—	—	..	0.10	—	1.48
Azerbaijan	2011	SPeeD	—	0.95	—	—	—	—	—	0.95
Bahrain	2010	Silva, Levin, and Morgandi 2013	—	1.14	—	—	—	—	—	1.14
Bangladesh	2014	Government of Bangladesh	0.09	0.24	0.44	0.05	0.21	0.05	—	1.09
Belarus	2013	SPeeD	—	2.66	—	—	..	0.22	—	2.89
Belize	2009	World Bank 2010b	—	0.17	0.08	0.01	—	1.46	0.09	1.82
Benin	2010	World Bank 2011d	—	—	..	0.29	0.03	—	..	0.32
Bhutan	2009	ADB 2009a	—	—	—	—	—	—	—	0.33
Bolivia	2013	Government of Bolivia	0.29	1.06	0.02	—	—	—	—	1.36
Bosnia and Herzegovina	2010–11	SPeeD	—	3.97	—	—	—	—	—	3.97
Botswana	2010	World Bank 2011a	—	0.31	0.53	—	0.29	—	0.30	1.43
Brazil	2011	LAC database	0.44	1.87	0.01	0.08	0.01	0.01	—	2.42
Bulgaria	2012	SPeeD	—	0.86	0.02	—	0.09	0.08	0.01	1.12
Burkina Faso	2010	World Bank 2011b	—	0.01	0.38	0.42	0.01	0.01	—	0.83
Burundi	2012	World Bank 2014b	—	0.65	1.44	0.54	1.44	0.10	0.05	4.21
Cabo Verde	2011	Helpage	—	0.93	—	—	—	—	—	0.93
Cambodia	2009	ADB 2009b	—	—	—	—	—	—	—	0.72
Cameroon	2010	World Bank 2011c	—	0.13	..	..	0.03	0.06	—	0.22
Central African Republic	—	—	—	—	—	—	—	—	—	—
Chad	—	—	—	—	—	—	—	—	—	—
Chile	2010	LAC database	—	1.20	0.04	0.33	0.09	0.34	—	2.00
China	2009	ADB 2009e	—	—	—	—	—	—	—	0.70
Colombia	2010	LAC database	0.35	0.47	0.04	—	—	0.03	—	0.89
Comoros	—	—	—	—	—	—	—	—	—	—
Congo, Dem. Rep.	—	—	—	—	—	—	—	—	—	—
Congo, Rep.	—	—	—	—	—	—	—	—	—	—
Costa Rica	2013	Government of Costa Rica	0.39	0.30	—	—	—	0.05	—	0.74
Côte d'Ivoire	—	—	—	—	—	—	—	—	—	—
Croatia	2011	SPeeD	—	3.63	—	—	—	—	—	3.63
Czech Republic	—	—	—	—	—	—	—	—	—	—

(Table continues next page)

Country/ economy/ territory	Year	Source	Conditional cash transfer	Unconditional cash transfer	Unconditional food and in kind	School feeding	Public works	Fee waivers	Other social safety nets	Total social safety nets
Djibouti	2014	Government of Djibouti; WFP 2015a	0.06	0.03	—	—	0.09	—	—	0.19
Dominica	—	—	—	—	—	—	—	—	—	—
Dominican Republic	2012–13	Government of Dominican Republic	0.05	0.03	0.34	0.15	—	0.18	—	0.76
Ecuador	2010	LAC database	0.97	0.61	0.03	0.03	..	0.09	—	1.73
Egypt, Arab Rep.	2010	Silva, Levin, and Morgandi 2013	—	0.17	—	—	—	—	—	0.17
El Salvador	2013	Government of El Salvador	0.05	0.14	0.14	0.08	0.07	0.32	0.05	0.85
Equatorial Guinea	—	—	—	—	—	—	—	—	—	—
Eritrea	2008	World Bank policy monitoring and reporting tools	—	—	—	—	—	—	—	2.50
Estonia	2012	SPeeD	—	2.18	0.21	—	..	—	0.60	2.99
Ethiopia	2013	Government of Ethiopia; WFP 2015b	—	..	0.34	0.03	0.77	—	—	1.13
Fiji	2010	ADB 2012c	0.07	0.53	0.21	—	—	0.02	—	0.84
Gabon	—	—	—	—	—	—	—	—	—	—
Gambia, The	2010	World Bank policy monitoring and reporting tools	—	—	—	—	—	—	—	1.00
Georgia	2012–13	SPeeD	—	5.74	—	—	—	1.25	0.02	7.00
Ghana	2013	ILO 2013	0.03	0.01	0.06	0.21	0.01	0.10	—	0.43
Grenada	—	—	—	—	—	—	—	—	—	—
Guatemala	2013	Government of Guatemala	0.39	0.12	0.05	—	—	—	—	0.56
Guinea	—	—	—	—	—	—	—	—	—	—
Guinea-Bissau	—	—	—	—	—	—	—	—	—	—
Guyana	2014	Helpage	—	1.04	—	—	—	—	—	1.04
Haiti	—	—	—	—	—	—	—	—	—	—
Honduras	2010–12	Government of Honduras	0.69	0.16	..	0.13	—	—	—	0.98
Hungary	2011	ESSPROS	—	—	—	—	—	—	—	3.40
India	2014	Government of India	—	0.09	—	0.11	0.29	0.23	—	0.72
Indonesia	2013	ADB	0.04	0.15	—	0.01	0.01	0.44	..	0.65
Iran, Islamic Rep.	—	—	—	—	—	—	—	—	—	—
Iraq	2012–13	Government of Iraq	—	0.38	2.23	—	—	—	..	2.60
Jamaica	2010–11	World Bank 2011f	—	0.11	0.11	0.21	—	—	0.59	1.02
Jordan	2009	Silva, Levin, and Morgandi 2013	—	0.56	—	0.11	—	0.01	—	0.68
Kazakhstan	2012	SPeeD	—	0.91	—	—	—	—	0.10	1.01

(Table continues next page)

Country/ economy/ territory	Year	Source	Conditional cash transfer	Unconditional cash transfer	Unconditional food and in kind	School feeding	Public works	Fee waivers	Other social safety nets	Total social safety nets
Kenya	2010, 2014	Government of Kenya	—	0.16	2.46	0.10	—	0.01	—	2.73
Kiribati	2010	World Bank policy monitoring and reporting tools	—	—	—	—	—	—	—	3.70
Kosovo	2013	SPeeD	—	1.18	—	—	—	—	0.03	1.21
Kuwait	2010	Silva, Levin, and Morgandi 2013	0.02	0.36	—	—	—	0.39	—	0.77
Kyrgyz Republic	2013	SPeeD	—	2.78	0.02	0.15	0.01	—	—	2.96
Lao PDR	2009	ADB 2009c	—	—	—	—	—	—	—	0.33
Latvia	2012	SPeeD	—	0.77	0.02	—	0.09	0.09	..	0.98
Lebanon	2013	Government of Lebanon	—	0.44	—	—	—	0.61	—	1.04
Lesotho	2010	World Bank 2012a	0.10	3.69	0.30	1.48	0.70	0.30	—	6.58
Liberia	2010–11	World Bank 2012g	—	0.06	1.03	1.00	0.12	—	—	2.21
Libya	—	—	—	—	—	—	—	—	—	—
Lithuania	2009	World Bank 2013a	—	—	—	—	—	—	—	2.12
Macedonia, FYR	2012	SPeeD	0.03	1.11	—	—	—	0.02	0.01	1.17
Madagascar	2010	World Bank 2012b	—	—	—	—	—	—	—	1.10
Malawi	—	—	—	—	—	—	—	—	—	—
Malaysia	2013	World Bank 2015	—	0.60	0.03	0.11	—	—	—	0.74
Maldives	2010–11	ADB 2012d	—	1.14	—	—	—	0.10	—	1.25
Mali	2009	World Bank 2011g	—	—	0.35	0.10	0.01	—	—	0.46
Marshall Islands	2009	ADB 2009f	—	—	—	—	—	—	—	1.05
Mauritania	2012	World Bank 2014a	—	0.36	0.84	0.10	—	—	—	1.30
Mauritius	2009	World Bank 2011h	—	2.95	0.24	0.02	—	0.13	—	3.34
Mexico	2010	LAC database	0.22	0.42	0.03	—	0.02	0.02	—	0.72
Micronesia, Fed. Sts.	—	—	—	—	—	—	—	—	—	—
Moldova	2013	SPeeD	—	1.49	—	—	—	—	—	1.49
Mongolia	2010	ADB 2012b	—	4.18	—	—	—	0.16	0.05	4.39
Montenegro	2012–13	SPeeD	—	1.62	0.07	—	—	—	0.09	1.77
Morocco	2009	World Bank 2011i	0.02	0.44	0.17	0.09	1.50	0.11	..	2.35
Mozambique	2010	World Bank 2011j	—	0.31	0.48	0.10	0.03	0.37	..	1.29
Myanmar	—	—	—	—	—	—	—	—	—	—
Namibia	2013–14	Government of Namibia	0.51	2.42	—	0.09	—	—	—	3.02
Nepal	2014	Government of Nepal	—	1.14	—	0.08	0.08	—	0.02	1.32
Nicaragua	2013	Government of Nicaragua	—	0.47	..	0.19	—	1.79	—	2.45
Niger	2008	World Bank 2009a	—	0.02	1.41	0.05	0.14	—	—	1.62
Nigeria	2014	Government of Nigeria	—	0.01	—	—	0.30	—	—	0.30
Oman	—	—	—	—	—	—	—	—	—	—

(Table continues next page)

Percent of GDP

Country/ economy/ territory	Year	Source	Conditional cash transfer	Unconditional cash transfer	Unconditional food and in kind	School feeding	Public works	Fee waivers	Other social safety nets	Total social safety nets
Pakistan	2009	Government of Pakistan	—	1.27	—	—	—	0.57	0.04	1.89
Palau	—	—	—	—	—	—	—	—	—	—
Panama	2013–14	Government of Panama	0.04	0.33	—	—	0.18	0.20	—	0.75
Papua New Guinea	2009	ADB 2009d	—	—	—	—	—	—	—	0.01
Paraguay	2010	ECLAC	0.03	0.43	—	—	—	—	—	0.46
Peru	2011–13	LAC database	0.16	0.16	0.09	0.32	0.02	0.07	—	0.82
Philippines	2013	Government of Philippines	0.40	0.03	0.03	..	..	0.11	0.01	0.57
Poland	2011	ESSPROS	—	—	—	—	—	—	—	1.60
Qatar	—	—	—	—	—	—	—	—	—	—
Romania	2012	SPeeD	—	2.80	0.08	—	..	—	0.15	3.12
Russian Federation	2010	Russian Federal State Statistics Service 2010	—	—	—	—	—	—	—	3.30
Rwanda	2011, 2014	World Bank 2012c; Government of Rwanda	—	1.29	0.03	—	0.28	0.52	0.03	2.14
Samoa	2014	Helpage	—	0.89	—	—	—	—	—	0.89
São Tomé and Príncipe	—	—	—	—	—	—	—	—	—	—
Saudi Arabia	2012	World Bank 2012e	..	0.71	—	..	—	—	—	0.71
Senegal	2011	World Bank 2013b	—	0.03	0.03	—	—	0.05	—	0.11
Serbia	2013	SPeeD	—	2.09	—	—	0.01	..	—	2.10
Seychelles	2012	World Bank 2013c	—	1.92	—	—	—	—	0.40	2.32
Sierra Leone	2011	World Bank 2012d	—	0.03	1.68	0.43	1.75	0.93	0.02	4.83
Slovak Republic	2011	ESSPROS	—	—	—	—	—	—	—	2.20
Slovenia	2011	ESSPROS	—	—	—	—	—	—	—	2.80
Solomon Islands	—	—	—	—	—	—	—	—	—	—
Somalia	—	—	—	—	—	—	—	—	—	—
South Africa	2013	Government of South Africa	—	3.10	0.01	0.14	0.24	—	0.01	3.51
South Sudan	—	—	—	—	—	—	—	—	—	—
Sri Lanka	—	—	—	—	—	—	—	—	—	—
St. Kitts and Nevis	2008	World Bank 2009b	—	—	—	—	—	—	—	1.60
St. Lucia	2011–13	LAC database	—	0.19	—	0.06	0.28	—	—	0.52
St. Vincent and the Grenadines	2008	World Bank 2010a	—	—	—	—	—	—	—	2.20
Sudan	2013	Government of Sudan	—	0.05	—	0.03	—	—	—	0.08
Suriname	2012	Helpage	—	1.62	—	—	—	—	—	1.62
Swaziland	2010	World Bank 2012f	—	1.43	0.21	0.10	0.08	0.25	..	2.07
Syrian Arab Republic	2010	Silva, Levin, and Morgandi 2013	—	—	—	—	—	—	—	1.00
Tajikistan	2012	SPeeD	0.03	0.49	—	—	—	—	0.10	0.62

(Table continues next page)

Appendix D. Spending on Social Safety Net Programs (Continued)
Percent of GDP

Country/ economy/ territory	Year	Source	Conditional cash transfer	Unconditional cash transfer	Unconditional food and in kind	School feeding	Public works	Fee waivers	Other social safety nets	Total social safety nets
Tanzania	2009	World Bank 2011k	0.02	—	0.22	0.03	0.02	—	—	0.29
Thailand	2010	ADB 2012a	—	0.34	0.08	0.08	—	—	—	0.50
Timor-Leste	2012	Government of Timor-Leste	0.06	3.15	—	0.17	0.54	—	—	3.93
Togo	2010	World Bank 2011e	—	..	0.37	0.04	—	0.18	—	0.60
Tonga	—	—	—	—	—	—	—	—	—	—
Trinidad and Tobago	2012	—	—	1.69	—	—	—	—	—	1.69
Tunisia	2013	World Bank 2013d	—	0.38	—	—	—	0.16	0.01	0.55
Turkey	2013	SPeeD	0.05	0.51	0.10	0.02	0.04	0.37	0.22	1.32
Turkmenistan	—	—	—	—	—	—	—	—	—	—
Tuvalu	—	—	—	—	—	—	—	—	—	—
Uganda	2013–14	Government of Uganda	0.15	0.16	0.45	0.05	0.15	..	0.07	1.02
Ukraine	2013	SPeeD	—	3.02	0.20	—	0.09	0.64	—	3.96
United Arab Emirates	—	—	—	—	—	—	—	—	—	—
Uruguay	2010	LAC database	0.43	0.61	0.01	—	0.03	—	—	1.07
Uzbekistan	—	—	—	—	—	—	—	—	—	—
Vanuatu	2009	ADB 2009g	—	—	—	—	—	—	—	0.28
Venezuela, RB	—	—	—	—	—	—	—	—	—	—
Vietnam	2010	Government of Vietnam	0.20	0.26	—	0.02	—	0.05	—	0.52
West Bank and Gaza	2014	Ministry of Social Affairs	—	4.69	0.10	—	—	0.63	—	5.42
Yemen, Rep.	2009	Silva, Levin, and Morgandi 2013	—	0.75	—	—	0.52	—	—	1.27
Zambia	2011	World Bank 2012h	—	0.07	0.06	0.04	0.01	0.34	—	0.53
Zimbabwe	2013	Government of Zimbabwe	—	0.09	0.07	—	..	0.22	0.01	0.40

Note: — = not available; .. = negligible.

References

ADB (Asian Development Bank). 2009a. *Kingdom of Bhutan: Updating and Improving the Social Protection Index*. Manila: Asian Development Bank.

———. 2009b. *The Kingdom of Cambodia: Updating and Improving the Social Protection Index*. Manila: Asian Development Bank.

———. 2009c. *The Lao People's Democratic Republic: Updating and Improving the Social Protection Index*. Manila: Asian Development Bank.

———. 2009d. *Papua New Guinea: Updating and Improving the Social Protection Index*. Manila: Asian Development Bank.

———. 2009e. *The People's Republic of China: Updating and Improving the Social Protection Index*. Manila: Asian Development Bank.

———. 2009f. *The Republic of Marshall Islands: Updating and Improving the Social Protection Index*. Manila: Asian Development Bank.

———. 2009g. *Republic of Vanuatu: Updating and Improving the Social Protection Index*. Manila: Asian Development Bank.

———. 2012a. *Kingdom of Thailand: Updating and Improving the Social Protection Index*. Manila: Asian Development Bank.

———. 2012b. *Mongolia: Updating and Improving the Social Protection Index*. Manila: Asian Development Bank.

———. 2012c. *Republic of Fiji: Updating and Improving the Social Protection Index*. Manila: Asian Development Bank.

———. 2012d. *Republic of Maldives: Updating and Improving the Social Protection Index*. Manila Asian Development Bank.

ILO (International Labour Office). 2013. *Rationalizing Social Protection Expenditure in Ghana* (draft). Geneva: International Labor Organization.

Russian Federal State Statistics Service. 2010. "Social Status and Standard of Living of the Russian Population." http://www.gks.ru/bgd/regl/b11_44/IssWWW.exe/Stg/d02/09-21.htm.

Silva, J., V. Levin, and M. Morgandi. 2013. *Inclusion and Resilience: The Way Forward for Social Safety Nets in the Middle East and North Africa*. Washington, DC: World Bank.

WFP (World Food Programme). 2015a. *Djibouti: WFP Activities*. World Food Programme, Rome. http://www.wfp.org/countries/djibouti/operations/current-operations.

———. 2015b. *Ethiopia: WFP Activities*. World Food Programme, Rome. https://www.wfp.org/countries/ethiopia/operations/current-operations.

World Bank. 2009a. *Niger: Food Security and Safety Nets*. Washington, DC: World Bank.

———. 2009b. "St. Kitts and Nevis: Social Safety Net Assessment." Policy Note, World Bank, Washington, DC.

———. 2010a. "St. Vincent and the Grenadines: Social Safety Net Assessment." Policy Note, World Bank, Washington, DC.

———. 2010b. *Belize: Issues and Options to Strengthen the Social Protection System*. Washington, DC: World Bank.

———. 2011a. *Botswana: Challenges to the Safety Net*. Washington, DC: World Bank.

———. 2011b. *Burkina Faso Social Safety Nets*. Washington, DC: World Bank.

———. 2011c. *Cameroun: Filets sociaux*. Washington, DC: World Bank.

———. 2011d. "Les filets sociaux au Bénin outil de réduction de la pauvreté." Working Paper. World Bank, Washington, DC.

———. 2011e. *Les filets sociaux au Togo: Rapport de synthèse*. Washington, DC: World Bank.

———. 2011f. *Jamaica Social Protection Assessment*. Washington, DC: World Bank.

———. 2011g. *Mali: Social Safety Nets*. Washington, DC: World Bank.

———. 2011h. *Mauritius: Social Protection Review and Strategy*. Washington, DC: World Bank.

———. 2011i. *Migration and Remittances Factbook 2011*. Washington, DC: World Bank.

———. 2011j. *Mozambique: Social Protection Assessment—Review of Social Assistance Programs and Social Protection Expenditures*. World Bank: Washington, DC.

———. 2011k. *Tanzania: Poverty, Growth, and Public Transfers*. Washington, DC: World Bank.

———. 2012a. *Lesotho: Inequality, Transfers and Safety Nets* (draft). Washington, DC: World Bank.

———. 2012b. *Madagascar—Three Years into the Crisis: An Assessment of Vulnerability and Social Policies and Prospects for the Future*. Washington, DC: World Bank.

———. 2012c. *Rwanda Social Safety Net Assessment: Draft Report*. Washington, DC: World Bank.

———. 2012d. *Sierra Leone: Social Protection Assessment*. Washington, DC: World Bank.

———. 2012e. "Social Assistance Cash Transfer Programs in the Kingdom of Saudi Arabia: A Review in Light of International (Benchmarking) Experience." Internal document, World Bank, Washington, DC.

———. 2012f. *Swaziland: Public Transfers and the Social Safety Net*. Washington, DC: World Bank.

———. 2012g. *World Bank 2012–2022 Social Protection and Labor Strategy: Resilience, Equity, and Opportunity*. World Bank: Washington, DC.

———. 2012h. *Zambia: Using Productive Transfers to Accelerate Poverty Reduction*. Washington, DC: World Bank.

———. 2013a. Europe and Central Asia Social Protection Database. Last updated Oct. 17, 2013. World Bank, Washington, DC.

———. 2013b. *Republic of Senegal: Social Safety Net Assessment*. Washington, DC: World Bank.

———. 2013c. "Seychelles—Second Sustainability and Competitiveness Development Policy Loan Project." World Bank, Washington, DC.

———. 2013d. *Vers une meilleure equite: Les subventions energetiques, le ciblage, et la protection sociale en Tunisie*. Washington, DC: World Bank.

———. 2014a. *Building on Crisis Response to Promote Long-term Development. A Review of Social Safety Net Programs in the Islamic Republic of Mauritania*. Washington, DC: World Bank.

———. 2014b. *Burundi: Assessment of Social Safety Nets*. Washington, DC: World Bank.

———. 2015. *Social Protection for a Productive Malaysia*. Washington, DC: World Bank.

Appendix E. Policies, Institutions, and Administration

Country/ economy/ territory	Y/N/P (Planned)	Policy and strategy			Institutions	Administration
		Strategy name	Initial year	Comment	Comment	Comment
Afghanistan	P	n.a.	n.a.	The previous social protection strategy, included in the Afghanistan National Development Strategy (ANDS) for 2008–13, was not updated as a result of the lengthy electoral and post-electoral processes in 2014. The new government embarked on developing a new social policy, which includes main elements of a social protection strategy, with particular focus on vulnerable groups.	An Interministerial Committee (IMC) on social protection, including ministries and agencies involved in social protection, has been formed.	Under the public pension scheme, a modern Management Information System (MIS) is being implemented. A similar system is planned for the Martyrs and Disabled scheme, the program with the largest share in the government social protection expenditure.
Albania	Y	Inter-sectorial Strategy on Social Inclusion	2007	The government has an overall social protection strategy, which was updated in 2013 for the period 2013–20.	—	The administration of the social protection system is currently paper-based, but the steps to automate the system have been finalized, with the establishment of a Management Information System in late 2013. The MIS is currently being tested and is expected to be operational in January 2014. Statistical monitoring information exists for all programs.
Algeria	Y	Government's Plan of Action for the Implementation of the President's Program	2009	The Ministry of National Solidarity has plans to revise the sector strategy.	The Ministry of National Solidarity is in charge of social assistance programs for most vulnerable groups.	Algeria has a monitoring and evaluation (M&E) plan for social assistance programs.
Angola	P	n.a.	n.a.	The government has made progress in developing a general framework for social protection, but faces the challenge of devising an effective strategy and putting it into operation.	The Basis of Social Protection Law states that the basic social protection scheme is under the responsibility of the Ministerio da Assistencia e Reinsercao Social (Minars).	—
Antigua and Barbuda	—	—	—	—	—	—
Argentina	Y	—	—	There is an overall social protection strategy that is dynamic, and has adapted in recent years to the reality of labor markets and social conditions.	ANSES, the National Social Security Administration, has the core role of coordination. Efforts have been made to formalize links between national and provincial governments.	ANSES began to publish a quarterly report on its main social assistance program, the Universal Child Allowance. However, there are no comprehensive reports or evaluation strategies, although some programs (mostly in labor) are being evaluated.
Armenia	Y	Poverty Reduction Strategy	2011	—	—	A new MIS will be developed as part of the Social Protection Administration Project (SPAP) 2, which will allow for the delivery of integrated monitoring of beneficiaries.

(Table continues next page)

| Country/ economy/ territory | Y/N/P (Planned) | Policy and strategy | | | Institutions | Administration |
		Strategy name	Initial year	Comment	Comment	Comment
Azerbaijan	Y	Poverty Reduction Strategy	2005	The social protection system consists of both targeted and categorical programs. Recently, there has been a slight shift toward programs without means-testing.	—	The Azerbaijan Ministry of Labor and Social Protection of Population (MLSPP) had commissioned technical assistance to build a comprehensive M&E system and build internal staff capacity. A list of 100 social protection indicators has been developed based on the review of international best practices. The project's next phase (after January 2014) will focus on Targeted Social Assistance (TSA) and social housing policy.
Bahrain	—	—	—	—	—	—
Bangladesh	P	National Social Protection Strategy (NSPS)	n.a.	The NSPS is still awaiting Cabinet approval.	The development of the National Social Protection Strategy is led by the Planning Commission. It will provide a framework for coordinating the existing 95 safety net programs.	The Statistics and Informatics Division is implementing the Bangladesh Poverty Database (BPD), which will allow safety net programs (and any other targeted programs) to adopt a more coordinated approach to targeting their beneficiaries more accurately.
Belarus	Y	Social and Economic Development of Belarus for 2006–2015	2006	The government has clearly formulated an objective of reducing poverty. This objective was translated into the overall strategy for social and economic development and the strategy documents for development of a social protection system.	—	Existing monitoring systems are able to track the number, types of beneficiaries, and budgets, but gaps remain. Evaluations are available for some programs.
Belize	P	n.a.	n.a.	Belize continues to have strongly formulated social protection objectives and has begun to put together the building blocks of a social protection strategy.	The government has begun a process of reorganizing institutional arrangements. The Ministry of Human Development, Social Transformation and Poverty Alleviation (MHD) and the Ministry of Education (MOE) will be in charge of implementing social protection programs. The CCT Working Group for the BOOST Program still exists.	A new monitoring and evaluation system in Belize was launched: the Inter-Agency Public Safety management information system (IPSMIS). This database tracks institutional and social indicators across the Statistical Institute of Belize, the Ministry of Education, the Ministry of Health, the Ministry of Human Development, and the Ministry of Economic Development. These ministries and the Institute are also sharing a common targeting tool to identify the poorest families. The MOE and MHD are using the Single Identification System of Beneficiaries (SISB).

(Table continues next page)

| Country/ economy/ territory | Y/N/P (Planned) | Policy and strategy | | | Institutions | Administration |
		Strategy name	Initial year	Comment	Comment	Comment
Benin	Y	Holistic Social Protection Paper	—	The Holistic Social Protection Policy Paper was adopted in early 2014.	The Comité Socle de Protection Sociale, chaired by the Ministry of Development, has been the main body in charge of coordinating social protection programs. The Committee has been active in promoting coordination of programs and the building of common safety net systems such as targeting and registry. With the adoption of the Holistic Social Protection Strategy paper by the Conseil des Ministres, the Comité Socle de Protection Sociale has evolved into the National Social Protection Committee (Comité National de Protection Sociale) under the direct leadership of the President of the Republic.	Progress has been made on implementing a national unified beneficiary database to be housed in the Ministry of Family and Social Affairs. It is expected that the database will be complete by the end of 2015, with support from the Ministry of Health through its results-based financing scheme.
Bhutan	P	National Social Protection Policy for Workers in Bhutan	n.a.	The government has drafted a national social protection and labor (SPL) strategy to make the social protection system more coherent. However, the strategy largely focuses on expanding labor rights and pension benefits to those in the formal sector but outside the civil service.	The draft social protection and labor strategy includes a discussion of which institutional arrangements are designed to formulate a broader social protection strategy and its coordination.	—
Bolivia	Y	Red de Protección Social y Desarrollo Integral Comunitario (RPS-DIC)	2007	The Ministry of Development Planning (MDP) has a strategy (RPS-DIC) under the National Development Plan.	MDP and the Unidad de Análisis de Políticas Sociales y Económicas (UDAPE) have responsibility for the direction, coordination, and monitoring of RPS-DIC.	UDAPE has been implementing the new Monitoring System of Social Programs since late 2013. MDP has started to implement a Beneficiary Registry of Social Programs. The first phase of the registry is the consolidation of beneficiary databases of four social programs (BJA, MPED, Renta Dignidad, and Juancito Pinto). The second phase, expected for 2015, is the identification of potential beneficiaries of social programs through a household survey in poor urban areas.
Bosnia and Herzegovina	N	n.a.	n.a.	—	Responsibility for social assistance is assigned to different levels of government: entity level (Federation of Bosnia and Herzegovina and Republika Srpska), cantonal level (FBH), and municipal level (FBH and RS).	Monitoring systems exist at the entity level, only. The administrative systems of the two entities are not shared and there is no coordination across programs, which could result in economies of scale and help identify gaps and duplication.

(Table continues next page)

| Country/ economy/ territory | Y/N/P (Planned) | Policy and strategy | | | Institutions | Administration |
		Strategy name	Initial year	Comment	Comment	Comment
Botswana	Y	Social Development Framework	2011	In 2011, Botswana, through Department of Social Services, adopted a Social Development Framework that covers the social protection aspects.	—	Botswana made important progress in establishing an overall M&E system for public policies and programs, and some progress has been made in developing information systems for specific social assistance programs within the Ministry of Local Government.
Brazil	Y	Brasil Sem Miséria Plan (BSM)	2011	—	The Ministry for Social Development and Fight Against Hunger (MDS) leads the BSM.	A secretariat (SAGI) is dedicated to M&E functions. It tracks performance of the main social protection programs, namely Bolsa Família and the many programs under the Brasil Sem Miséria plan. MDS has promoted the use of the Single Registry (Cadastro Único) as a platform and targeting mechanism for all social programs.
Bulgaria	Y	—	—	Bulgaria has adopted a number of strategic documents and action plans related to the accomplishment of the Europe 2020 strategy, including strategic directions and measures related to employment, social protection, and social inclusion, as well as multisectoral strategies such as the Strategy on Aging and Demographic Developments.	—	Existing monitoring systems are able to track basic data across all social protection programs.
Burkina Faso	Y	Strategy for Growth and Sustainable Development	2011	In 2011, the government, with the support of the development partners, developed an action plan to implement the social protection strategy. The plan still needs to be operationalized.	In 2013, the government put in place a National Permanent Secretariat for Social Protection (Conseil National de la Protection Sociale, CNPS) to serve as an interministerial coordination mechanism for social protection and social safety nets. The CNPS is chaired by the prime minister at the highest political level and includes a safety net coordinating body chaired by the Ministry of Social Action (MASSN) and a social insurance coordinating body chaired by the Ministry of Public Service.	In 2013/14, the government started a project to develop an M&E system for the new cash transfer program and to undertake impact evaluations. In 2014, the government (CNPS) also started to prepare a national targeting approach to use to improve the efficiency and effectiveness of targeting safety net and emergency programs to poor and vulnerable groups and to build a registry of households to improve coordination of the system.

(Table continues next page)

Country/ economy/ territory	Y/N/P (Planned)	Policy and strategy			Institutions	Administration
		Strategy name	Initial year	Comment	Comment	Comment
Burundi	Y	National Social Protection Policy (PNPS)	2011	A PNPS was adopted in April 2011.	A National Social Protection Commission (CNPS) was set up by a presidential decree in August 2012. This commission is chaired by the president. A Permanent Executive Secretary and a Technical Committee for the CNPS started operations in early 2014.	—
Cabo Verde	Y	National Strategy of Social Protection	2009	The government has developed a National Strategy of Social Protection, which is well articulated with the pillar of Social Cohesion of the country's Third Growth and Poverty Reduction Strategy (GPRSP III, 2012).	The Ministry of Youth, Employment and Human Resources Development is responsible for government coordination in this sector, and for the implementation of many of its programs.	To monitor the performance of the system, the government has developed an M&E system (Sistema de Seguimento e Avaliacao, SISA), which covers 80 percent of the government budget. The system integrates budget and financial execution information with physical execution. It also contains a logic framework for all programs included in the budget, which provides result and outcome indicators. The recent creation of the unique registry will allow greater monitoring of the sector.
Cambodia	Y	National Social Protection Strategy (NSPS, 2009–2013)	2010	The government formulated and adopted the National Social Protection Strategy (NSPS) in 2012. The Action Plan for implementing the NSPS (2012–15) assigned responsibilities, time frames and budgets. A Mid-Term Review of the NSPS took place in 2014.	The mandate was expanded for the Council for Agricultural and Rural Development to coordinate the development and implementation of the NSPS, including ensuring that effective interministerial coordination mechanisms are in place.	The Monitoring Framework of the National Social Protection Strategy has been developed. A central targeting mechanism, ID-Poor, will continue to be the main tool for registering the poor across Cambodia. It is fully managed by the Ministry of Planning.
Cameroon	P	n.a.	n.a.	The government is in the process of preparing a social protection strategy.	—	—
Central African Republic	N	n.a.	n.a.	—	Programs are implemented under the leadership of the Ministry of Planning.	Some policy action has been taken to coordinate social assistance programs.
Chad	P	Stratégie Nationale de Protection Sociale (SNPS)		A National Social Protection Strategy was prepared and validated by a technical committee established by the government. The SNPS is yet to be approved by the Council of Ministers before the official adoption by the National Assembly.	The Ministry of Social Action, National Solidarity and Family has the role of coordinating and monitoring the implementation of programs in partnership with other departments and with the support of nongovernmental organizations (NGOs). The SNPS includes a set of proposals to establish new institutional arrangements to improve coordination, supervision, and implementation of social protection and labor policies.	—

(Table continues next page)

Appendix E. Policies, Institutions, and Administration (Continued)

Country/ economy/ territory	Y/N/P (Planned)	Policy and strategy			Institutions	Administration
		Strategy name	Initial year	Comment	Comment	Comment
Chile	Y	Intersectoral Social Protection System	2009	In 2009, Congress established the Intersectoral Social Protection System to coordinate, monitor, and evaluate the implementation of current subsystems (extreme poverty, early childhood development) and to create new subsystems when needed.	A variety of specific mechanisms and arrangements have been developed to promote coordination, including interinstitutional agreements, national budgeting procedures, and an integrated social information system.	—
China	Y	12th Five Year Plan (2011–2015)	2011	The 12th Five Year Plan includes an overall strategy for a set of social protection programs. In November 2014, the Chinese Communist Party's 18th third plenum outlined a reform proposal to deepen reforms so as to address the second generation issues of social protection and labor.	In 2012, a leading group composed of MOHRSS, MOF, NDRC, ACFTU, and NSSF was formed to take various measures to coordinate within social assistance programs and between social assistance and insurance programs.	In 2012, the Ministry of Civil Affairs began to establish social assistance (SA) centers at both the national and subnational levels, aiming to improve the monitoring and evaluation for social assistance programs.
Colombia	Y	National Development Plan	2010	—	The Ministry of Social Protection operated from 2002 to 2012. It was subsequently divided into the Ministry of Labor and Ministry of Health and Social Protection. The government has a new entity to lead the national strategy against extreme poverty, UNIDOS.	The government is working to better align two major information systems: RUAF (registry of beneficiaries) and SISBEN (targeting identification system).
Comoros	P	Social Protection Policy	n.a.	The government, under the leadership of the Ministry of Health and Solidarity, started a participatory process in early 2014 to develop a social protection policy. The policy is now ready to be presented to the cabinet for endorsement.	The Commissariat General au Plan coordinates all policies. The Ministry of Health and Solidarity is in charge of coordinating safety net programs.	—
Congo, Dem. Rep.	P	n.a.	n.a.	Efforts are underway to develop a Social Protection Note as an initial building block toward a comprehensive policy.	A Social Protection Thematic Group has been established and meets regularly under the leadership of the Ministry of Social Affairs and the Ministry of Employment.	—
Congo, Rep.	Y	National Social Protection Action Plan (PNAS, 2012–2016)	2012	There is currently a strategy for social protection and policy, the National Social Protection Action Plan (PNAS), to be implemented from mid-2012 to 2016. In 2013, the Ministry of Social Affairs demonstrated strong commitment to have the PNAS approved by the parliament. With the development of the LISUNGI project, the PNAS is expected to be approved soon.	The Ministry of Social Affairs provides the core institutional home for social protection. A multisectorial steering committee on social protection was established and the first meeting was held in November 2014. The steering committee is expected to meet every six months.	A framework for monitoring and evaluation of programs' performance is in place, as described in the PNAS, but the main change was expected to happen in 2014 while LISUNGI is being implemented.

(Table continues next page)

| Country/ economy/ territory | Y/N/P (Planned) | Policy and strategy | | | Institutions | Administration |
		Strategy name	Initial year	Comment	Comment	Comment
Costa Rica	Y	Plan Nacional de Desarrollo (2010–2014)	2010	The government has an overall social protection strategy and a set of programs that deliver some elements of prevention, protection, and promotion for large groups of the population.	Social protection programs are mainly implemented by IMAS (Instituto Mixto de Ayuda Social) for the social assistance component, and Caja del Seguro Social for social insurance.	Beneficiaries are all captured by a unique registry (SIPO).
Côte d'Ivoire	Y	Social Protection Strategy	2014	The country gained momentum following analytical work and a process put in place (with a multisectoral national social protection team working group and a multidonor coordination mechanism), leading to the development of a social protection strategy and an action plan. These were approved by the Council of Ministers in May 2014.	Following the approval of the social protection strategy, the government established a technical team within the Ministry of Employment, Social Affairs and Vocational Training with the mandate to work on the design of a social safety net operation. The project is under preparation and will be submitted to the board in the fourth quarter of Fiscal Year (FY) 2015.	—
Croatia	Y	Strategy of Social Welfare Development	2011	—	The Department of Social Policy is leading the social protection coordination and proposing policy reforms.	The contributory and noncontributory programs have separate beneficiary registries, although significant advances have been made with their interconnectivity at the national level to avoid errors of inclusion. A one-stop-shop was designed for all national social benefit programs for full deployment in mid-2014.
Czech Republic	—	—	—	—	—	—
Djibouti	Y	Social Protection Strategy	2012	The government formulated a Social Protection Strategy in 2012. The government is working on scaling up the existing social safety net through the Djiboutian Social Development Agency (ADDS) and on designing new programs based on a forthcoming Poverty and Social Impact Analysis.	Given the cross-sectorial nature of the programs, ADDS coordinates with other partners, including the Ministry of Health and Ministry of Education.	The sectorial strategy aims at enhancing program and donor coordination through the development of a social registry of the poor and vulnerable. In the absence of a comprehensive national identification system, the social registry will rely on biometric information to reduce double counting and misuse of resources.

(Table continues next page)

Country/ economy/ territory	Y/N/P (Planned)	Policy and strategy			Institutions	Administration
		Strategy name	Initial year	Comment	Comment	Comment
Dominica	Y	Growth and Social Protection Strategy (GSPS)	2012	The GSPS lacks comprehensiveness and attention to improvements in the social protection system. This is being partially addressed through the development of an Integrated Social Protection Strategy (ISPS).	The Planning and Public Investment Unit (PPIU) of the Ministry of Finance (MoF) has oversight in implementing the GSPS, including forging the necessary interministerial and interagency coordination. This is complemented by attempts to improve coordination in the social protection system outlined in the ISPS.	A National Beneficiary Information System (NBIS) was designed for the Public Assistance program, but its use was discontinued because of concerns about the targeting tool. It still provides the Ministry of Social Services, Community Development and Gender Affairs with an internal tool for program monitoring. The ISPS seeks to address these challenges by laying out a framework for revising and rolling out the NBIS and for developing M&E systems for main social assistance programs.
Dominican Republic	P	n.a.	n.a.	The government is calling for a new social protection strategy in order to accelerate results in terms of poverty reduction, coordination, coverage, and results-orientation. The process for designing such a strategy is just beginning.	In 2009–10, important institutional improvements were made in terms of creating new cross-sectoral coordination mechanisms with education and health services to help identify and monitor the reduction of supply-side gaps in basic social services.	The targeting system, SIUBEN—used to target the CCT, energy subsidies, and subsidized health insurance regime—was expanded and updated in 2012 through a socioeconomic survey, now covering about 1.7 million households. A major objective for 2014 was the application of the results of the SIUBEN 2 survey to the registries of key social programs (CCT, targeted subsidies) and services (subsidized health insurance, National Health Insurance Authority, or SENASA). The government is defining the mechanisms to update the rosters of beneficiaries for its targeted programs to reflect the updated 2012 SIUBEN socioeconomic survey.
Ecuador	Y	National Plan 2013–2017	2013	The constitution and the new National Plan for the second period of the current administration reinforce access to social security without discrimination and extend its coverage to additional groups. Such extensions have served to underline the need for reform to establish a coherent and sustainable contributory and noncontributory social insurance (SI) system.	The Ministry Coordinator of Social Development (MCDS) leads the institutional framework in charge of the Social Protection Policy, and jointly with the National Secretary for Planning (SENPLADES) leads the National Strategy for Poverty Reduction. Ecuador is moving toward integrating different safety net programs into the Vice-Ministry of Social Protection and Mobility, consolidating the cash transfer program, Bono de Desarrollo Humano (BDH), as the centerpiece of the country's social safety net.	The MCDS is leading the monitoring process through two main information systems: the Social Registry (proxy-means test), and the Registry of the Social Programs (RIPS). In terms of evaluation, the MCDS and SENPLADES share the responsibility for evaluating the main programs and the second impact evaluation of the BDH.

(Table continues next page)

Appendix E. Policies, Institutions, and Administration *(Continued)*

| Country/ economy/ territory | Y/N/P (Planned) | Policy and strategy | | | Institutions | Administration |
		Strategy name	Initial year	Comment	Comment	Comment
Egypt, Arab Rep.	Y	—	—	The government has clearly formulated an objective of reducing poverty and has formulated some subsectoral social protection strategies, such as the one on youth employment. A set of programs exists, which delivers elements of prevention, protection, and promotion.	Five ministries administer the system. The Ministry of Manpower and Migration (MOMM) directly oversees a network of employment offices providing job intermediation, but no active labor market policies (ALMP). The Ministry is also in charge of the migration agenda. The Social Fund for Development (SFD) is a semi-autonomous governmental agency under the direct supervision of the prime minister and provides a training program for unemployed youth and redundant workers, and a microcredit program. Social insurance is overseen by the Ministry of Finance, the Ministry of Investments, and the Ministry of Health. The Ministry of Social Solidarity is in charge of the social safety net system; its main elements are food and fuel subsidies and cash transfers.	—
El Salvador	Y	Universal Social Protection System	2013	As part of the National Development Plan 2010–2014, the government has set up the Universal Social Protection System (SPSU) as the cornerstone of its social policy strategy. A new legislation is currently being discussed in congress, the Ley de Desarrollo y Proteccion Social, aiming to provide a social protection as stated in the SPSU strategy.	The Technical Secretariat of the Presidency (STP), oversees the SP system.	The government has started implementation of the single registry of beneficiaries (RUP). The STP is also strengthening its M&E system: the CCT already has an impact evaluation, as well as the Temporary Income Support Program (PATI).
Equatorial Guinea	Y	Horizon 2020	2007	The National Economic Development Plan, Horizon 2020, seeks to reduce poverty and diversify the economy. The Plan includes three strategic objectives related to social protection (nos. 21–23).	—	—
Eritrea	N	n.a.	n.a.	—	—	—
Estonia	—	—	—	—	—	—
Ethiopia	Y	Social Protection Policy	2014	The National Social Protection Policy was approved by the Council of Ministers in November 2014. The policy has the broad objective of providing an overall social protection system and creating an enabling environment in which Ethiopian citizens have equitable access to all social protection.	The Ministry of Labor and Social Affairs (MOLSA) and Ministry of Agriculture (MOA) continues to play a central coordination function among stakeholders.	Significant work is being undertaken to develop management information systems for social protection and safety nets in Ethiopia.

(Table continues next page)

Country/ economy/ territory	Y/N/P (Planned)	Policy and strategy			Institutions	Administration
		Strategy name	Initial year	Comment	Comment	Comment
Fiji	N	n.a.	n.a.	"Build a Better Fiji for All" is a national initiative that was launched in 2007 through a People's Charter for Change, Peace and Progress (PCCPP). The reduction of poverty to negligible levels is one of the pillars of the Charter.	The Department of Social Welfare (DSW), under the Ministry of Social Welfare, Women and Poverty Alleviation, is primarily responsible for alleviating poverty by providing welfare support and empowering people who are disadvantaged in all the vulnerable sections of the community, and administering poverty alleviation programs.	The monitoring arrangements are in place to track the number and type (category) of program beneficiaries and budgets. The government has been taking steps to modernize the system, including the transition from the e-Welfare to e-Gov system. These efforts still need to be fully accomplished.
Gabon	N	n.a.	n.a.	Although the health insurance and social protection fund were launched, there is currently no formal social protection policy in Gabon.	—	In 2008, the government carried out a census of vulnerable people.
Gambia, The	P	First National Social Protection Policy	2015	In the last year, the government has made significant efforts toward creating a national Social Protection Strategy. A validation workshop for the First National Social Protection Policy, organized by the government and the United Nations (UN) system, was conducted in July 2014. The Strategy is a ten-year document from 2015 to 2025.	Given the relatively small size of the country, coordination takes place under the auspices of the Vice President, who is also the Minister of Women Affairs, and in her capacity as Vice President oversees the government activities in education, health, nutrition, and social protection.	—
Georgia	Y	Poverty Reduction Strategy	2013	Overall, Georgia has a good social protection strategy and system. There has been significant progress, relative to many other countries in the region, in streamlining different social benefit schemes, targeting to the poor, and maintaining a fiscally sustainable family of social protection programs.	Within the Ministry of Health, Labor and Social Affairs (MoHLSA), the Social Services Agency (SSA) is responsible for the administration and delivery of Georgia's social protection program, including health and pensions. With a widespread network of 68 regional and local offices, and a sophisticated MIS system, the SSA outperforms other countries in terms of monitoring its expenditures with up-to-date tracking facilities.	The Social Information Management System is in an implementation/testing stage to help improve the targeting effectiveness of social assistance and enable beneficiaries to access benefits faster.

(Table continues next page)

Country/economy/territory	Y/N/P (Planned)	Policy and strategy			Institutions	Administration
		Strategy name	Initial year	Comment	Comment	Comment
Ghana	P	National Social Protection Strategy	n.a.	The government is devising a roadmap for completing the National Social Protection strategy and strengthening the coordinating capabilities of the Ministry of Gender, Children and Social Protection (MoGCSP).	The MoGCSP has been granted cabinet approval to coordinate and oversee the social protection sector.	The new MoGCSP is also initiating preliminary discussions on designing a results framework and M&E system for social protection programs in the country. It has adapted the Common Targeting Mechanism as a basis to create a national targeting system. To further strengthen coordination, the MoGCSP received cabinet approval to develop a Ghana National Household Registry (GNHR). Through this initiative, a national household registry for social protection programs to effectively and efficiently target beneficiaries will be developed.
Grenada	Y	Social Safety Net Policy Framework	2013	This framework builds on the 2009 Social Safety Net Assessment. This framework was approved by the cabinet in August 2013.	The cross-sectoral technical coordination committee for the Support for Education, Empowerment and Development (SEED) Program has been revived. It is made up of experts in health, education, housing, finance, and social protection and is taking an active role in decision making about SEED, as well as social programs.	Monitoring and evaluation systems are in the process of being developed. M&E is a critical area stressed under the new Social Safety Net Policy Framework, thus allowing policy makers to make more informed decisions about existing programs. Efforts are being made to develop greater coordination among programs through the creation of memorandums of understanding (MOUs) and regular intersectoral meetings.
Guatemala	N	n.a.	n.a.	—	—	The recently approved and functioning Single Registry (RUU) can serve as a step in enhancing coordination across social programs. The RUU includes more than 108 social programs from different ministries, enabling the identification of beneficiaries receiving different program benefits.
Guinea	P	n.a.	n.a.	The government formed a multisector group to oversee the development of a social protection strategy. However, legal documents for the establishment of this group are not yet operational.	The Ministry of Social Affairs and Promotion of Women and Children is in charge of interventions for the protection of poor and vulnerable people.	Monitoring and evaluation are periodic and tend to be project-based.

(Table continues next page)

| Country/ economy/ territory | Y/N/P (Planned) | Policy and strategy | | | Institutions | Administration |
		Strategy name	Initial year	Comment	Comment	Comment
Guinea-Bissau	N	Poverty Reduction Strategy	n.a.	The government has social protection policies but has yet to formulate a social protection strategy. Social protection policies described in the National Poverty Reduction Strategy include a few programs targeting vulnerable groups, notably war veterans, the handicapped, and senior citizens.	—	—
Guyana	N	n.a.	n.a.	—	—	An MIS system is operational.
Haiti	Y	Thinking and Fighting for a Haiti Without Poverty: Action Plan for Accelerating the Reduction of Extreme Poverty (PAARP)	—	In May 2014, the Prime Minister's Office launched its new plan, "Thinking and Fighting for a Haiti Without Poverty: Action Plan for Accelerating the Reduction of Extreme Poverty" (Penser et Lutter Vers une Haïti Sans Pauvreté: Plan d'Action pour Accélérer la Réduction de l'Extrême Pauvreté, PAARP).	As part of PAARP, coordination mechanisms are being put in place. The Ministry of Social Affairs (MAST) has the institutional mandate for social protection.	A national targeting system, a unique beneficiary registry that can be used by various social programs, and an integrated service delivery model at the communal level are all being developed.
Honduras	Y	National Social Protection Policy	2013	In March 2012, the government approved a comprehensive National Social Protection Policy. The Policy is expected to consolidate a large number of programs (about 80).	Social protection initiatives and programs continue to be dispersed among eight or more different implementation ministries and decentralized institutions.	The Unique Registry Participants (RUP) has been revamped. The RUP database is composed of beneficiaries of most social programs. In October 2014, a presidential decree was issued to mandate the use of RUP as the targeting instrument for all social interventions, starting with 9 major programs (including Bono Vida Mejor), with a planned target of reaching 18 by the end of 2014.
Hungary	—	—	—	—	—	—
India	N	n.a.	n.a.	India has a strong legal framework, including Right to Food and the Mahatma Gandhi National Rural Employment Guarantee Act acts. India also has the Directive Principles of State Policy, although a coherent social protection policy framework is not yet in place.	—	Initiatives such as the Unique Identification (UID) hold the potential of improving coverage, implementation, and coordination across programs in the future. In addition, there are many state-level initiatives aimed at increasing performance of social protection programs utilizing information technology (IT) and innovations in administration.

(Table continues next page)

Country/ economy/ territory	Y/N/P (Planned)	Policy and strategy			Institutions	Administration
		Strategy name	Initial year	Comment	Comment	Comment
Indonesia	N	n.a.	n.a.	Recently, the government released a Master Plan for Poverty Reduction (MP3KI) as a comprehensive long-term poverty reduction strategy for 2012–25. The strategy is not a comprehensive social protection strategy.	In 2010, the president elevated oversight of the poverty strategy to the National Team for the Acceleration of Poverty Reduction (TNP2K), which is chaired by the Vice President and supported by a secretariat housed in his office.	The TNP2K Secretariat established a M&E Working Group in 2010 responsible for establishing a single monitoring system with data from poverty reduction programs. It also created a national registry of 25 million poor and vulnerable households. A unified social protection card was issued to 15.5 million households entitling them to unconditional cash transfers (BLSM), the Rice Subsidy for the Poor (Raskin), and scholarship for poor students (BSM) benefits. An M&E working group established in the TNP2K Secretariat aims to improve M&E activities and collate data that can be used to track the performance of all social safety net programs.
Iran, Islamic Rep.	—	—	—	—	—	—
Iraq	Y	National Development Plan	2013	The government began to reform the social protection policies in alignment with the National Development Strategy and implementation of these reforms through the Emergency Social Protection Project (ESPP). The reforms included expanding the social safety net programs.	—	The new law has had a number of positive outcomes, such as improving targeting, introducing conditional cash transfers (CCTs) and linkages with health and education, involving civil society organizations, and improving the management information system (MIS) for registry and monitoring. The Iraqi government is also considering upgrading its MIS and applying proxy-means-testing.
Jamaica	Y	Social Inclusion Policy	2013	In 2014, the government developed a social protection strategy. The challenge in the next few years will be to make it operational.	The Ministry of Labor and Social Security is progressively implementing a case management system, which will improve coordination among social assistance programs through improved reference and cross-reference systems.	A beneficiary recertification process is underway to ensure accuracy of targeting, and resources are being invested in M&E to improve tracking and program effectiveness. The government is developing a graduation strategy for the Programme of Advancement through Health and Education (PATH) beneficiaries that will entail tight collaboration and well-functioning articulation with other programs.

(Table continues next page)

| Country/ economy/ territory | Y/N/P (Planned) | Policy and strategy | | | Institutions | Administration |
		Strategy name	Initial year	Comment	Comment	Comment
Jordan	Y	National Agenda	2007	The government has developed a comprehensive strategy for social protection as part of its National Agenda, as well as subsequent updates and strategies, including the National Employment Strategy (2012) and the Poverty Reduction Strategy (2013).	Institutional mechanisms are planned as part of the development of a National Unified Registry.	There are systems to monitor performance of safety nets and labor market programs. The government is developing a National Unified Registry, which ultimately will be the main coordinating mechanism for social safety nets and subsidy reform in the country.
Kazakhstan	Y	Strategic Development Plan 2020	2010	The government has a strategy for social protection integrated in a set of documents covering employment, pensions, safety nets, and social services.	—	Existing monitoring systems can track numbers and types of beneficiaries, spending, average benefits, and the like. The Household Budget Survey is periodically used for analysis of social protection programs. An indicator framework for social protection was developed and is used for reporting of results.
Kenya	Y	National Social Protection Policy (NSNP)	2012	Legal changes on social protection were launched in 2013. A new Social Assistance Bill was submitted to the National Assembly that aims to further provide a legal and policy framework for social protection.	The NSNP is being implemented and forms the basis for harmonization and consolidation of the main cash transfer programs in the Ministry of Labor, Social Security and Services (MLSSS) and the Ministry of Devolution and Planning. In 2014, the programs within the NSNP developed a Program Consolidation Strategy, which will lead to increased coordination of institutions and functions involved in delivering government cash transfer programs It is anticipated that the NSNP will form the basis for a fully coordinated social protection system at the national scale.	The upgrading of the management information systems for the main cash transfer programs in the NSNP was completed in 2014. These upgrades ensure better fiduciary controls in the programs and also more flexible delivery of payments, if the need should arise. The government has procured a new payment service provider, which will offer biometric payment mechanisms and an option to use bank accounts. The development of a Single Registry is at an advanced stage and is expected to be launched in 2015.
Kiribati	Y	Kiribati Development Plan 2012–2015	2012	Kiribati has one of the most extensive social assistance programs in the East Asia and Pacific region. While there is no specific social protection strategy, the Kiribati Development Plan 2012–2015 acknowledges the need for providing protection to vulnerable groups such as women and children.	Various agencies field an array of programs providing protection, prevention, and promotion of social services to households.	Improving updates of statistics and relevant information for planning and policy formulation is one of the strategies mentioned to help economic growth and poverty alleviation in the Kiribati Development Plan 2012–2015.

(Table continues next page)

| Country/ economy/ territory | Y/N/P (Planned) | Policy and strategy | | | Institutions | Administration |
		Strategy name	Initial year	Comment	Comment	Comment
Kosovo	P	n.a.	n.a.	A White Paper (Social Protection Strategy) was developed in 2008, but has not yet been adopted. An interagency Working Group was established with the objective of developing a new social protection strategy.	—	Existing monitoring systems can track the number and types of beneficiaries and budgets. New social assistance and employment registries were introduced in early 2012.
Kuwait	—	—	—	—	—	—
Kyrgyz Republic	Y	National Social Protection Development Strategy and Action Plan 2012–2014	2011	The Strategy lays down measures to strengthen the social safety net, reform the system of social care, step up child protection, and improve social security for the elderly. The government is in the process of developing a new pension policy, which provides for better protection of the elderly from destitution and strengthens old-age insurance.	—	Existing monitoring systems can track numbers and types of beneficiaries, spending, average benefits, and the like. The Kyrgyz Integrated Household Survey is used to analyze social protection programs, with support from Development Partners. A registry of social assistance beneficiaries, being rolled out by the Ministry of Social Development, is expected to improve coordination among the programs administered by the ministry.
Lao PDR	P	n.a.	n.a.	The government continues to have poverty reduction among its declared objectives but has not yet formulated a social protection strategy. Various UN agencies have in their development plan a goal of helping the government establish a social protection framework and have it finalized by 2015, linked to the 7th National Socio-Economic Development Plan (NSEDP).	—	—
Latvia	—	—	—	—	—	—
Lebanon	Y	National Social Development Strategy	2011	The government has poverty reduction among its declared objectives and has developed a Social Sector Strategy. Some policies have been implemented, including its National Poverty Targeting Program (NPTP).	—	—

(Table continues next page)

Country/ economy/ territory	Y/N/P (Planned)	Policy and strategy			Institutions	Administration
		Strategy name	Initial year	Comment	Comment	Comment
Lesotho	Y	National Social Protection Strategy	2014	The government recently approved a National Social Protection Strategy that sets out to "provide comprehensive inclusive social protection that reduces poverty, vulnerability and inequality, increases resilience to risks and shocks, promotes access to services and to the labor market, and stimulates economic growth and social stability."	The Ministry of Social Development leads and coordinates the social protection agenda.	The National Information System for Social Assistance (NISSA) serves as a national registry for beneficiaries of safety net programs.
Liberia	Y	Social Protection Strategy and Policy	2012	The Social Protection Strategy and Policy provides a solid framework for addressing vulnerabilities over the next 17 years covered by the country's long-term plan.	—	In 2013, a single-set of indicators for a common MIS was developed and a MIS database was populated with beneficiary information from the country's largest social safety net programs (excluding school feeding).
Libya	—	—	—	—	—	—
Lithuania	—	—	—	—	—	—
Macedonia, FYR	Y	National Strategy for Alleviation of Poverty and Social Exclusion (2010–2020)	2010	The government has developed an overall strategy for social protection, the National Strategy for Alleviation of Poverty and Social Exclusion, and a set of programs that aim to improve resilience, opportunity, and equity for large groups of the population.	The Inter-ministerial Working Group is responsible for preparing the annual programs, as well as coordinating and reporting on implementation of the strategy to the government.	A unique registry of social cash beneficiaries, the Cash Benefits Management Information System (CBMIS), was developed and is an important tool in defining policies to improve the functioning of the system. Recently the social assistance database was linked with the administrative registries in the Employment Service Agency, Cadastre Agency, and the Pension and Disability Insurance Fund.
Madagascar	P	n.a.	n.a.	The social protection policy is expected to be finalized by June 2015.	The Ministry of Population, Social Protection and Gender is making a big effort to initiate the coordination of key social protection programs. The Ministry has created the Ad Hoc Committee for Social Protection.	The Ministry of Social Protection has proposed to build an M&E system for the social protection sector under the planned World Bank-financed Social Safety Net Project. This IT-based system would enable the ministry to effectively monitor and evaluate the performance of key social protection programs.

(Table continues next page)

Country/economy/territory	Y/N/P (Planned)	Policy and strategy			Institutions	Administration
		Strategy name	Initial year	Comment	Comment	Comment
Malawi	Y	Social Support Policy	2013	The government approved the Social Support Policy in July 2012. By April 2013, the National Social Support Programme was also approved to operationalize the policy.	Coordination is under the Ministry of Finance Economic Planning and Development, within its Directorate of Poverty Reduction and Social Protection. The ministry has the structure in place to coordinate the many interventions in place in the country through the National Steering Committee (NSC), a high-level committee comprising principal secretaries and development partners.	The government has a central M&E department in the Ministry of Economic Planning and Development that captures information from the district level, where the programs are implemented.
Malaysia	N	n.a.	n.a.	—	Seven ministries implement 39 social safety net programs.	Existing monitoring systems can track the number and types of beneficiaries and budgets of individual programs.
Maldives	Y	Social Protection Act	2014	The Social Protection Act was introduced in early 2014 to provide a legal framework for a number of existing social protection schemes, as well as a broad vision for the national social protection system. Specific regulations are being prepared, but the implementation plan for the Act has not been fully developed.	The major agencies delivering social protection and labor programs are the National Social Protection Agency (NSPA), the Maldives Pension Administration Office (MPAO), and Ministry of Youth and Sports (MoYS). A coordination mechanism is yet to be formalized.	Most programs have functioning monitoring mechanisms to track the number and types of beneficiaries, as well as expenditures. There have been efforts to develop shared administrative systems, including common and improved targeting and monitoring systems.
Mali	Y	National Action Plan for the Extension of Social Protection	2011	In August 2011, the government adopted a National Action Plan for the Extension of Social Protection, which aims at improving the resilience, equity, and opportunity for large groups of the population.	A National Strategic Steering Committee for Social Protection (Conseil National d'Orientation Strategique de la Protection Sociale, CNOS-PS) to coordinate the social protection programs was scheduled to be created in early 2012. However, the political situation put a hold on the creation of the committee.	Existing monitoring systems can track basic data. Evaluations are available for some programs.
Marshall Islands	N	n.a.	n.a.	—	The Marshall Islands Social Security Administration (MISSA) administers old-age and disability benefits via the Republic of the Marshall Islands (RMI) Social Security Retirement Fund, and works together with the Ministry of Health in collecting Health Fund contributions.	—

(Table continues next page)

| Country/ economy/ territory | Y/N/P (Planned) | Policy and strategy | | | Institutions | Administration |
		Strategy name	Initial year	Comment	Comment	Comment
Mauritania	Y	National Social Protection Strategy	2013	The strategy was adopted by the Council of Ministers in June 2013. Implementation of the strategy began in 2014.	The government has placed responsibility for the strategy's implementation with the Ministry of Economic Affairs and Development, which has established a technical unit tasked with coordinating the implementation of the strategy. There is a functioning Interministerial Steering Committee to pilot the strategy, and an associated Technical Committee to validate the design of interventions.	The Ministry of Economic Affairs and Development directly implements the national social registry, to ensure that it is a tool that can be used by all programs, irrespective of their institutional bases. The actual launch of the registry is scheduled for the first half of 2015. The first wave of data collection in 2015 is expected to register 30,000 households. The social registry will provide information and facilitate targeting for all social programs in Mauritania, starting with the national social transfer program.
Mauritius	Y	Social Protection Review and Strategy	2010	The government completed a Social Protection Review and Strategy in 2010.	The Ministry of Social Security implements the main social assistance program, Social Aid.	The government is rolling out a single registry (the Social Register of Mauritius, SRM), which started by integrating databases for Social Aid and the National Empowerment Foundation (NEF) programming, with the aim of improving integrated service delivery and coordination. The NEF is currently developing a comprehensive monitoring and evaluation framework.
Mexico	Y	National Development Plan	2013	Mexico has a well-defined national policy for social development, together with a comprehensive strategy to reduce poverty.	—	In 2013, the Social Ministry (SEDESOL) started taking steps to develop a unified social information system that would capture information on beneficiaries (and potential beneficiaries) of existing social programs, and on the benefits they are receiving.
Micronesia, Fed. Sts.	N	n.a.	n.a.	—	—	—
Moldova	N	n.a.	n.a.	—	—	Each government agency has its own MIS that is able to track the number and types of beneficiaries. The social assistance MIS is being enhanced to keep track of a broader set of performance indicators. It is developing links with social insurance agency data as well as other public registries to simplify the application process for beneficiaries and verify eligibility.

(Table continues next page)

| Country/ economy/ territory | Y/N/P (Planned) | Policy and strategy | | | Institutions | Administration |
		Strategy name	Initial year	Comment	Comment	Comment
Mongolia	N	n.a.	n.a.	—	Some institutional arrangements promote coordination of programs and policies within the social protection system.	Monitoring arrangements are in place to track the number and type (category) of program beneficiaries, as well as budgets. An intersectoral database of poor households and registry of beneficiaries is being developed.
Montenegro	Y	Strategy for Social and Child Protection (2008–2012)	2008	Montenegro implemented a Strategy for Social and Child Protection (2008–2012), and is now implementing a Strategy for Integration of People with Disabilities (2008–2016), a National Action Plan for Gender Equality, and a set of programs that will deliver the basic elements of prevention, protection, and promotion for vulnerable population groups.	The strategy and policies for social assistance are elaborated at the central level by the Ministry of Labor and Social Welfare (MLSW). The implementing agencies include Centers for Social Work (decentralized bodies of MLSW) and their branch offices.	Existing monitoring systems can track the number and types of beneficiaries and budgets. Evaluations are available for some programs. The programs are largely integrated. The social assistance and child protection programs, along with some social care services, are accessed with the same or similar eligibility criteria.
Morocco	N	n.a.	n.a.	—	—	—
Mozambique	Y	National Strategy for Social Protection	2010	The National Strategy for Social Protection was initially defined for a five-year period (2010–14). The government has started an evaluation process for the strategy, which will facilitate the development of the Strategy for 2015–19.	Coordination within the Basic Social Protection Susbsector falls under the Coordination Council for the Basic Social Protection Subsystem, which became operational in 2013 and aims to increase coordination between the four prongs of the Basic Social Protection Subsector.	By end-2014, a proper management information system was expected to be operational.
Myanmar	P	n.a.	n.a.	In 2013, the Social Protection Sector Working Group (SPSWG), chaired by the Ministry of Social Welfare, Relief and Resettlement (MSWRR), was established and tasked with developing a social protection strategy through dialogue with relevant ministries. A draft strategy was produced toward the end of 2014 and is in the process of being endorsed by the government.	—	A first step in the establishment of monitoring and evaluation systems in social assistance programs is being initiated through pilots, such as for the Ministry of Education's School Stipends program.
Namibia	Y	Vision 2030 Strategy	2004	The government's overall social protection strategy is articulated in the long-term Vision 2030 Strategy, which sets goals for protecting the vulnerable (including orphans, the elderly, and the disabled) and promoting the welfare of youth and women in the context of reducing poverty.	—	Basic data (such as numbers of beneficiaries, services delivered, and spending) are tracked. Evaluations are conducted for some programs.

(Table continues next page)

Appendix E. Policies, Institutions, and Administration *(Continued)*

| Country/ economy/ territory | Y/N/P (Planned) | Policy and strategy | | | Institutions | Administration |
		Strategy name	Initial year	Comment	Comment	Comment
Nepal	P	National Social Protection Strategy	n.a.	The government began preparing a 10-year national social protection strategy/ framework in 2011 but has not yet finalized it.	Different government entities—including the National Planning Commission, Ministry of Finance, Ministry of Federal Affairs and Local Development, Ministry of Education, and the Poverty Alleviation Fund—have begun working together, under the auspices of the Ministry of Finance, to ensure the coordination of social protection schemes across different ministries.	In 2013, the Ministry of Federal Affairs and Local Development (MoFALD) established a MIS for its cash transfer programs, which was rolled out in 2 districts, to be expanded to an additional 12 districts. The government had already been delivering cash via banks in all urban areas. An electronic database, combined with electronic transfers and the development of "poverty identity cards," is expected to improve transparency of the fund flow and enhance efficiency of transfers.
Nicaragua	Y	National Human Development Plan (NHDP) 2012–2016	2012	The government developed the NHDP 2009–2013 and created the National Social Welfare System in 2008. In 2013, the government undertook a review of these two instruments to align different approaches into a systemic social assistance strategy. Starting in 2013, the updated version of the NHDP 2012–2016 was put in place.	The national welfare system is overseen by the Social Cabinet for the Family and Solidarity, consisting of a coordinator and the Ministers of Finance, Health, Education, and the Family, Youth and Children.	The Ministry of the Family, Adolescents and Children (MIFAN) completed the design of its unified registry of beneficiaries of social programs and continues to advance in creating interfaces with the MIS of the Ministry of Health to share information about beneficiaries. MIFAN has used this registry to roll out its model with family grants in 2013 and is designing the impact evaluation of this program.
Niger	Y	National Social Protection Strategy	2011	In October 2013, the government held its first national social protection forum, aimed at operationalizing the National Social Protection Strategy, and leading to stronger ownership of this strategy by key stakeholders.	The Consultative Interministerial Committee on Social Protection created in August 2013 to coordinate SP interventions is still in place. However, program coordination efforts continue to be sector-specific.	The system can monitor and evaluate the impact of the main safety net programs.
Nigeria	P	National Social Protection Policy Framework (draft)	n.a.	The new policy framework is expected to be presented to the National Assembly immediately after the forthcoming national elections.	The social protection policy framework is expected to bring the current social safety net interventions in the country into a better coordinated system.	The National Planning Commission has M&E systems for all targeted SSN interventions. The introduction of a National Identity Card system is planned. The system is expected to be coordinated with the targeting and identification system for the social protection administrative and coordinating system.
Oman	—	—	—	—	—	—

(Table continues next page)

Country/ economy/ territory	Y/N/P (Planned)	Policy and strategy			Institutions	Administration
		Strategy name	Initial year	Comment	Comment	Comment
Pakistan	Y	National Social Protection Strategy	2007	In 2007, the government approved its National Social Protection Strategy. Under the leadership of the Federal Planning Commission, the government started consultations with the provinces and embarked on the process of developing a National Social Protection Framework.	—	Most social protection programs can track the number and types and benefits received by their beneficiaries. The payment delivery for Benazir Income Support Programme (BISP) is being improved, moving away from reliance on the postal service to technology-based payment mechanisms such as debit cards, smartcards, and mobile phones. The BISP targeting system is being shared with over 20 federal and provincial social protection programs.
Palau	—	—	—	—	—	—
Panama	N	n.a.	n.a.	—	Secretaría Técnica del Gabinete Social	The Social Development Ministry (MIDES) has implemented a Unified Registry of Beneficiaries (RUB) of MIDES programs, which is functional.
Papua New Guinea	P	Social Protection Policy	n.a.	A first draft of the Social Protection Policy has been submitted to the Department for Community Development (DfCD), with the elderly and disabled as the initial target beneficiaries. In 2014, the DfCD, with support from the World Bank, UNICEF, and the United Nations Capital Development Fund (UNCDF), drafted an umbrella Social Protection Policy.	—	The government is working to complete the e-Identification system. Work has already begun to input beneficiary data into a database, which will greatly help identify beneficiaries. However, this project may not be ready when implementation of the Social Protection Policy begins in 2015.
Paraguay	N	n.a.	n.a.	—	A Social Cabinet competes with the Technical Secretary for Planning to coordinate the sector.	The Single Registry of Beneficiaries has not yet been operationalized.
Peru	Y	Crecer para Incluir (Growth for Inclusion)	2011	Implementation of the strategy has continued, with revisions of some programs and expansions of others.	The Ministry of Development and Social Inclusion (MIDIS) has been tasked with coordinating the implementation of the five most important social protection programs.	Implementation of the M&E system has advanced, and more data is available at MIDIS. Further work is necessary to expand it and open it to public access. All social programs are expected to use the national target system. A unique registry of beneficiaries is being developed, along with an integrated complaints and redress mechanism.

(Table continues next page)

| Country/ economy/ territory | Y/N/P (Planned) | Policy and strategy | | | Institutions | Administration |
		Strategy name	Initial year	Comment	Comment	Comment
Philippines	Y	Social Protection Operational Framework and Strategy	2012	The Social Protection Strategy and Policy is defined by the Social Protection Operational Framework, which was developed in a participatory manner through extensive consultations with government, agencies, civil society, and development partners. It was approved by the National Economic and Development Authority (NEDA) in 2012.	In 2009, the Social Development Committee (SDC) of the NEDA approved the creation of a Subcommittee on Social Protection. It is co-chaired by the Department of Social Welfare and Development and NEDA.	All major agencies involved in the design and implementation of social protection policies have established record keeping and monitoring systems. A data sharing software/tool will be launched soon to increase awareness and use of the National Household Targeting System for Poverty Reduction (NHTSPR) database by national agencies, local governments, the private sector, and nongovernmental organizations that implement their own assistance programs.
Poland	Y	Social Assistance Law	2004	The government has an overall social protection strategy and a well-designed set of programs, both on the contributory and the noncontributory side. In 2014, the government made a number of important reforms. Parliament passed an ambitious pension reform.	The Ministry of Labor and Social Policy is responsible for developing policy in social assistance, social insurance, and labor market policies.	The ministry has a sophisticated administrative system to administer its programs and track results of the main programs.
Qatar	—	—	—	—	—	—
Romania	Y	Social Assistance Reform Strategy	2011	In early 2011, Romania approved a new Law on Pensions, a Labor Code, and a Social Assistance Strategy for social assistance benefits. In late 2011, Romania approved a Framework Law on Social Assistance. In 2013, Romania drafted or approved several sectorial strategies. In 2014, the Ministry of Labor aimed to finalize two other key strategies (ex ante conditionalities for absorbing European Funds): the Strategy of Social Inclusion and the Active Aging Strategy.	The Ministry of Labor effectively coordinates the delivery of most social assistance programs, social services, and labor market policies.	All the social protection sectors have well developed IT systems, which allow a good monitoring and evaluation of beneficiaries and funds. Regular monitoring of performance indications has begun. The implementation of impact evaluations is not yet fully institutionalized.
Russian Federation	N	Concept of Long-Term Socio-Economic Development of the Russian Federation until 2020	n.a.	A comprehensive poverty reduction strategy, which would include specific social protection interventions, has not been developed yet; however, the first attempts at formulating a poverty reduction strategy were made in the Concept of Long-Term Socio-Economic Development of the Russian Federation until 2020.	—	—

(Table continues next page)

| Country/ economy/ territory | Y/N/P (Planned) | Policy and strategy | | | Institutions | Administration |
		Strategy name	Initial year	Comment	Comment	Comment
Rwanda	Y	National Social Protection Strategy (NSPS)	2011	An NSPS was developed through a consultative process.	A sector working group (SWG) established in 2008 has fostered increased coordination of the social protection sector, regularly bringing together government, development partners, and civil society organizations to discuss policy/strategy and implementation issues, review progress, and make recommendations. The Ministry of Local Development (MINALOC) serves as the coordinator for SP in Rwanda, with its Local Development Agency (LODA) as the main implementing body.	Rwanda is developing an integrated management information system (MIS) that includes a unified registry. The MIS design work was completed in 2012, and implementation piloting began in October 2013.
Samoa	N	n.a.	n.a.	—	The Ministry of Women, Community and Social Development remains as the main coordination point for social protection programs in Samoa.	—
São Tomé and Príncipe	Y	National Social Protection Policy and Strategy (PENPS)	2014	—	Some public social protection programs exist under the responsibility of two institutions. The National Institute of Social Security (INSSS) manages social security contributions from formal employment in the private and public sectors. The Directorate of Social Protection of the Ministry of Labor and Solidarity assists vulnerable people through social programs funded by the state budget.	—
Saudi Arabia	—	—	—	—	—	—
Senegal	Y	National Social Protection Strategy	2005	The government has developed an overall strategy for social protection, which was recently approved and endorsed by the different sectors and development partners.	The newly created Délégation Générale à la Protection Sociale et la Solidarité Nationale is responsible for the coordination of the sector.	The Délégation Générale has been tasked with the overall monitoring and evaluation of the sector and a unique registry of programs. The government has implemented a unique registry (with 75,000 households in 2013) that will be used to target multiple programs and articulate interventions and should increase coordination.

(Table continues next page)

Country/ economy/ territory	Y/N/P (Planned)	Policy and strategy			Institutions	Administration
		Strategy name	Initial year	Comment	Comment	Comment
Serbia	Y	Social Welfare Development Strategy	2005	The government has strategies and action plans for the basic elements of social protection social insurance, a labor market policy, social assistance, and social services, including the National Strategy for the Development of Social Protection.	—	The Ministry of Labour, Employment, Veteran and Social Policy (MLESP) is in the process of completion of a centralized management information system that will help improve coordination between the Centers for Social Work, social care institutions, and MLESP.
Seychelles	Y	—	—	Seychelles has a comprehensive social protection system.	The Agency for Social Protection (ASP) was created in 2012 by merging the Social Security Fund and Social Welfare Agency (SWA) to improve the efficiency and governance of the social protection system.	The ASP rolled out the integrated management information system for the SWA and has made progress on establishing automated cross-checks with relevant government agencies to support the implementation of the means test.
Sierra Leone	Y	National Social Protection Policy (Agenda for Prosperity)	2013	The social protection agenda is detailed in the country's third-generation Poverty Reduction Strategy Paper (PRSP) (2013–2018), dubbed Agenda for Prosperity.	In 2012, a National Social Protection Authority was created by parliament to lead coordination in the sector. The National Social Protection Secretariat has been established and is hosted at the National Commission for Social Action (NaCSA).	The quality of M&E systems continues to vary across programs, though information on number and types of beneficiaries and budgets is generally available. A growing number of impact evaluations are being carried out.
Slovak Republic	—	—	—	—	—	—
Slovenia	—	—	—	—	—	—
Solomon Islands	N	n.a.	n.a.	The Solomon Islands has a Social Welfare Act, but no current social protection strategy framework is being implemented.	—	—
Somalia	—	—	—	—	—	—
South Africa	Y	White Paper for Social Welfare	1997	South Africa has put in place a well-developed publicly provided social protections system that consists of two main pillars of social grants and social insurance.	—	A new electronic biometric card payment system was successfully rolled out in 2014 to all social benefit beneficiaries.
South Sudan	P	South Sudan Development Plan (SSDP)	n.a.	The SSDP 2011–2013 includes social protection interventions under the Social and Human Development Pillar. A draft National Social Protection Policy Framework is yet to be finalized.	The government has created a Social Protection Core Team led by the Ministry of Gender, Child and Social Welfare to coordinate and facilitate the development of a comprehensive social protection policy.	—

(Table continues next page)

Appendix E. Policies, Institutions, and Administration *(Continued)*

| Country/ economy/ territory | Y/N/P (Planned) | Policy and strategy | | | Institutions | Administration |
		Strategy name	Initial year	Comment	Comment	Comment
Sri Lanka	P	n.a.	n.a.	The Department of National Planning at the Ministry of Finance and Planning has embarked on developing a social protection strategy.	The government has been interested in coordinating several social assistance programs and schemes using the Divineguma program. The Divineguma Act was presented and debated by Parliament and has been certified into law.	The government intends to transform its extensive social safety net system into an integrated one, which will not only provide relief against deprivation but also prevent deprivation and promote capability and productivity.
St. Kitts and Nevis	Y	National Social Protection Strategy	2011	St. Kitts and Nevis provides numerous social assistance, social insurance benefits, and labor market programs, now guided by an overall Social Protection Strategy that has been approved by the cabinet.	The recent approval of the social protection strategy and a move to its implementation phase is expected to establish coordination mechanisms.	The social protection strategy will facilitate improved M&E through the development of information systems and capacity building.
St. Lucia	P	n.a.	n.a.	The reform process is divided into four phases. Phase I, which is being implemented, includes the formulation of a National Social Protection Policy.	—	M&E of social protection and labor (SPL) programs will also improve once the MIS for social programs has been developed under the current reform. A proxy-means-test, Saint Lucia's National Eligibility Test (SL-NET), has been developed.
St. Vincent and the Grenadines	N	n.a.	n.a.	The government has a variety of social assistance programs, ALMPs, and a social insurance system, but lacks an overall social protection strategy that defines objectives and principles for the sector.	—	Most programs collect basic information; however, this is not always systematically collated.
Sudan	N	n.a.	n.a.	The government has completed the preparation of an Interim Poverty Reduction Strategy Paper (I-PRSP). It recognizes the importance of social protection, but the social protection section of the I-PRSP is brief on current activities and does not identify challenges, or strategy and priority actions.	The Ministry of Welfare and Social Security is in charge of the overall coordination of the social protection initiatives.	The government is introducing electronic payments through collaboration with Sudan's Central Bank.
Suriname	—	—	—	—	—	—
Swaziland	P	n.a.	n.a.	The government intends to establish an interministerial committee to oversee the development of a safety net strategy.	The Department of Social Welfare has been housed in the Deputy Prime Minister's Office since 2009. It is responsible for Swaziland's largest cash transfer programs and is also responsible for overseeing social care services.	—
Syrian Arab Republic	—	—	—	—	—	—

(Table continues next page)

Appendix E. Policies, Institutions, and Administration *(Continued)*

| Country/ economy/ territory | Y/N/P (Planned) | Policy and strategy | | | Institutions | Administration |
		Strategy name	Initial year	Comment	Comment	Comment
Tajikistan	P	n.a.	n.a.	Tajikistan is in the process of consultations with various stakeholders and development partners on the new social protection strategy.	In 2014, the social protection function was transferred to the Ministry of Health.	The government is establishing a consolidated registry for social protection programs. It is expected that the system will be launched in mid-2015. The new MIS registry system is expected to substantially improve the capacity of the government to plan and monitor implementation of its key poverty-related interventions.
Tanzania	P	n.a.	n.a.	The government is finalizing a draft of a National Social Protection Framework (NSPF), which aims to improve coordination and speed up the implementation of social protection policies designed to improve the lives of the poor and most vulnerable groups. The process includes the preparation of an Action Plan for operationalizing the Framework.	The government created a supervisory agency for the pension industry that will regulate all pension-related issues—except financial issues, which will be regulated by the central bank. The Social Security Regulatory Agency (SSRA), covering all pension schemes and health insurance services, was recently formed to enforce the Act.	A national monitoring system exists for capturing performance of the National Strategy for Growth and Reduction of Poverty (NSGRP II). Social protection indicators have been developed and incorporated in the national monitoring system. Most programs can track numbers of beneficiaries and budgets.
Thailand	Y	Eleventh National Economic and Social Development Plan	2012	The government has an overall strategy for social protection and a set of programs that deliver prevention, protection, and promotion services for large groups of the population. The government is working toward developing a universal social protection system by 2017, called the Welfare Society, a policy announced under the previous government.	The Ministry of Social Development and Human Security (MOSDHS) is the core agency responsible for coordinating all social protection programs.	Existing monitoring systems track the number and type of beneficiaries and budgets devoted to programs.
Timor-Leste	N	n.a.	n.a.	There is no overarching government-wide social assistance policy.	—	The Ministry of Social Solidarity will incorporate an M&E module into its MIS, which is currently under development.
Togo	P	n.a.	n.a.	A Social Protection Strategy and a budgeted action plan were validated in November 2013 by the main national stakeholders. The government has not yet adopted this strategy document.	The National Social Protection Promotion Committee provides directions and coordinates all social protection activities in Togo. The Ministry of Employment and Social Security is the lead structure for social protection, in collaboration with the Ministry of Social Action.	Monitoring & evaluation systems exist for most programs. Discussions have started with the technical and financial partners and the government to develop a national targeting system, which is the first step toward a national registry, in order to streamline social protection interventions.

(Table continues next page)

Country/ economy/ territory	Y/N/P (Planned)	Policy and strategy			Institutions	Administration
		Strategy name	Initial year	Comment	Comment	Comment
Tonga	P	n.a.	n.a.	Tonga does not have an overall social protection strategy. However, the government is making progress toward addressing this. The 2014–15 budget specifically refers to developing clear policy-based and financially affordable social protection schemes, to support vulnerable groups such as the elderly and disabled.	—	—
Trinidad and Tobago	P	National Poverty Reduction Strategy	n.a.	For fiscal year 2013–14, the Ministry of the People and Social Development set as objectives the development of a National Poverty Reduction Strategy.	—	The main social protection programs have monitoring and information systems and collect the main information. The country implements a Multiple Indicator Cluster Survey to monitor Millennium Development Goals. It also implements a periodical Survey of Living Conditions. The latest version was conducted in 2013.
Tunisia	Y	—	—	Tunisia has developed a comprehensive social protection and labor (SPL) system.	Tunisia has taken steps toward consolidating its main social assistance programs under a single Directorate of Social Promotion.	In 2012, the government launched a new project to develop a unified registry and improved monitoring of beneficiaries.
Turkey	N	n.a.	n.a	The government has an overall strategic approach for social protection and a comprehensive set of programs, but this strategy has not been documented as a formal strategy paper.	Social assistance programs are provided through the Social Assistances General Directorate in Ministry of Family and Social Policies (MoFSP).	The government intends to implement an alternative proxy-means-test for all its programs in 2015. The MoFSP has an active and well-staffed research department that carries out analysis of the social assistance system (as well as primary data collection). This research is used to inform policy changes. However, research is not made publicly available; as a result, the quality of this research is not known.
Turkmenistan	Y	Social Protection of the Population Code	2012	The government has an overall framework for social protection (2012 Code).	—	—

(Table continues next page)

Country/ economy/ territory	Y/N/P (Planned)	Policy and strategy			Institutions	Administration
		Strategy name	Initial year	Comment	Comment	Comment
Tuvalu	Y	Te Kakeega II (National Strategies for Sustainable Development 2005–2015)	2005	While there is no formal national social protection strategy, the government's national development strategy, Te Kakeega II (National Strategies for Sustainable Development 2005–2015) includes many areas that target improvement in life for all.	The Department of Community Affairs in the Ministry of Home Affairs and Rural Development (MHARD) focuses on monitoring and developing a social policy to address poverty and hardship. It also lobbies and coordinates the activities of other departments within MHARD and other stakeholders in social development.	—
Uganda	Y	Social Protection Strategy, within the Uganda National Development Plan	2012	The Ministry of Gender Labor and Social Development, with the support of development partners, has launched a social protection sector review to develop an effective and efficient social protection system and strengthen the strategy.	Social assistance programs are coordinated under the Ministry of Gender, Labor and Social Development— with the exception of the Public Sector Pension Fund and the Armed Forces Pension Fund.	A national monitoring system exists to capture performance of the National Development Plan. Most programs can track numbers of beneficiaries and budgets. Evaluations are carried out in large programs like the Northern Uganda Social Action Fund (NUSAF) and the cash transfer program, but are not carried out systematically across programs.
Ukraine	Y	National Poverty Reduction Strategy 2010–2015	2010	The government has clearly formulated an objective of reducing poverty, which was translated into its overall strategy for social and economic development and presidential strategy for economic development.	—	Existing monitoring systems can track the number and types of beneficiaries and budgets, but gaps remain.
United Arab Emirates	—	—	—	—	—	—
Uruguay	Y	Social Equity Plan	2007	The Social Cabinet coordinates policies, within the framework of the Social Equity Plan, which aims at eliminating extreme poverty and increasing equality.	The National Social Policies Council unites the Ministries of Finance, Labor, Social Development, Health, Education, and the Banco de Previsión Social (BPS). This council holds interministerial meetings and also has operational committees that work on implementation issues.	The two main institutions, BPS and Ministry of Social Development (MIDES), have strong monitoring systems that produce and disseminate performance indicators on a regular basis. Data are shared among institutions through a single system (SIIAS) that is managed collaboratively by all agencies. The new SIIAS system will also produce cross-sector monitoring reports.
Uzbekistan	Y	Welfare Improvement Strategy for 2012–2015	2012	The government has an overall policy for social protection as part of its broader strategy to improve the well-being of the population.	Importantly, the same ministry is in charge of both labor and social assistance policies.	M&E information is very basic and could improve to capture standard performance indicators such as coverage, targeting, and poverty impact. The government has expressed an interest in establishing a registry of beneficiaries. Common administrative systems are used for all cash transfer programs.
Vanuatu	N	n.a.	n.a.	—	—	—

(Table continues next page)

| Country/ economy/ territory | Y/N/P (Planned) | Policy and strategy | | | Institutions | Administration |
		Strategy name	Initial year	Comment	Comment	Comment
Venezuela, RB	N	n.a.	n.a.	No social protection strategy is in place, though poverty reduction is clearly stated as an objective in national development plans.	—	—
Vietnam	Y	National Social Protection Strategy (2011–2020)	2011	In 2012, the government adopted a resolution on social protection that will guide government policy until 2020. It covers labor market policy, social insurance, social assistance, social services, and poverty reduction.	The Ministry of Labor, Invalids and Social Affairs has begun promoting greater harmonization and reduced fragmentation of SSN programs.	—
West Bank and Gaza	—	—	—	—		—
Yemen, Rep.	P	Social Protection Strategy	n.a.	A new legal and policy framework is being implemented. The government has initiated an overall Social Protection Strategy and accompanying policies for protection of the population.	The Republic of Yemen has not yet institutionalized a system of coordination.	The major safety net programs have a well-developed database and MIS, which are supporting management processes and decision making. This information system was instrumental in making the safety net program more responsive to the recent political and economic crisis.
Zambia	Y	National Social Protection Policy, chapter in the Fifth National Development Plan	2014	The cabinet approved a new Social Protection Policy in June 2014.	Some attempt has been made to coordinate social assistance programs, with the Ministry of Community Development, Mother and Child (MCDMC) providing overall coordination.	The National Social Protection Policy should provide a basis for harmonization of programs and also a comprehensive monitoring and evaluation system. Work on a Single Registry of Beneficiaries was initiated in 2014, and has proceeded up to the stage of defining a road map for its development.
Zimbabwe	P	n.a.	n.a.	The government began developing a National Social Protection Policy in 2014.	Coordination and monitoring of social protection programs is mainly through the Ministry of Public Service Labor and Social Welfare decentralized at the provincial and district level.	The government developed a MIS for key social safety net programs. The system records and updates beneficiary data and accommodates add-on case management software. The ministry is in the process of integrating the MIS to accommodate all social safety net programs and link it to all provincial and district offices.

Source: World Bank, based on a World Bank internal monitoring tool.

Note: "Initial year" refers to either the year the social protection strategy was approved or the year of its effectiveness; ACFTU = All-China Federation of Trade Unions; ALMP = active labor market policy; CCT= conditional cash transfer; CT = conditional transfer; IT = information technology; M&E = monitoring and evaluation; MIS = management information system; MOF = Ministry of Finance; MOHRSS = Ministry of Human Resources and Social Security; N = no strategy available; n.a. = not applicable (the country does not have a national strategy or policy in place); NDRC = National Development and Reform Commission; NSSF = National Council for Social Security Fund; P = planned; PRSP = Poverty Reduction Strategy Paper; SA = social assistance; SI = social insurance; SP = social protection; SPL = social protection and labor; SSN = social safety net; UN = United Nations; Y = strategy available; — = not available.

Appendix F. Performance Indicators (All Social Safety Nets)

Country/economy/territory	Survey year	Coverage		Benefit incidence	Adequacy		Gini inequality reduction (%) (all hh)	Poverty headcount reduction (%) (all hh)	Poverty gap reduction (%) (all hh)
		Poorest 20%	Total	Poorest 20%	Poorest 20%	Total			
Afghanistan	2007	23.6	15.3	6.7	41.3	27.6	0.2	1.0	2.2
Albania	2008	45.8	33.2	14.3	6.4	6.3	1.6	6.6	15.6
Algeria	—	—	—	—	—	—	—	—	—
Angola	—	—	—	—	—	—	—	—	—
Antigua and Barbuda	—	—	—	—	—	—	—	—	—
Argentina	2010	21.8	9.4	40.0	19.2	11.0	0.8	2.9	7.1
Armenia	2009	34.0	23.0	32.4	33.1	17.0	4.8	13.0	31.4
Azerbaijan	2008	87.0	87.5	18.0	75.5	36.0	31.1	59.2	81.8
Bahrain	—	—	—	—	—	—	—	—	—
Bangladesh	2010	24.8	14.6	24.7	6.1	4.9	1.0	3.8	8.6
Belarus	2010	68.9	58.3	29.2	18.5	7.2	6.8	17.8	36.1
Belize	2009	18.5	16.3	18.7	23.4	8.6	0.2	0.7	2.2
Benin	2003	—	—	—	—	—	—	—	—
Bhutan	2007	1.6	1.0	15.3	3.0	2.1	..	0.1	0.2
Bolivia	2007	73.3	54.4	9.3	35.2	7.8	1.1	8.4	9.9
Bosnia and Herzegovina	2007	21.8	20.5	13.2	27.7	17.1	3.2	12.0	22.1
Botswana	2009	89.5	70.3	16.6	20.1	7.1	3.0	15.4	31.3
Brazil	2009	53.2	21.1	33.2	24.1	14.5	2.0	8.5	20.0
Bulgaria	2007	57.6	39.5	24.5	16.9	9.5	5.3	14.2	26.0
Burkina Faso	2009	—	—	—	—	—	—	—	—
Burundi	—	—	—	—	—	—	—	—	—
Cabo Verde	2008	25.3	21.9	14.8	19.3	7.1	1.3	7.6	14.7
Cambodia	2008	0.5	0.5	0.2	0.3	10.5	-0.1	..	..
Cameroon	2007	0.2	1.4	0.8	28.3	18.4	..	0.6	1.2
Central African Republic	—	—	—	—	—	—	—	—	—
Chad	—	—	—	—	—	—	—	—	—
Chile	2009	95.6	83.2	24.1	17.0	7.2	3.4	17.2	29.0
China	—	—	—	—	—	—	—	—	—
Colombia	2012	61.1	41.7	21.3	13.1	5.2	0.7	4.2	8.9
Comoros	2004	—	—	—	—	—	—	—	—
Congo, Dem. Rep.	2005	4.7	5.5	4.5	9.0	5.4	..	..	0.1
Congo, Rep.	2005	1.0	0.9	10.5	136.7	74.6	0.3	1.3	5.6
Costa Rica	2009	69.6	44.6	—	—	—	—	—	—
Côte d'Ivoire	2002	3.3	5.8	—	—	—	—	—	—
Croatia	2008	46.3	23.6	41.8	16.1	7.7	2.7	7.3	20.3
Czech Republic	—	—	—	—	—	—	—	—	—
Djibouti	2012	30.9	10.8	53.8	20.9	11.9	0.9	2.4	7.6
Dominica	2002	10.6	8.0	2.4	31.2	21.0	0.5	4.4	4.8
Dominican Republic	2009	35.2	23.7	25.7	10.9	5.0	1.0	5.7	8.7
Ecuador	2010	85.6	64.7	27.9	25.1	11.4	3.1	13.3	23.4
Egypt, Arab Rep.	2008	54.9	44.9	17.6	5.0	3.6	1.4	5.8	11.7
El Salvador	2009	67.2	42.6	43.9	9.3	6.2	0.3	1.4	2.9
Equatorial Guinea	—	—	—	—	—	—	—	—	—
Eritrea	—	—	—	—	—	—	—	—	—
Estonia	—	—	—	—	—	—	—	—	—

(Table continues next page)

Country/economy/ territory	Survey year	Coverage		Benefit incidence	Adequacy		Gini inequality reduction (%) (all hh)	Poverty headcount reduction (%) (all hh)	Poverty gap reduction (%) (all hh)
		Poorest 20%	Total	Poorest 20%	Poorest 20%	Total			
Ethiopia	2010	16.2	13.2	—	—	—	—	—	—
Fiji	2008	11.2	9.6	13.7	30.3	14.0	1.0	5.7	11.2
Gabon	2005	49.1	44.8	5.8	14.0	21.1	0.2	0.8	1.9
Gambia, The	1998	1.1	2.9	2.1	6.3	4.0	..	0.5	0.4
Georgia	2011	51.6	31.3	37.0	48.8	22.6	5.4	12.8	35.4
Ghana	2013	6.2	6.1	11.7	69.5	29.7	..	0.1	0.4
Grenada	—	—	—	—	—	—	—	—	—
Guatemala	2006	61.0	48.3	19.5	22.7	7.9	2.9	11.8	23.7
Guinea	—	—	—	—	—	—	—	—	—
Guinea-Bissau	—	—	—	—	—	—	—	—	—
Guyana	—	—	—	—	—	—	—	—	—
Haiti	2001	1.0	0.8	5.7	1.1	0.6	..	..	..
Honduras	2011	63.0	49.3	17.3	18.2	4.2	0.7	5.0	7.1
Hungary	2007	81.6	59.6	34.1	36.9	13.9	12.7	29.5	53.8
India	2009	20.8	17.2	—	—	—	—	—	—
Indonesia	2009	65.0	41.1	—	—	—	—	—	—
Iran, Islamic Rep.	—	—	—	—	—	—	—	—	—
Iraq	2006	86.4	80.0	18.2	4.3	2.3	2.0	8.6	14.9
Jamaica	2010	85.5	67.3	44.1	9.3	4.6	1.2	7.3	10.5
Jordan	2010	83.3	65.7	22.7	6.9	4.0	3.0	10.4	24.8
Kazakhstan	2007	42.3	29.1	22.4	5.1	3.3	1.0	4.9	8.1
Kenya	2005	34.4	20.0	7.9	5.1	8.0	0.1	1.7	3.4
Kiribati	2006	4.8	4.6	8.8	8.9	5.6	0.1	0.9	1.2
Kosovo	2006	16.2	7.0	38.8	48.3	34.0	4.0	7.5	26.4
Kuwait	—	—	—	—	—	—	—	—	—
Kyrgyz Republic	2006	15.7	8.5	36.2	53.1	26.0	2.7	8.9	21.4
Lao PDR	2007	—	—	—	—	—	—	—	—
Latvia	2008	40.1	40.2	17.0	20.2	7.8	3.1	10.0	22.6
Lebanon	2004	3.2	4.8	—	—	—	—	—	—
Lesotho	2014	64.1	51.6	17.3	—	—	—	—	—
Liberia	2007	63.0	61.2	..	—	6.9	..	..	..
Libya	—	—	—	—	—	—	—	—	—
Lithuania	2008	68.1	58.7	24.6	18.5	6.5	4.4	14.6	29.8
Macedonia, FYR	—	—	—	—	—	—	—	—	—
Madagascar	2010	2.2	0.9	8.9	17.3	24.1	-0.1	0.2	0.7
Malawi	2010	19.4	20.2	10.8	8.2	4.1	..	0.2	0.7
Malaysia	2008	93.8	82.8	20.8	6.5	1.7	1.3	6.3	13.3
Maldives	2004	3.1	3.8	25.7	34.4	7.4	0.1	0.2	1.7
Mali	2009	—	—	—	—	—	—	—	—
Marshall Islands	1999	—	—	—	—	—	—	—	—
Mauritania	2008	30.3	33.5	7.2	56.7	44.1	4.8	18.7	33.8
Mauritius	2006	44.7	40.6	14.2	41.4	24.9	10.2	31.1	54.6
Mexico	2010	74.2	48.9	29.6	41.9	17.9	5.2	18.8	36.1
Micronesia, Fed. Sts.	2000	4.6	6.3	3.6	50.6	20.0	0.9	6.9	12.0
Moldova	2010	41.7	33.8	26.8	21.9	9.0	4.1	13.9	28.0

(Table continues next page)

Country/economy/territory	Survey year	Coverage		Benefit incidence	Adequacy		Gini inequality reduction (%) (all hh)	Poverty headcount reduction (%) (all hh)	Poverty gap reduction (%) (all hh)
		Poorest 20%	Total	Poorest 20%	Poorest 20%	Total			
Mongolia	2007	91.7	83.2	22.6	15.5	6.3	6.0	22.3	36.2
Montenegro	—	—	—	—	—	—	—	—	—
Morocco	2009	50.1	36.8	—	—	—	—	—	—
Mozambique	2008	7.7	5.4	—	—	—	—	—	—
Myanmar	—	—	—	—	—	—	—	—	—
Namibia	2003	19.3	9.8	—	—	—	—	—	—
Nepal	2010	47.7	38.7	15.7	3.7	2.6	0.7	4.8	7.1
Nicaragua	2005	66.0	47.2	—	—	—	—	—	—
Niger	2011	2.6	2.7	—	—	—	—	—	—
Nigeria	2010	1.3	1.7	11.1	5.0	2.2	..	0.1	0.3
Oman	—	—	—	—	—	—	—	—	—
Pakistan	2009	13.7	12.6	11.6	12.1	12.2	1.1	6.6	11.8
Palau	2006	8.7	2.9	25.2	8.3	10.5	0.1	0.9	1.8
Panama	2008	79.0	52.0	48.7	9.5	2.7	0.3	1.3	4.5
Papua New Guinea	2009	1.9	3.4	2.3	2.1	1.7	..	0.1	0.1
Paraguay	2009	58.9	40.1	39.7	18.8	13.5	0.2	1.5	3.0
Peru	2009	84.6	57.0	56.4	16.5	11.0	0.8	3.0	8.9
Philippines	2013	57.3	27.4	45.2	20.9	11.6	2.4	12.5	27.3
Poland	2005	71.0	50.6	41.9	48.9	14.2	12.2	25.5	57.6
Qatar	—	—	—	—	—	—	—	—	—
Romania	2008	79.5	55.4	31.7	18.6	8.3	6.9	17.8	36.3
Russian Federation	2007	46.8	28.2	—	—	—	—	—	—
Rwanda	2005	0.4	1.4	0.9	2.4	3.2	..	..	..
Samoa	—	—	—	—	—	—	—	—	—
São Tomé and Príncipe	—	—	—	—	—	—	—	—	—
Saudi Arabia	—	—	—	—	—	—	—	—	—
Senegal	2011	7.3	10.3	3.6	5.5	6.2	−0.1	1.2	2.2
Serbia	2007	21.8	11.9	30.7	20.4	12.6	1.9	6.1	13.0
Seychelles	—	—	—	—	—	—	—	—	—
Sierra Leone	2011	34.6	30.2	15.1	..	..	..	..	..
Slovak Republic	2009	95.6	83.2	38.4	14.4	4.4	7.1	15.8	28.9
Slovenia	—	—	—	—	—	—	—	—	—
Solomon Islands	2005	1.1	1.6	4.0	25.5	13.0	..	0.3	0.5
Somalia	—	—	—	—	—	—	—	—	—
South Africa	2010	83.4	58.5	—	—	—	—	—	—
South Sudan	—	—	—	—	—	—	—	—	—
Sri Lanka	2006	52.1	29.7	32.5	6.7	4.0	1.3	5.8	12.1
St. Kitts and Nevis	—	—	—	—	—	—	—	—	—
St. Lucia	—	—	—	—	—	—	—	—	—
St. Vincent and the Grenadines	—	—	—	—	—	—	—	—	—
Sudan	—	—	—	—	—	—	—	—	—
Suriname	—	—	—	—	—	—	—	—	—
Swaziland	2010	70.9	51.6	13.7	21.7	15.7	2.8	11.7	27.7
Syrian Arab Republic	2003	—	—	—	—	—	—	—	—

(Table continues next page)

Country/economy/ territory	Survey year	Coverage		Benefit incidence	Adequacy		Gini inequality reduction (%) (all hh)	Poverty headcount reduction (%) (all hh)	Poverty gap reduction (%) (all hh)
		Poorest 20%	Total	Poorest 20%	Poorest 20%	Total			
Tajikistan	2011	13.0	9.8	7.6	1.3	2.4	..	0.4	0.7
Tanzania	2008	79.1	77.4	4.1	4.5	6.9	-0.1	1.2	1.2
Thailand	2009	85.4	70.4	7.4	2.5	3.7	..	0.1	0.1
Timor-Leste	2007	23.5	26.3	0.9	1.2	9.8	1.1	9.2	17.8
Togo	2006	—	—	—	—	—	—	—	—
Tonga	—	—	—	—	—	—	—	—	—
Trinidad and Tobago	—	—	—	—	—	—	—	—	—
Tunisia	—	—	—	—	—	—	—	—	—
Turkey	2012	57.5	21.2	38.4	10.5	7.7	1.2	3.5	9.9
Turkmenistan	—	—	—	—	—	—	—	—	—
Tuvalu	—	—	—	—	—	—	—	—	—
Uganda	2009	75.7	66.8	—	—	—	—	—	—
Ukraine	2006	53.5	47.4	23.3	15.9	7.2	4.7	15.4	29.3
United Arab Emirates	—	—	—	—	—	—	—	—	—
Uruguay	2009	84.6	42.2	41.5	12.8	6.3	2.2	9.4	20.0
Uzbekistan	—	—	—	—	—	—	—	—	—
Vanuatu	—	—	—	—	—	—	—	—	—
Venezuela, RB	2006	5.0	4.7	—	—	—	—	—	—
Vietnam	2006	43.3	20.9	13.8	20.5	16.5	1.8	6.7	14.0
West Bank and Gaza	2007	22.5	11.5	38.5	2.5	1.6	0.1	..	1.2
Yemen, Rep.	2005	17.0	13.4	22.9	6.5	3.3	0.4	2.0	3.6
Zambia	2010	1.0	0.6	—	—	—	—	—	—
Zimbabwe	—	—	—	—	—	—	—	—	—

Source: ASPIRE.

Note: Indicators are calculated using national representative household surveys and are available at www.worldbank.org/aspire. When interpreting ASPIRE indicators, it is important to note that the extent to which information on specific transfers and programs is captured in the household surveys can vary considerably across countries. As a consequence, ASPIRE indicators are not fully comparable across program categories and countries; however, they provide approximate measures of social protection systems performance. "Poorest 20%" refers to households in the bottom quintile of the national consumption or income distribution. hh = household; — = not available; .. = negligible.

Appendix G. Coverage of Social Safety Nets, by Program Type

Percent of households in the poorest quintile of the national consumption or income distribution

Country/economy/ territory	Survey year	Unconditional cash transfers	Conditional cash transfers	Social pensions	Food and in-kind	School feeding	Public works	Fee waivers	Other SSNs
Afghanistan	2007	0.5	—	—	0.4	1.4	23.3	—	—
Albania	2008	16.8	—	0.4	—	—	0.1	—	36.2
Algeria	—	—	—	—	—	—	—	—	—
Angola	—	—	—	—	—	—	—	—	—
Antigua and Barbuda	—	—	—	—	—	—	—	—	—
Argentina	2010	—	18.7	—	—	—	2.5	—	1.6
Armenia	2009	23.4	—	—	14.6	0.2	—	—	2.6
Azerbaijan	2008	86.4	—	—	3.2	—	—	8.0	22.1
Bahrain	—	—	—	—	—	—	—	—	—
Bangladesh	2010	0.3	14.6	9.4	0.7	—	0.8	0.2	0.8
Belarus	2010	42.9	—	—	—	—	—	—	53.4
Belize	2009	3.3	—	5.2	—	03.3	n.a.	1.1	9.2
Benin	—	—	—	—	—	—	—	—	—
Bhutan	2007	—	—	—	—	—	—	—	1.6
Bolivia	2007	—	69.3	10.7	—	—	—	—	—
Bosnia and Herzegovina	2007	3.5	—	18.7	—	—	—	—	—
Botswana	2009	0.3	—	1.5	—	85.7	—	—	32.5
Brazil	2009	—	52.1	1.9	—	—	—	—	—
Bulgaria	2007	40.9	—	21.4	—	—	5.4	13.2	2.5
Burkina Faso	—	—	—	—	—	—	—	—	—
Burundi	—	—	—	—	—	—	—	—	—
Cabo Verde	2007	..	—	21.5	—	—	—	—	4.6
Cambodia	2008	—	—	—	—	—	—	—	0.5
Cameroon	2007	0.1	—	—	—	—	—	—	0.1
Central African Republic	—	—	—	—	—	—	—	—	—
Chad	—	—	—	—	—	—	—	—	—
Chile	2009	64.1	26.5	12.5	84.4	66.1	—	44.8	22.5
China	—	—	—	—	—	—	—	—	—
Colombia	2012	1.4	34.0	4.1	—	37.2	—	2.2	3.8
Comoros	—	—	—	—	—	—	—	—	—
Congo, Dem. Rep.	2005	4.4	—	—	—	—	—	—	0.3
Congo, Rep.	2005	—	—	—	—	—	—	—	1.0
Costa Rica	2009	7.5	18.1	—	15.0	55.1	—	6.8	22.4
Côte d'Ivoire	2002	1.0	—	—	—	—	—	—	2.3
Croatia	2008	45.8	—	0.2	1.7	—	—	1.0	0.8
Czech Republic	—	—	—	—	—	—	—	—	—
Djibouti	2012	5.8	—	—	27.0	—	—	..	—
Dominica	2002	10.6	—	—	—	—	—	—	—
Dominican Republic	2009	35.2	—	—	—	—	—	—	—
Ecuador	2010	—	52.4	0.1	73.4	39.9	—	—	24.5
Egypt, Arab Rep.	2008	8.6	—	—	51.8	—	—	—	—
El Salvador	2009	16.4	—	—	34.1	62.9	—	1.0	45.3
Equatorial Guinea	—	—	—	—	—	—	—	—	—
Eritrea	—	—	—	—	—	—	—	—	—
Estonia	—	—	—	—	—	—	—	—	—
Ethiopia	2010	—	—	—	3.6	—	14.0	—	—

(Table continues next page)

Percent of households in the poorest quintile of the national consumption or income distribution

Country/economy/ territory	Survey year	Unconditional cash transfers	Conditional cash transfers	Social pensions	Food and in-kind	School feeding	Public works	Fee waivers	Other SSNs
Fiji	2008	7.1	—	—	—	—	—	—	4.1
Gabon	2005	—	—	0.2	47.3	—	—	—	2.3
Gambia, The	1998	—	—	—	—	—	—	—	1.1
Georgia	2011	34.6	—	0.7	8.7	—	—	37.4	1.6
Ghana	2013	0.2	—	—	—	—	—	4.7	1.3
Grenada	—	—	—	—	—	—	—	—	—
Guatemala	2006	—	—	—	56.7	14.2	—	10.0	2.6
Guinea	—	—	—	—	—	—	—	—	—
Guinea-Bissau	—	—	—	—	—	—	—	—	—
Guyana	—	—	—	—	—	—	—	—	—
Haiti	2001	—	—	—	0.3	—	—	0.8	—
Honduras	2011	—	9.6	1.1	0.6	57.1	—	9.6	0.1
Hungary	2007	76.9	—	0.3	0.3	—	—	22.2	9.4
India	2009	—	—	—	—	—	20.8	—	—
Indonesia	2009	—	—	—	—	—	—	65.0	—
Iran, Islamic Rep.	—	—	—	—	—	—	—	—	—
Iraq	2006	83.2	—	—	14.6	—	—	—	0.2
Jamaica	2010	10.0	42.3	12.3	—	63.0	—	46.7	2.3
Jordan	2010	18.0	—	—	—	—	—	—	79.5
Kazakhstan	2007	2.7	—	36.7	0.2	—	—	—	6.7
Kenya	2005	24.3	—	—	21.4	—	—	—	2.0
Kiribati	2006	4.8	—	—	—	—	—	—	—
Kosovo	2006	14.9	—	—	2.6	—	—	—	—
Kuwait	—	—	—	—	—	—	—	—	—
Kyrgyz Republic	2006	14.3	—	—	—	—	—	—	1.7
Lao PDR	—	—	—	—	—	—	—	—	—
Latvia	2008	34.8	—	0.8	1.3	—	—	4.7	5.7
Lebanon	2004	—	—	—	—	—	—	—	3.2
Lesotho	2014	3.7	2.2	17.9	4.2	48.7	12.4	—	4.7
Liberia	2007	—	—	—	19.7	18.1	3.9	54.6	—
Libya	—	—	—	—	—	—	—	—	—
Lithuania	2008	62.5	—	6.8	—	—	—	—	6.9
Macedonia, FYR	—	—	—	—	—	—	—	—	—
Madagascar	2010	0.2	—	—	—	—	—	—	2.0
Malawi	2010	0.4	—	—	3.4	14.7	2.0	—	0.4
Malaysia	2008	93.6	—	—	—	—	—	—	9.1
Maldives	2004	2.0	—	—	—	—	—	1.6	—
Mali	—	—	—	—	—	—	—	—	—
Marshall Islands	—	—	—	—	—	—	—	—	—
Mauritania	2008	—	—	—	—	—	—	—	30.3
Mauritius	2006	7.4	—	38.7	—	—	—	2.0	5.2
Mexico	2010	2.8	45.0	4.2	7.1	—	0.2	57.3	3.0
Micronesia, Fed. Sts.	2000	4.6	—	—	—	—	—	—	—
Moldova	2010	23.5	—	9.1	—	—	—	23.4	9.9
Mongolia	2007	91.7	—	—	—	—	—	—	2.0
Montenegro	—	—	—	—	—	—	—	—	—

(Table continues next page)

Percent of households in the poorest quintile of the national consumption or income distribution

Country/economy/ territory	Survey year	Unconditional cash transfers	Conditional cash transfers	Social pensions	Food and in-kind	School feeding	Public works	Fee waivers	Other SSNs
Morocco	2009	0.8	0.6	—	45.3	13.4	—	—	2.9
Mozambique	2008	7.7	—	—	0.1	—	—	—	—
Myanmar	—	—	—	—	—	—	—	—	—
Namibia	2003	—	—	19.3	—	—	—	—	—
Nepal	2010	0.1	—	16.0	5.9	—	10.2	—	28.1
Nicaragua	2005	—	—	—	15.1	63.0	—	—	0.8
Niger	2011	2.6	—	—	—	—	—	—	—
Nigeria	2010	—	—	—	0.4	—	0.3	—	0.6
Oman	—	—	—	—	—	—	—	—	—
Pakistan	2009	12.3	0.1	—	2.3	—	—	—	2.1
Palau	2006	8.7	—	—	—	—	—	—	—
Panama	2008	2.4	27.1	—	5.5	74.5	—	—	19.6
Papua New Guinea	2009	1.9	—	—	—	—	—	0.1	—
Paraguay	2009	—	8.2	—	45.5	46.8	—	—	0.1
Peru	2009	—	29.7	—	78.1	45.3	—	—	13.7
Philippines	2013	2.3	50.8	—	10.1	—	1.4	—	9.7
Poland	2005	60.3	—	4.1	—	—	—	15.3	25.5
Qatar	—	—	—	—	—	—	—	—	—
Romania	2008	76.8	—	5.7	—	—	—	—	24.7
Russian Federation	2007	39.6	—	3.7	0.7	—	—	8.7	3.8
Rwanda	2005	0.4	—	—	—	—	—	—	—
Samoa	—	—	—	—	—	—	—	—	—
São Tomé and Principe	—	—	—	—	—	—	—	—	—
Saudi Arabia	—	—	—	—	—	—	—	—	—
Senegal	2011	—	—	—	3.5	—	—	2.3	1.8
Serbia	2007	21.3	—	0.6	—	—	—	—	0.1
Seychelles	—	—	—	—	—	—	—	—	—
Sierra Leone	2011	0.1	—	3.5	31.5	—	—	—	1.3
Slovak Republic	2009	86.0	—	28.0	—	7.5	—	3.5	20.0
Slovenia	—	—	—	—	—	—	—	—	—
Solomon Islands	2005	1.1	—	—	—	—	—	—	—
Somalia	—	—	—	—	—	—	—	—	—
South Africa	2010	71.6	—	38.1	—	—	—	1.2	0.1
South Sudan	—	—	—	—	—	—	—	—	—
Sri Lanka	2006	51.2	—	4.0	—	—	—	—	—
St. Kitts and Nevis	—	—	—	—	—	—	—	—	—
St. Lucia	—	—	—	—	—	—	—	—	—
St. Vincent and the Grenadines	—	—	—	—	—	—	—	—	—
Sudan	—	—	—	—	—	—	—	—	—
Suriname	—	—	—	—	—	—	—	—	—
Swaziland	2010	4.0	—	34.7	—	—	—	—	55.0
Syrian Arab Republic	—	—	—	—	—	—	—	—	—
Tajikistan	2011	0.3	—	0.6	—	—	—	6.7	7.0
Tanzania	2008	—	—	—	3.5	77.9	0.4	—	1.1
Thailand	2009	4.3	—	60.6	—	60.2	—	—	1.3

(Table continues next page)

Percent of households in the poorest quintile of the national consumption or income distribution

Country/economy/ territory	Survey year	Unconditional cash transfers	Conditional cash transfers	Social pensions	Food and in-kind	School feeding	Public works	Fee waivers	Other SSNs
Timor-Leste	2007	—	—	—	23.3	—	0.2	—	—
Togo	—	—	—	—	—	—	—	—	—
Tonga	—	—	—	—	—	—	—	—	—
Trinidad and Tobago	—	—	—	—	—	—	—	—	—
Tunisia	—	—	—	—	—	—	—	—	—
Turkey	2012	18.5	—	9.9	29.1	—	—	47.5	2.7
Turkmenistan	—	—	—	—	—	—	—	—	—
Tuvalu	—	—	—	—	—	—	—	—	—
Uganda	2009	3.1	—	—	6.6	7.3	—	—	71.3
Ukraine	2006	29.1	—	—	—	—	—	2.5	32.7
United Arab Emirates	—	—	—	—	—	—	—	—	—
Uruguay	2009	—	79.6	—	15.8	39.4	0.9	—	—
Uzbekistan	—	—	—	—	—	—	—	—	—
Vanuatu	—	—	—	—	—	—	—	—	—
Venezuela, RB	2006	—	0.3	—	—	—	—	—	4.7
Vietnam	2006	2.4	—	12.6	—	—	—	26.4	34.2
West Bank and Gaza	2007	8.1	—	—	15.4	—	—	—	—
Yemen, Rep.	2005	11.1	—	3.3	0.1	3.0	0.4	1.1	0.4
Zambia	2010	1.0	—	—	—	—	—	—	—
Zimbabwe	—	—	—	—	—	—	—	—	—

Source: ASPIRE.

Note: Indicators are calculated using national representative household surveys and are available at www.worldbank.org/aspire. When interpreting ASPIRE indicators, it is important to note that the extent to which information on specific transfers and programs is captured in the household surveys can vary considerably across countries. As a consequence, ASPIRE indicators are not fully comparable across program categories and countries. However, they provide approximate measures of social protection systems performance. Social pensions refer to periodic cash transfers to the elderly outside or supplemental to the contributory pension system; the transfers include veteran and disability noncontributory pensions. n.a. = not applicable; — = not available; SSN = social safety net.